INFRASTRUC
DELIVERY PLA
An effective practice approach

Janice Morphet

for
Dylan

First published in Great Britain in 2016 by

Policy Press
University of Bristol
1-9 Old Park Hill
Bristol BS2 8BB
UK
+44 (0)117 954 5940
pp-info@bristol.ac.uk
www.policypress.co.uk

North America office:
Policy Press
c/o The University of Chicago Press
1427 East 60th Street
Chicago, IL 60637, USA
t: +1 773 702 7700
f: +1 773 702 9756
sales@press.uchicago.edu
www.press.uchicago.edu

British Library Cataloguing in Publication Data
A catalogue record for this book is available from the British Library.

Library of Congress Cataloging-in-Publication Data
A catalog record for this book has been requested.

ISBN 978 1 44731 679 4 paperback
ISBN 978 1 44731 678 7 hardcover
ISBN 978 1 44731 682 4 ePub
ISBN 978 1 44731 681 7 Mobi

Cover design by Andrew Corbett
Front cover: image kindly supplied by Getty
Printed and bound in Great Britain by CMP, Poole
Policy Press uses environmentally responsible print partners

Contents

Contents

List of figures, tables and boxes

Figure

Tables

Boxes

Abbreviations

BRICS	Brazil, Russia, India, China, South Africa
CA	combined authority
CEC	Commission of the European Communities
CIL	Community Infrastructure Levy
CLLD	Community Led Local Development
CO_2	carbon dioxide
CoR	Committee of the Regions
DCO	Development Consent Order
DG	Directorate General
EC	European Commission
ECJ	European Court of Justice
EEA	European Economic Area
EIB	European Investment Bank
EP	European Parliament
ERM	exchange rate mechanism
ESDP	European Spatial Development Perspective
ESIF	European Structural and Investment Funds
ETS	emissions trading scheme
EU	European Union
FDI	foreign direct investment
FE	further education
FEA	functional economic area
FIT	Fields in Trust
GATT	General Agreement on Tariffs and Trade
GDP	gross domestic product
GIS	geographical information system
GOR	Government Offices of the Regions
GPA	Government Procurement Agreement
HST	high speed train
ICT	information and communications technologies
IDP	infrastructure delivery plan
IEA	International Energy Agency
IFRS	International Financial Reporting Standard
IMF	International Monetary Fund
IPC	Infrastructure Planning Commission
ITI	Integrated Territorial Investment
JTW	journey to work
LEPs	Local Enterprise Partnerships
LSE	London School of Economics and Political Science
MEPs	Members of the European Parliament
MLEI	mobilising local energy investment

MLG	multilevel governance
NIPA	National Infrastructure Planning Association
NPPF	National Planning Policy Framework
NPS	National Policy Statements
NSIP	Nationally Significant Infrastructure Project
OECD	Organisation for Economic Co-operation and Development
PA	Partnership Agreement
PFI	Private Finance Initiative
PPP	public–private partnership
PWLB	Public Works Loan Board
R&D	research and development
RDS	Regional Development Strategy
SDP	Strategic Development Plan
SEM	Single European Market
SEP	Strategic Economic Plan
SGEI	services of general economic interest
SNR	subnational review
SRO	senior responsible officer
SUDS	sustainable urban drainage systems
SUMP	Sustainable Urban Mobility Plan
TEEB	The Economics of Eco-systems and Bio-diversity
TEN	Trans-European Networks
TEN-E	Trans-European Networks – Energy
TEN-T	Trans-European Networks – Transport
TIF	tax increment financing
TOD	transport oriented development
TP	Territorial Pact
UN	United Nations
UNEP	United National Environmental Programme
WEF	World Economic Forum
WTO	World Trade Organization
XML	Extensible Markup Language

About the author

Janice Morphet has had a career in local and central government and as an academic and consultant. She has degrees in sociology, planning, management, politics and literature. Janice has been a planner for over 45 years and has worked in a range of local authorities including London boroughs, county, district and unitary councils and was secretary of SERPLAN. She was head of a UK planning school and has been a professor of planning for over 30 years. She is now a visiting professor in planning at University College London where she teaches management for built environment professionals. Janice was a member of the ODA planning committee for London 2012 and she has been centrally involved in infrastructure delivery planning since 2007. Her latest research has been on the practices and geographies of devolution. Janice has written extensively on planning, local government and the EU.

Preface

Infrastructure has always been at the heart of planning. In the post-war years decisions about locations and scale of provision were supported by the application of public service standards – how far should a five-year-old be expected to walk to school? How quickly should an ambulance respond to an emergency call? How many car spaces are required for a new development or town centre? Service providers were funded to deliver to these standards. Planners applied these standards to identify where there were gaps in provision and used their regular plan reviews to identify how any deficits in service provision could be met through land allocation, policies or other development options.

After 2000, these national standards were removed and despite government guidance that evidence-based local standards should be provided by planners, this has largely not occurred. Planners were uncertain about taking on this new role of defining service provision and access standards. They had few direct links with service providers to discuss their operational and longer-term needs. Planners moved to safer ground where their role was more defined. They became focused on the infrastructure required for new development. They moved away from thinking of communities as a whole and their changing requirements for social, economic and environmental infrastructure and then proactively planning for its provision.

This book is an attempt to raise these issues and provides some approaches to infrastructure delivery planning in the future. This requires planners to return to a comprehensive view of their areas and then to engage with delivery through plan making and development. I have been involved in infrastructure delivery planning from my first days in planning – finding out the relative rates of burials to cremations in order to identify new cemetery provision, examining library catchment areas and reviewing the whole of the housing waiting lists to estimate how many older people needed to down-size into purpose-built accommodation. This was in the late 1960s and we were preparing for our first local plan. Later I became responsible for highways, town centres, open space, car parks, schools and provision for older people. All of these services need more funding than is ever available and decisions always have to be made about prioritisation based on evidence of need, distribution of services and changing methods of provision. One of the key elements in making these recommendations for provision rested on understanding how infrastructure was funded – who could provide it? How did other organisations make their decisions? Were there any benefits in bringing organisations together to improve provision? There were also questions of how new facilities were going to be funded – who would pay for the running costs of the community centre or how would a swimming pool or sports centre manage its energy bills once built?

The introduction of spatial planning in England in 2004, where plan making and delivery combine, provided an opportunity to consider infrastructure delivery planning again in a more systematic way. Through a research project that I led on behalf of University College London and Deloitte for the Royal Town Planning Institute, Greater London Authority, Joseph Rowntree Foundation and Department of Communities and Local Government, infrastructure delivery plans accompanying each local plan were proposed. These were not 'wish lists' but founded on existing commitments in capital programmes and bringing together all those organisations responsible for infrastructure provision in any area. They focused on developing standards for existing areas as well as new provision based on sustainable principles. Following the use of training and support programmes funded through the Planning Advisory Service the vast proportion of English local authorities now have infrastructure delivery plans and are keeping them up to date. They are included in local plan preparation and are now spreading to Neighbourhood Plans.

In writing this book, I have drawn upon the experience of many different local authorities, consultants and infrastructure providers that I have learned about in training and consultancy work across the country. This local reorientation has not always been easy to understand, particularly the inclusion of needs and deficits in existing areas as well as those in new developments. There have also been challenges where there is enough existing capacity, but communities would prefer new facilities or where individual organisations in the same town want their own facilities even where these may be expensive to run, reduce the viability of all similar services and only meet partial community needs. For some facilities, such as schools or health, understanding the mechanisms of finance have been difficult, not least as the government has changed funding models on a regular basis. Working within local authorities to deliver provision for services such as schools can sometimes be more challenging than working with external bodies.

I hope that this book gives planners both useful techniques and improved confidence to continue their work on infrastructure delivery planning and to restore its role as a central feature of the planning process.

I have worked with many colleagues on delivering infrastructure planning and my thanks go to Alan Wiles, Richard Blyth, Marco Bianconi, John Pounder, Jackie Leask, Gilian MacInnes and Tim Marshall together with the many other people I have worked with on this issue. The usual thanks go to my family for the many interesting and informative discussions we have had about these issues over a long period of time.

Janice Morphet
February 2016

ONE

The role of infrastructure in society

Introduction

Infrastructure is a means and not an end. Societies rely on infrastructure for all that they do – how they live, generate economic activity, safeguard the environment and manage risks. Infrastructure implementation represents a major financial commitment and is funded as capital investment for periods of 30 years or more. Much infrastructure is provided directly by the state or within state-managed regulatory frameworks. Spatial planning, with its emphasis on delivery, is central to the adequate provision of infrastructure that is a core component of the social, economic and environmental functioning of society.

The provision and use of infrastructure is contextualised within the objectives for any place and the plans that are made to achieve them. These objectives are primarily set by local democratic leaders and the wider community. They will be framed by the priorities that have been adopted by governments concerned with strategic infrastructure provision such as energy security and transport networks. Some strategic plans will also be made by infrastructure providers, managing their own investment and future capacity whether for water or school places. Infrastructure delivery planning brings together the sectoral demands of providers with the locality's priorities and needs. It identifies the gaps between supply and demand and how these can be managed and mitigated within a sustainable context. This is an essential feature of the spatial planning process.

Infrastructure delivery planning requirements will vary between different spatial scales and territories. Functional economic areas (FEA) or subregions, whether urban or rural, may be focused on physical infrastructure such as transport and telecommunications and major social and community provision such as universities, theatres and hospitals. At the local scale, there will be a concern for schools, walking, cycle paths, and community services. In some cases, a national infrastructure project, such as a road or major energy plant, will impact on all spatial scales including the local.

Policy context

Infrastructure delivery planning operates within a policy context that includes societal objectives and their means of implementation including government commitments, legislation, regulation and funding. While individual infrastructure providers have a primary focus on their own service, this cannot be delivered without reference to the democratically determined objectives that will be translated into their operating policies. Within the European Union (EU), these objectives and policy frameworks, including those that promote economic, social and territorial cohesion, are agreed by the member states (Barca, 2009; CEC, 2013b), although the range and role of these agreements may be little understood in their application within a domestic context. This is particularly the case within the UK but may also be the case elsewhere (Morphet, 2013a). In this book, where the EU has a legal role in the development and delivery of infrastructure planning, this is set out.

The EU's policies, legislation and programmes also influence the countries that surround and trade with it, particularly where these are members of the European Economic Area (EEA), such as Norway, or where a state is embedded within the EU and has all its border with members, for example Switzerland. In the EEA, EU legislation is adopted without the participation of the EEA member state in its formulation and agreement. In Switzerland, which lies outside the EEA, much of the EU's legislation is applied in order to facilitate trade and movement of goods. The standards adopted by the EU are required to be applied by any state outside as well as within the EU if there is trade between them.

The EU's objectives are developed and implemented through spatial plans, strategies and programmes based on assessments of gaps between the fulfilment of these objectives, existing capacity and future requirements. The EU's social, economic and territorial objectives are shown in Box 1.1

> **Box 1.1: EU thematic objectives for social, economic and territorial cohesion**
> 1. strengthening research, technological development and innovation;
> 2. enhancing access to, and use and quality of, ICT;
> 3. enhancing the competitiveness of SMEs, of the agricultural sector and of the fishery and aquaculture sector;
> 4. supporting the shift towards a low-carbon economy in all sectors;
> 5. promoting climate change adaptation, risk prevention and management;
> 6. preserving and protecting the environment and promoting resource efficiency;
> 7. promoting sustainable transport and removing bottlenecks in key network infrastructures;
> 8. promoting sustainable and quality employment and supporting labour mobility;
> 9. promoting social inclusion, combating poverty and any discrimination;
> 10. investing in education, training and vocational training for skills and lifelong learning;
> 11. enhancing institutional capacity of public authorities and stakeholders and efficient public administration. (CEC, 2013b, Article 9)

The application of these EU objectives will be supplemented by those determined at other governance scales and are interpreted to apply in local circumstances. The territorial expression of this process, including the proposed policies and projects to meet these gaps or transform places, is at the heart of spatial planning (Morphet, 2011a). In most localities these changes may be small or incremental but there are times when major territorial reshaping is required to support responses to environmental conditions including carbon reduction, unexpected flooding or lagging economies (Krawczyk and Ratcliffe, 2005; Urry et al, 2014; Williams, 2014). This reshaping can be undertaken in a variety of ways including densification, dispersal, design, retrofitting and redevelopment and the options are considered within the spatial planning process.

Spatial planning processes include infrastructure investment that adds value and privilege to specific locations (Adams and Watkins, 2014). This approach can be included within the wider definition of placemaking that seeks to promote the positive features of places through formal and informal local leadership (Collinge and Gibney, 2010). Infrastructure provision at all scales can also be contested by communities opposing change or cities seeking competitive advantage that such investment might bring.

In the UK, the system of spatial planning was adopted in 2003 in Scotland, 2004 in England and Wales and 2015 in Northern Ireland. While there have been legal refinements and changes in emphasis since the initial adoption in the UK, the fundamental principles of spatial planning as a means of plan-making, regulation and delivery continue. As in other countries, spatial planning operates within the wider government policy context that considers capacity, sustainability, interoperability and security. Infrastructure has to be resilient against overload, damage or attack (McDaniels et al, 2008). Spatial planning is concerned with placeshaping and delivery, plan-making, policy, regulation and implementation (Waterhout, 2008; Morphet, 2011a) and active integration between institutions and providers to achieve these ends (Stead and Meijers, 2009). While transport, energy or telecommunications infrastructure is primarily viewed within sectors and provided by a multiplicity of organisations, the role of spatial planning is to achieve the integration of this provision in ways that serve society's economic, environmental and social objectives in specific locations, and is mutually beneficial to society and serves future or changing needs

This active engagement also means working between the scales of the state where different types of infrastructure are provided. Spatial planning is therefore concerned with multilevel governance (MLG) frameworks and practices (Adshead, 2014). This will require joint institutions stretching across scales of governance and geographies with operational programmes for delivery, defining specific responsibilities (Barca, 2009). Within the EU, this is frequently referred to as achieving horizontal and vertical integration. These practices may take time to deliver and may be driven by external factors including economic competition, government incentives or wider security issues (Stead, 2014).

When infrastructure, such as energy, is provided by the private sector, the market is regulated by the state in a way that will include the costs of expanded supply, maintenance of existing facilities and profit for the provider. There are other regulatory requirements such as interconnectivity between suppliers and, in some cases, between different types of infrastructure. Multiple service providers for the same type of infrastructure can be in open competition with each other. In some markets, competition may lead to wasteful externalities such as where older buses duplicate routes at lower passenger fares but add public costs through increased air pollution (Defra, 2011a; Preston and Almutairi, 2013).

While some infrastructure might be free at the point of its use, much is funded through general taxation or specific fees and charges levied to offset the costs of its provision and maintenance. Physical infrastructure is also defined as services that are subject to competition within the EU and the treaties individual member states have signed with the World Trade Organization (WTO). These agreements include access to markets and fair competition rules within and between the states that have signed these treaties. In the EU, it is the European Commission (EC) that assesses the compliance of member states to these treaties (Meunier, 2005) and any instances that are deemed to be in breach will be referred to the European Court of Justice (ECJ). Referrals may also come from any member state against the actions of another state. The EC can also take cases against individual or groups of companies if there is evidence that they might have acted singly or together to distort competition.

Within the EU, some infrastructure is defined as 'services of general economic interest' (SGEI) (CEC, 2012a) that defines the competition frameworks for their provision. The competition for these services is regulated, particularly against the provision of state aid and has a core role in economic competition. The EC can also take action against any public body if it is found that state aid has been provided – that is public resources including land, finance or special terms to support any specific project and distort competition (Franchino and Mainenti, 2013).

Categories of infrastructure

Infrastructure is considered within three main categories – physical, environmental/ green and social/community – in this book. All three categories of infrastructure contribute to economic, social, environmental and territorial objectives. Physical infrastructure includes investment in transport networks, nodes and hubs, energy, waste, telecommunications and water. These are planned over long periods of time and they are provided by the public or private sector. They are defined as SGEI within the EU which means that their provision and pricing to users are regulated by government. These regulations will include the standards for connections, requirements for interoperability and quality of service within and between states. The regulator will also approve the terms of competition and in some cases the price of service.

In each country, there have been historic periods of concentrated investment in particular types of physical infrastructure. This investment may be speculative such as the provision of railways (Martí-Henneberg, 2013) or metro systems (Börjesson et al, 2012; Halliday, 2013a). Infrastructure may be provided in response to changing business demands such as the provision of internet cabling and Wi-Fi and in turn this may influence building design or relocation. Much infrastructure has been provided in response to public health concerns such as the provision of sewers (Halliday, 2013b), clean water supply and public housing (Álvarez et al, 2014).

Environmental and green infrastructure serves a variety of roles in providing benefits for mental and physical health (Tzoulas et al, 2007; Barton et al, 2003) and also capacity to maintain biodiversity (Hostetler et al, 2011), air quality (Pugh et al, 2012), carbon reduction (Wilson and Piper, 2010), manage environmental risks such as flooding (Lennon et al, 2014), and provide food and energy. Green infrastructure can be located within urban and rural environments (Gill et al, 2007) and through the use of footpaths, cycleways and waterways can create corridors between places that also support biodiversity.

Finally, the provision of social infrastructure is important for communities and wider society. This includes provision of facilities for health (Agénor and Moreno-Dodson, 2006), education, and social facilities for specific age groups including the elderly and young (Kunzmann, 2004; Fobker and Grotz, 2006). Social infrastructure also supports leisure and sport, arts and culture, and community facilities (Bigotte and Antunes, 2007; Brown and Barber, 2012) and has an influence on local social capital (Veenstra, 2005; Roskruge et al, 2011). Some social infrastructure is located in nodes or hubs such as city, town or village centres and will include meeting spaces such as cafes, pubs and bars, shops and other services (Graham, 2000; Caragliu et al, 2011). Finally some social infrastructure will be distributed within communities such as places of worship, day care for children and older people, post offices and local community meeting places within a polycentric model (Schmitt et al, 2013).

Role of spatial planning

Planning has a role in identifying the need for the provision of new infrastructure but also has to take into account the capacity and condition of existing infrastructure when considering locations for development. While some developers might prefer the ease of building on greenfield sites, this may not be a sustainable approach where there is brownfield land that is already serviced by infrastructure including energy, water and transport (Dixon et al, 2011). Greenfield sites require services to be installed for the first time. In the UK, these services are funded by all users through payment for supply. In other countries, such as the Netherlands, the government provides a lead on infrastructure in order to capture and direct these contributions (Brueckner, 2000; Alpkokin, 2012; van der Krabben and Jacobs, 2013). Brownfield sites are more sustainable and may result in lower costs for other users and, although they may require site remediation, this can be offset against other infrastructure costs (Mashayekh et al, 2012; Adams and Watkins, 2014).

A central feature in any infrastructure planning is the legacy of the past. Those cities that have played a leading economic role have benefited from this accrued investment in physical networks for energy, transport and other services (Burns et al, 1999; Turok, 2004). Infrastructure has been constructed and maintained over long periods of time and any changes to the distribution of infrastructure will be additional rather than wholesale change. The exceptions to this are those cities that are shrinking (Schilling and Logan, 2008; Martinez-Fernandez et al, 2012) or that have changed their fundamental role. Elsewhere, infrastructure may be improved, supplemented, adapted or filled in. This legacy of infrastructure has a dominant effect on places and the ways they function.

A major consideration on the discussion in infrastructure delivery planning is whether the definitions used have any implications for the process. Planning for infrastructure in different ways may have effects on the outcomes. Planning by sector has inherent challenges (Tett, 2015). If transport is planned by sector, for example, integration between different transport modes including roads, public transport and air will be difficult in practice as investment for each mode will be assessed within its own institutional confines. Separation within transport and other infrastructure types such as energy has been a target for a more integrated approach, and implementing this can be a challenge at the local level. This can be equally problematic at national or state scales, where sectors are the responsibility of a range of government departments with differing policy priorities, as in the UK's national infrastructure policy approach (Rhodes, 2014)

Even where national infrastructure plans have been made, these may be little more than a 'cut and paste' of different sectoral plans without an integrating policy narrative or common criteria binding them together, detracting from the benefits of a more integrated approach (Hansman et al, 2006), This criticism can also be addressed to the UK's sector-led approach to infrastructure planning since 2008 where the state strategy is on the implementation of specific sectoral projects not on the needs of investment, nor the added value that might be generated from taking an integrated approach (HMT, 2014) or any spatial planning. In part, this may be a legacy of market liberalisation, when formerly owned public infrastructure was exposed to competition following the implementation of the GATT agreement in 1976. Since then, the state has been a regulator and its leadership in integrating public policy spatially has been weak. This is confirmed by Barca's (2009) assessment that the UK is the only EU member state not to have a national spatial plan.

The provision of most infrastructure is by hybrid institutions that are a mixture of public and private organisations and funding (Grimsey and Lewis, 2007; Marshall, 2009d). In some sectors this may vary between types of provision, whereas in others the whole provision is set within a regulated structure. The provision of community infrastructure might be entirely from the private sector including shops, leisure centres, cinemas, theatres, cafes and other sports and social clubs. Although community infrastructure may be funded from the private sector, it depends on the (public) spatial planning system in a number of ways. First, the planning system identifies locations where infrastructure providers can be close to other facilities, and supports public transport and accessibility. Second, the planning system regulates nuisance and other amenity issues that may cause problems for local residents and place users. Third, the planning system will also consider the quality of provision so that the market is not saturated with similar providers. Spatial planning also defines town and local centres where these uses are welcomed and are protected (Guy, 2006). Thus the private sector operates with its own capital but also within a predictable and protected market created by the planning system (Adams and Watkins, 2014).

The provision of infrastructure is complex although it has to operate in a coordinated way at the point of delivery. Public policy-making may be considered too complex to understand or comprehend all the dimensions of decision making (Cairney, 2015). Concepts such as 'joined up' or 'holistic' policies create a sense of order even where there is no expectation that such arrangements will work (Kavanagh and Richards, 2001). Conversely, the notion of complexity might be a counsel of despair and suggest that the forces that maintain the status quo are stronger than any that might be engaged in change. While those managing any existing system are likely to have a strong sense of retaining the status quo, unless it is in their perceived interests, unexpected change or external influences can have unintended consequences that force change (Morphet, 2013a). In other cases a step-change in policy may be the only means of achieving integrated change such as the policy to stop smoking in public places (Levy et al, 2004).

Infrastructure and the economy

The relationship between infrastructure and the economy is fundamental (OECD, 2011a). While this might focus on physical infrastructure investment such as energy, telecommunications and transport, softer infrastructure including cafes, shops, consumer and public services are all important features of efficient and effective workplaces and innovation hubs (WEF, 2014). Without these, employees may be less attracted to particular organisations or locations. The role of social facilities has been seen to be a major benefit in specific areas where it has encouraged spatial agglomerations as in San Francisco and Cambridge (Athreye, 2000) or online games development in Dundee (Clarke and Beaney, 1993).

The relationship between infrastructure capacity and investment and the economy has become a focus of economic analysis to underpin longer-term growth (OECD, 2011a). This has included widening investment models incorporating hybrid institutional governance frameworks to provide funding (Hare, 2013). However, infrastructure provision is not only concerned with different modes of transport, for example, but how they link and serve each other. There is an increased emphasis on hubs, gateways and inland ports to supplement existing provision (Rodrigue et al, 2013) so that over time, investment will reinforce existing infrastructure provision and supplement it through filling in some of gaps between existing networks. This might point to new investment in hubs including multimodal rather than single mode access. The accompanying economic development around the hubs may have its own growth potential with investors and governments wanting to promote clusters of economic activity (Centre for Cities, 2014). This approach also reinforces the role of spatial and territorial characteristics in infrastructure investment and the potential negative outcomes where strategic access is poor (Wilcox, 2014).

Much of the economic geography since Christaller has depended on central place theory (Getis and Getis, 2008; Mulligan et al, 2012), with those working in the centre living in the periphery or in more suburbanised locations. Central place theory is supported by public infrastructure investment in transport, energy and water. These theories have been reinforced by investment patterns and property markets (Healey, 2004) and the application of sustainability principles, particularly since the UN Earth Summit in 1992. In Italy, the focus has turned to what is termed the 'inner city', that area within a one-hour travel to work area but not the central area. In the UK this might be described as the suburban periphery or the FEA or subregion.

However, a changing public sensibility towards more sustainable living has encouraged a second trend of resettling in city centres, reducing journeys to work and increasing personalised healthy travel modes such as walking and cycling (Pucher et al, 2010). These trends are associated with creative and high-tech industries and emerging differences in household structures. As income levels in dual-career families equalise, journey to work reduces for both partners (Pickup, 1978). Greater distance from work is characterised by a larger disparity in income between the two partners (Wheatley, 2011). Couples may prefer to minimise their travelling time, leading to greater revival of inner city housing, services and jobs (Karsten, 2003; Hjorthol and Vågane, 2014). This has played a significant role in gentrification in cities in many countries (Rérat and Lees, 2011; Rérat, 2012; Skaburskis, 2012; Goodsell, 2013; Boterman and Karsten, 2014).

There have also been other spatial patterns emerging. Increased car-dependency was a core determinant of peripheral business parks and retail malls (Herbert and Thomas, 2013). This trend can be defined as 'edge city' (Garreau, 2011) and encouraged an enclosed and defined relationship between workplace and home dependent on a combination of personal rather than public transport (Lang and LeFurgy, 2003). The development of these more distributed development patterns were neo-liberal government policy preferences in the UK in the period from the 1980s (Thornley, 1991), and earlier in the United States.

In the UK, the proliferation of edge and out of town development, reliant on cars for access to housing, has undermined existing settlements. This has placed severe pressure on town centres and their economic viability (Erkip et al, 2013; Rae, 2013). Peripheral locations are less efficient and economic to serve by public transport. Now as employers become more aware of their environmental responsibilities and the transport costs to and from their businesses this has made edge of town locations less attractive. Changes in lifestyle now mean that out of town retailers, particularly food megastores, are becoming less used by shoppers and may be redeveloped (Kohijoki, 2011; Armstrong, 2015). In the US, shopping malls that are no longer viable are being used for other purposes including university and further education campuses (Stabiner, 2011).

The return to more urban and concentrated living and working locations has been supported by the new economic geography. Krugman (1991) found that while most national trade policies in the West were focused on growth through external trade between nations, as much growth was generated from trade within regions. Policy makers and later Krugman (2004, 2011) developed initiatives to support this internal growth through the designation of FEAs that could be defined by journey to work areas used in transport models. FEAs can be identified through a defined travel time, usually on public transport of 50 minutes to an hour between home and work. The use of this theory to support policy has returned to some of Christaller's central place theories and their associated policies such as investment in public transport and reinforcement of its use through behaviour change or 'nudge' approaches (Thaler and Sunstein, 2009).

The application of FEA theory and associated policy is now being implemented in OECD countries including the US, Australia and the EU (Gurria, 2014). Further research has found that alignment between the boundary of the FEA and its governance has produced more GDP for the area and the state (OECD, 2014). Existing administrative boundaries are based on historic factors or natural features such as rivers or land ownership. The alignment of administrative boundaries with FEAs is now emerging as a proliferating model of governance in these countries (Gurria, 2014). In England this is through the establishment of combined authorities (CAs) as governance institutions to manage the planning and provision of infrastructure for the FEAs.

An essential feature of working within this new economic geography that ties governance with economic space is also an emphasis on integration within and between organisations, institutions and places. In particular there is an emphasis on closer working between democratic bodies at different spatial scales through MLG policies. This is particularly prevalent within the EU and emerging as critical policy shaping approaches in other countries. In federal states including Canada (Conteh, 2013) and Australia (Bishop, 2014) there are new debates about the respective responsibilities and infrastructure funding between different governance scales with new institutional arrangements and plans to develop these.

A further element is the OECD push towards more compact cities (2012) where urban areas are growing rapidly. This is the case in some EU cities, and while the definition of 'compact' varies between locations, the impact of this approach on economic growth has been found in different city locations (Westerink et al, 2012; Salvati, 2013). In Korea, the OECD (2014a) recommended spatial development and infrastructure policies to assist in the growth of urbanisation within the country and a means of conserving resources and maximising economic growth. In particular there was a focus on transport oriented development (TOD) is a common approach in OECD recommendations for spatial policy.

There are other definitions of FEAs. Brenner for example uses the term 'new state spaces' (2004) and describes these FEAs as being manufactured by the state as a means to destabilise existing governance patterns through fuzzy governance systems (de Roo and Porter, 2009; Haughton et al, 2010). These critics argue that the introduction of fuzzy governance means that it is less accountable and makes it easier for the state to implement its policies through the reduction of local democratic processes. Pemberton and Morphet (2014) argue that this 'fuzziness' is, rather, a process of territorial transition that will result in new democratic structures although it is clear that the influence of central government action within the process of devolving policy decisions and funding remains a concern.

The fashion for more urban living – with edge being replaced by 'edgy' – has started to change other behaviours. People living in cities may use car clubs or bicycle schemes and public transport rather than owning their own cars, or use them less. In Paris the city government is implementing a car-free area in the centre when pollution levels are high whereas in Italy in some towns, cars are only allowed on specific days (Masiol et al, 2014). Public investment in transport infrastructure together with incentives to switch modes or to promote car pooling through specific road lanes for cars with more than two passengers have had a strong influence on other behaviours. Convenience stores and coffee shops by stations have taken the place of the pub. People are shopping by the day rather than weekly and some out of town stores are now underperforming or being abandoned before being opened.

Can housing be defined as infrastructure?

While most infrastructure provision can be understood and defined relatively easily, the provision of housing as infrastructure remains a contested debate within public policy. However, it is clear from the research of Adams and Watkins (2014) that planning for housing is an essential component of the infrastructure delivery planning system and its relationship with investment is central and critical (Dolphin and Griffith, 2011; Cox, 2014). Policy interventions in the provision of housing have been economic, social and environmental and these are each considered in turn:

Housing as economic infrastructure

The case for housing as a core component of economic infrastructure has been made on the basis of its contribution to supporting labour supply and mobility as well as its role as an important economic sector in its own right (Regeneris Consulting and Oxford Economics, 2010). The provision of housing has also been identified as a central component in place competitiveness and in the attraction of foreign direct investment (FDI) within localities (Phelps and Fuller, 2000). While many job moves do not require a change in housing location, the opportunities to improve employment may be reduced by relative immobility associated with tenure and low pay (OECD, 2011a). Secure social housing, for example, may not be willingly exchanged for more insecure tenure despite the prospect of a better-paid job elsewhere. While the notion of moving to find employment may be possible, other factors such as the working patterns of partners, family or other childcare may mitigate against labour mobility. Housing infrastructure is as stratified in its type and the role of specific elements of provision as other types of infrastructure (Kushner, 2010; Clarke et al, 2014). As economies have grown, the locations for industries and services have attracted an incoming migrant workforce that has required housing near to these workplaces.

The development of housing has became a major economic indicator in the UK as starts, completions and bricks used are reported regularly for government and in the financial press (Cox, 2014). Both the EU, through the growth and stability pact (CEC, 2010), and the OECD (André, 2011) have pressured the UK to provide more infrastructure investment. The role of planning in identifying the requirements for housing supply in relation to the economy of an area has been a central feature of the planning process. However, the role of housing in creating secure pension investment following the failure of private pension schemes, as a means of transmitting secure intergenerational wealth and generating income through creating 'buy to let' portfolios have all acted in different ways on the housing market (Barker, 2014).

The return of public housing providers to support the economic role of housing has emerged through the widening of local authority powers for development in the 2011 Localism Act, the application of International Financial Reporting Standards (IFRS) from 2014 and a re-presentation of policy through a government-backed review (Lyons, 2007, 2011). In other countries, such as Ireland, the role of housing in EU macroeconomic policy is a critical element of economic and financial stability and the operational environment for the economy (Agnello and Schuknecht, 2011; Van der Heijden et al, 2011). It is also a significant in consideration of economic growth and recovery policies. The availability of housing, and its effects on labour mobility and economic recovery have become a central issue in future planning approaches for the state (OECD, 2011a; Hughes, 2014).

Housing as social infrastructure

The most active period of social housing supply in the UK, particularly by local authorities, was in the period 1945-85 when post-war reconstruction was a major focus of social policy. In some cases this united with the role of housing as economic infrastructure through the new towns programme, but much of the new social housing replaced Victorian and Edwardian dwellings identified as being unfit. Houses built for a more middle-class population that had now left areas or at too low a density to be regarded as an efficient use of land and resources, was replaced with social housing. This became the major and mainstream sector providing housing for working-class people and was seen to be at the top of the housing market for those in privately rented furnished or unfurnished accommodation. Social housing provided security of tenure and in many places community facilities.

While the quality of the space within the dwelling was always high, unlike other countries such as Germany, less attention was paid to the maintenance of the developments and the estates outside the dwelling. Most social housing had resident caretakers but pressure on public sector funding removed many of these to be replaced by a non-resident contracted service and later the mix in social housing was changed through the Thatcherite Right to Buy policies where social housing units were lost to the social housing sector and entered the private sector market.

Although some attempts to provide additional stock and meet social housing needs has been provided by housing associations and the housing movement, these organisations have been required to diversify to provide housing across all sectors, and public funding to provide social housing has been reduced. A renewal of Right to Buy incentives in 2014 has also served to reduce supply in this sector although there has been no accompanying evidence that the need for social housing has changed in character and has possibly been increased through the pressures of the economic downturn and economic migration increasing the UK birth rate. The role of social housing as part of the overall provision has also been identified as a policy area that needs urgent public sector investment (Schmuecker, 2011) as part of general public policy and that of specific regions including those that are economically lagging (Dayson et al, 2013). Housing also has an effect on people's lives including that of children (Harker, 2007; Feinstein et al, 2008), older people and those who fall into homelessness.

Housing as infrastructure – a discussion of its institutional role

Within the UK spatial planning system, housing is primarily considered as local infrastructure to support community needs based on demographic projections. The role of housing as economic infrastructure has been reasserted particularly at the subregional scale or as part of the operation of FEAs, where there hitherto had been a separation of the roles of housing and the economy in the planning system. Cox (2014) argues that policies for equity and growth in less prosperous areas also need to be served by these combined policies as well as those that are growing. What is also of interest in Cox's argument is a stronger role to be played by the planning process in managing land supply for economic and housing uses together rather than at different spatial scales.

Including housing as part of national infrastructure suggests that different approaches to its provision and funding may be required. The current approach, primarily reliant on private sector funding within a system of need defined by local authorities and regulated by the planning system, may not be adequate. In other types of infrastructure the funding of supply is hybrid but within a controlled system. Competition is managed within quasi rather than free markets. The provision of housing is outside this framework. Land can be optioned without commitment or certainty and through the winning of specific consents for housing on specific sites.

The market for housing, where activity is within the spatial planning system and profit levels managed by an independent regulator, would bring the housing sector into the same regime as other SGEI. This would allow new entrants to the provision of housing infrastructure and also secure public providers. It is unlikely that private sector providers could or would provide enough housing to meet national requirements, 'For UK house-builders, limited production makes sense both as an economic calculation and as a business strategy – the growth in the underlying cost of land makes house-building less profitable, while the control of supply and limited expansion of production helps maintain prices and profit margins' (Dolphin and Griffith, 2011, p 41).

Griffith and Jeffreys (2013) argue that a radical change in the policy approach and mix is required although many of the policies suggested are those that have been used before and had been discarded or fallen from use. However, the underlying message is that housing infrastructure needs further public investment and a wider, more interventionist policy approach.

The EU (Monti, 2010; CEC, 2012c) regards the provision of housing in the same economic terms as the OECD (2011a, 2011b) and the UK government has agreed to address its housing market as an impediment to economic growth by 2020. So can central government define housing as infrastructure without being directly involved in its provision through formal and procedural decision-making processes? Housing was initially excluded for consideration as a major infrastructure as defined by the UK national infrastructure regime created in 2008. Under this system, national infrastructure applications are separated from the local planning system. Parliament approves policy and the consideration of specific infrastructure proposals is undertaken by the Planning Inspectorate. The planning approach is not concerned with the principle of the location of the development but the details of the site and the development considerations. Excluding housing from infrastructure definitions has not been advanced as government policy although calls to change this approach have been growing (Cox, 2014) based on economic rather than social arguments. The government announced its intention to include housing in the national infrastructure planning regime following the general election in 2015 and this may be included in the work of the Infrastructure Planning Commission also launched in 2015.

Economists argue that housing is part of infrastructure provision, particularly when there is a shortage within an area that is undertaking economic expansion; there are contrasting views that housing is a local social rather than an economic good. While housing is a social good, the provision of an adequate supply of housing is part of economic infrastructure but related to appropriate governance scales. This tension between national, subregional and local scales has existed within UK planning since the 1930s (Barlow Report, 1940) and remains one that policy makers and politicians have found difficult to resolve.

Infrastructure, social access and equity

One of core concerns in the provision of infrastructure is social, physical and economic access to it. As Lewis (2014) has shown, having split-second advantages over pricing can mean a high economic return. While cities and major hubs seek to improve their transport provision as part of their economic policy, access to services for people who live within urban and rural areas is vital. A study by the Centre for Cities (Clayton, 2011) found that access to public transport reduced the opportunities that poorer people had to obtain work. They may also have longer journeys to hospitals and other services. Other studies such as those for obesity and public health have found that poor access to shops selling fresh food and a concentration of hot food takeaways in poorer areas or near school gates can encourage obesity (GLA, 2012; PHE, 2014). Access to sports and social facilities, safe walking and open spaces can all make a different to the health of the community (PHE, 2013). Access is at the core of social equity and spatial planning has the responsibility to address this through defining service access standards (DCLG, 2012) and implementing them through its role in infrastructure delivery planning.

Approaching infrastructure delivery planning

The approach taken in this book is to consider infrastructure delivery planning at different spatial scales. The focus on different infrastructure types becomes apparent at all scales but all infrastructure types are of some policy interest at each level. The use of scales to structure the book reflects a shift from the predominance of infrastructure sectors over the last 30 years. Different types of infrastructure have their own provenance and each has been through its own processes of change in institutional structure, funding and management.

Infrastructure definitions

This book uses the major categorisation of physical, environmental and social infrastructure. These definitions are drawn from those prepared by the author for local infrastructure delivery planning (PAS, 2009; Morphet, 2011a) and their subsequent use in practice and are shown in Tables 1.1, 1.2 and 1.3.

Table 1.1: Infrastructure categories: physical infrastructure

Physical	Subcategories	Indicative lead spatial scales
Transport	Road	National Local
	Rail	National
	Bus	Local
	Taxis	Local
	Airports	National FEA
	Port/harbours	National FEA
	Cycle and pedestrian facilities	Local
	Car parking	Local
	Fuel connectors	Local
	Canals	National FEA Local
Energy	Centralised power generation	National
	Transmission and distribution systems for gas and electricity	EU National
	Biomass processing	Local
	District heating and cooling	Local
	Wind power	National Local
Water and drainage	Water supply	National Local
	Waste water	National Local
	Drainage	Local
	Flood defences	National Local
Waste	Collection Disposal	Local Local
Itc	Broadband and wireless Public phones	National
Public realm	Footways Street furniture	Local
Historic legacy	Listed buildings	National Local

Table 1.2: Infrastructure categories: green infrastructure

Green infrastructure	Subcategories	Indicative lead spatial scales
Open space		Local
	Children's play areas	Local
	Sports pitches and courts	Local
	Country parks	Local
	Green public realm	Local
	National parks and other area management	National
Rivers	River corridors	FEA
Coast	Littoral	National Local
Historic landscapes	Historic sites	National Local

Table 1.3: Infrastructure categories: social and community infrastructure

Social and community	Subcategory	Indicative spatial scale
Affordable housing	100% affordable Intermediate	Local
Education	Nursery and preschool	Local
	Primary	Local
	Secondary	Local
	Further education	FEA
	Higher education	National FEA
Health	Hospitals	National FEA
	Health centres/GP surgeries	Local
	Public health and prevention	Local
Gypsies and travellers	Sites and facilities	Local
Post offices	Main post offices Sub post offices Sorting offices Parcels	National Local
Community services	Libraries	Local
	Community centres	Local
	Youth	Local
	Social services/over 50s/support	Local
	Police	FEA
	Fire	FEA
	Ambulance	FEA
	Cemeteries and crematoria	Local

Social and community	Subcategory	Indicative spatial scale
	Courts	National
	Prisons	National
	Places of worship	National Local
Culture	Museums/galleries	National FEA Local
	Theatres	FEA Local
	Cinemas	Local
Leisure	Sports centres	Local
	Swimming pools	Local
	Festivals and town centre programmes	Local
	Markets	Local

Conclusions

The role of infrastructure in society is significant and spatial planning has a core role in its use, management and provision. This chapter has demonstrated the importance of infrastructure for economic, environmental and social reasons but also reinforced the role of infrastructure in the service of wider societal objectives. Infrastructure has no specific purpose of its own although specific infrastructure projects and sectors can sometimes narrow and dominate this wider perspective. Spatial planning's role is to deliver these wider objectives in an integrated and sustainable way.

TWO

Delivering infrastructure

Introduction

Infrastructure delivery planning can be considered by sector, funding, location or delivery method. While these are all important components of infrastructure delivery planning, the approach that is advocated here as being most effective is a focus on place. Without this, infrastructure delivery planning can be producer-driven and disconnected from society's needs. Consideration of infrastructure delivery planning can also be undertaken at varying spatial scales appropriate for different types of infrastructure. Areas have their own requirements for infrastructure and this investment impacts on places influencing the quality of life for residents and business.

A major challenge for infrastructure delivery planning is the integration of producer and user interests to create added value. This can be achieved through a spatial vision incorporating standards of access, quality of service and efficiency in delivery. Different providers of infrastructure are not required to work together, even as part of regulatory and consent regimes. Spatial planning's role is to bring together the strategy, policy, programmes and projects in ways that are beneficial for the areas and its population. This does not suggest that spatial planning has specific delivery roles or powers over all infrastructure delivery decisions. However, spatial planning has a role in understanding the combined effects of existing and planned infrastructure that can be of significant benefit to investors and localities. Much of what spatial planning can achieve will be through its role in advocacy, agenda setting and framing investment decisions.

Role of spatial planning

Spatial planning is concerned with both the development of plans and programmes and their delivery. Morphet (2011a) discusses the role and provenance of spatial planning as a dominant mode in practice, arguing that planning, from its inception, was always concerned with delivering change as well as managing it. While this has been a consistent practice within mainland Europe, with a particular focus on state-led delivery, this approach was disrupted in the UK during the Thatcher period, particularly between 1979 and 1986, when a more laissez-faire market-driven approach was adopted. This was accompanied by a reduction in public sector-led development both by the state, that did not invest in infrastructure, and local authorities, who no longer contributed a significant share of housing development each year. This period was also characterised by the application of commitments to open the public sector to competition as agreed by the UK, in common with many other countries, with the GATT in 1976 (that later became the WTO in 1995) (Morphet, 2013a). In some cases, the shift in the delivery of public services was accompanied by the introduction of state regulators that represented the national interests in setting service objectives and the competitive framework for utilities. This incorporated incentives for changes within the supply market including pricing, provision of new facilities, maintenance and reducing consumption such as in energy and water metering. The local authorities' role in the supply of housing was not replaced and was further drained by Right to Buy policies despite the government being recommended to do so by their own adviser (Barker, 2004).

In 1991, the laissez-faire approach to planning was reformed to be replaced by a plan-led system. This was intended to provide investment certainty to the market and was to be exercised through the adoption of a national coverage of local plans across the UK. However, this intention was disrupted by three major factors. The first was that as local authorities had become acculturated to a defensive mode in their planning practice, with many decisions being made through the planning appeal system, they did not have the will or capacity to prepare plans that were positive in their style. They further assumed that future actions from the development industry would not be influenced by positive planning and, despite new locations being identified in plans, the industry would seek to extend these through the planning application system. This view was exacerbated in the short term by an economic downturn in the early 1990s when local authorities had no funding for staff to prepare these plans.

Second, the adoption of the Maastricht Treaty, negotiated and led by the UK prime minister John Major, led to a change in the ways in which the economic and social cohesion policies of the EU were to be delivered. The application of regional policies and selective assistance, introduced when the UK joined the EU in 1973, could no longer be sustained in its existing form as EU membership was expanded to the east. Further, while there were political and economic benefits of enlargement there were also deficiencies in infrastructure and communications to be addressed. While parts of the EU may have had skill deficits, their infrastructure links, within and between countries, had been improving. In the accession states, skills were better but communication was very poor, particularly with western Europe.

This refocusing on the larger geography of the EU space meant the creation of an EU-wide plan and considering ways in which the new member states could be integrated with the existing. This led to the establishment of the European Spatial Development Perspective (ESDP) (CEC, 1999) and mega regional strategies *Europe 2000* (CEC, 1991b) and *Europe 2000+* (CEC, 1994) with their focus on macro-regions and cross-border working. The Trans-European Networks (TEN) were also adopted in 1996. This approach was also coupled with the application of greater subsidiarity as agreed in the Maastricht Treaty.

This widening and deepening of spatial policy and responsibilities had twin effects in the UK. First, it supported the move to greater devolution in Scotland

and Wales and provided a basis for the potential for a new peace agreement in Northern Ireland. However, this was less welcome in England where there was little appetite for devolution to local authorities. The creation of Government Offices of the Regions with a strategic planning role enabled the government to suggest more devolved approaches in England while in effect controlling much of the decision making. Regional planning guidance was prepared by government offices and even when this was transposed into Regional Spatial Strategies there was still central government dominance in their preparation and adoption. These regional plans provided the framework for local authorities and their plans (Glasson and Marshall, 2007).

Third, when the UK left the exchange rate mechanism (ERM) on Black Wednesday in 1992 this was initially considered as a temporary move. The UK agreed conditions to rejoin the ERM, and later the euro, based on the achievement of specific convergence conditions which included the structure of the economy. While the UK had made progress towards these by 1997, the housing market was identified as being a continuing concern and the reason identified for not joining the eurozone. The continuing challenge of the functioning of the housing market in the UK has remained a macroeconomic concern for the UK, with the OECD, IMF and EU all identifying this as a matter for action. The pressure to act on housing has primarily been on the role of planning to achieve greater supply without the additional funding for public sector building or interventions in the management of the market and demand side initiatives by successive governments. In practice this has meant a growing pressure on housing delivery targets and numbers through the planning system. The regional planning system became imbalanced in its focus on housing numbers. The provision of housing grew as a heightened political issue and there were some perceived benefits in having a top-down system that local politicians could blame. However it also meant that there was little consideration of the rest of the regional strategy and the investment required for infrastructure. This was still undertaken by separate government departments each with their own priorities and programmes.

Spatial planning is now an accepted part of the overarching economic narrative of place that has become a policy focus of international economic organisations particularly the OECD (OECD, 2015) and translated into reform programmes through its members in Europe (Salet et al, 2003). Within the EU, this approach has been combined with policies that support subsidiarity and substate governance that have been increasingly important since 1992 (Morphet, 2013a). The underlying theory rests on the role of FEAs (functional economic areas) and city subregions as central drivers of economic growth and GDP in national economies. This is found to be further enhanced when the boundaries of administrative and economic areas are co-terminus (Ahrend et al, 2014).

The implementation of these changes has often been through state-led 'nudged' approaches (Thaler and Sunstein, 2009) that have incentivised local authorities and other stakeholder organisations into working together in new FEA or city groupings without reforming the underlying formal systems. New institutions are brought about through alliances and shared or combined formations. These processes of institutional re-formation have been recognised (Albrechts et al, 2003) but not fully understood by those being incentivised to shift their governance constructions and have frequently been described as informal (Mäntysalo et al, 2015) or fuzzy (de Roo and Porter, 2009). Spatial planning has also frequently been associated with attributes that have focused on softer forms of governance and criticised as a neo-liberal agent in weakening democratic state institutions (Haughton et al, 2010) without recognising the development of new democratic bodies and spatial planning's role of integration, implementation through MLG (multilevel governance). Since 1992, spatial planning has become embedded within the planning systems of EU member states (Waterhout, 2008; Dühr et al, 2010; Faludi, 2010) and increasingly its focus has been on the relationship between places, strategy and delivery. This spatial planning turn is central to wider changes in the governance and implementation of infrastructure. While the introduction of competition into the public services agreed through the GATT Treaty in 1976 has focused on the delivery of infrastructure within a competitive market, the role of the government as client has been developed in different ways.

Introduction of spatial planning in the UK

The introduction of spatial planning in 2004 was the first attempt to move beyond the silo practices (Tett, 2015) of government departments and to enable local authorities to consider the ways in which multiple infrastructure investment was coordinated in their localities. This spatial planning turn was marked in the UK through a series of planning system revisions in each of the four nation states that commenced in Scotland in 2003 and was then adopted in England and Wales in 2004 and in Northern Ireland in 2015. During this period there have been other changes to the planning system in operation including the introduction of the National Planning Policy Framework (NPPF) (2012) in England and strategic planning in Scotland (2006) but the fundamental principles of spatial planning have remained. This shift to spatial planning, with its focus on delivery, has led to the introduction of infrastructure delivery planning at all spatial scales across the UK (Morphet, 2011c; Clifford and Morphet, 2015). These new practices have been introduced in different ways and have not been framed as a consistent policy by any of the national governments responsible for planning. Infrastructure delivery planning has now been incorporated as a core component of spatial planning.

In the UK the government has, until recently, regarded its client role through its regulatory functions and dealt with this at arm's length. However, there has been an increased focus on the UK's poor performance in infrastructure delivery compared with other nations as it lies 27th in the WEF (World Economic Forum) league table (Rhodes, 2014; Schwab, 2014). This relatively poor performance is in marked comparison with its position as the fifth largest international economy. This poor performance has brought the UK government back into a stronger and more direct client role as evidenced by new national infrastructure legislation in 2008, establishing a purpose-built organisation in Infrastructure UK and publishing the UK infrastructure plan (HMT, 2014). This has marked a strong re-engagement by the state in the planning and delivery of infrastructure (Helm, 2015).

Another pressure on the UK government has been the concern for energy security. This is related to the age and poor environmental performance of the UK's power stations and increased threats of loss of supply to other EU member states from geopolitical instability. The EU is addressing this through the establishment of an EU Energy Union as a major priority for the period to 2020 (CEC, 2015a). The UK's response is for government to exercise a stronger client role and place less reliance on the market.

The reform of regulatory processes in the UK has not seen a return to the pre-competition era, with state control of infrastructure. Rather there is a range of reforms that fit this government-led role into the new legal framework created by the implementation of the agreed EU principle of subsidiarity within the UK state (CEC, 2007c; Morphet, 2013a). Spatial planning is one of the means of delivering these changes through separation of responsibilities for infrastructure at different spatial scales and the reform of existing institutions to meet these requirements. In the UK, the Highways Agency had responsibilities for roads at all scales until 2015. The Agency has been restructured to have responsibility only for national level roads with the other functions being devolved. The same is the case for the organisation concerned with regeneration, the Homes and Communities Agency, that is responsible for managing and developing the state owned land. This has reinforced its national over local role.

Finally there has been a reinforcement of infrastructure delivery planning at all spatial scales – national, subregional, local and neighbourhood. The national infrastructure planning system was been introduced in 2008, the subregional approach was included in the Strategic Economic Plans (SEPs) prepared by LEPs (Local Enterprise Partnerships) in 2013, local plans from 2004 (Morphet, 2011a; Holt and Baker, 2014) and neighbourhood plans from 2011. While local and neighbourhood plans have to be in alignment, the national infrastructure plan is sectoral rather than spatial and the SEPs are not prepared within a democratic process. Nevertheless they need to be considered together as they all impact on the locations where the projects are to be delivered.

Effective practice in infrastructure delivery planning

Infrastructure delivery planning is complex and the challenges of integration including delivering objectives, programming, funding and creating added value across spatial scales are considerable. The approach set out here is based on business planning methods adapted for spatial planning. It is consistent with the approach included within the EU Regulation on Cohesion (CEC, 2013b) that identifies the roles of strategic Integrated Territorial Investment (ITI) plans and Community Led Local Development (CLLD) approaches within these. It is also consistent with approaches used across local authorities in England to prepare their spatial plans from 2004 onwards (Morphet, 2011a, 2011b, 2013b), Scotland (2006), Wales (2004, 2015) and Northern Ireland (2015).

Vision

Spatial plans represent the vision for an area agreed by democratically accountable leaders. This vision may be set out in a community strategy or plan for the area that encompasses a range of objectives or targets for a defined period of 10–30 years. These strategies are prepared following wide consultation and agreement on the vision. Spatial plans are one means of delivering this vision. Where spatial plans are prepared in isolation or in competition with other strategies they will have difficulties in achieving acceptance; commitment to resource commitment and delivery may be reduced and confused while the spatial plan may be more of an impediment than part of the delivery of this vision.

The vision may reflect aspirations for the area, based on evidence of expected change or set to achieve wider objectives such as climate change (Krawczyk and Ratcliffe, 2005; Zonneveld and Waterhout, 2005). Visions are generated using community and stakeholder involvement to set priorities (Morphet et al, 2007; Sheppard et al, 2011) and are framed by social, economic and environmental objectives. As part of the spatial plan, infrastructure delivery planning is a means of realising this vision through identifying and supporting ways that it can be implemented.

All infrastructure delivery plans will depend on the vision for direction, priorities and focus. The vision also provides a means of assessing proposals individually and together. It creates a framework for organisations to locate their projects and proposals by helping them to identify likely benefits and challenges. Without a vision, there are risks that infrastructure investment may be duplicated, delayed or diverted. There may be a variety of ways that the vision can be implemented and these will be considered and mediated through the spatial planning process.

Policy and legislative context

All visions and their strategies are framed by a policy and legislative context set by governments. Policies and legislation for all types of infrastructure including transport, water, waste, energy, telecommunication and green infrastructure will be as agreed within the EU for all member states, including the UK. In some cases, the EU will also identify specific investment projects including through the programmes for Trans-European Networks for transport (TEN-T) and energy (TEN-E). The EU legal and policy framework identifies the way that programmes and projects are selected including the use of environmental assessment, Sustainable Urban Mobility Plans (SUMPs) (CEC 2013g; www.eltis. org) and cohesion. Member states agree these policies and adopt the legislation together. This is also supplemented by specific legal rulings such as those on state aid that will then influence the application of specific national policies such as that for Community Infrastructure Levy (CIL).[1]

While the EU develops policy within a continuous flow, the UK uses an episodic style with new initiatives appearing following a general election or cabinet reshuffle. Much of UK policy and legislation is the delivery of EU agreed policies within a domestic political narrative (Morphet, 2013a). This means that engaging with wider EU policy making can be helpful in anticipating UK initiatives when formulating spatial plan policies and programmes. The range of policy areas that the UK has pooled within the EU is shown in Box 2.1.[2]

Box 2.1: UK–EU pooled policy areas

- economy
- trade
- employment/skills
- youth
- energy
- water
- air
- habitats
- ICT
- rural/agriculture
- public health
- culture/heritage
- regeneration
- waste
- transport – all modes and scales
- ports.

Governance

All visions and their strategies will be set by those responsible for an area. These are primarily directly elected politicians and their paid officials responsible for the government of the locality but may also be extended to include stakeholder organisations such as business, universities and charities and community representatives that comprise the wider governance of the area. The vision for any locality will be expressed through its policy documents, plans and strategies but also in the practical delivery of priorities and projects. An important consideration will be the way that project funding and human resources are used to support specific programmes and their delivery, and the way that some projects are privileged over others. It is through the leadership of place that these priorities can be expressed and managed (Lyons, 2007). Without these there are dangers of fragmentation (Merk, 2014) and cross-border competition (Monti, 2010).

Within all areas, there needs to be a governance framework for the infrastructure delivery planning programme and implementation. This is most likely to be effective if it is led by the owners of the vision and strategy and not set up separately, detached from these processes (Mills and Keast, 2009). The infrastructure delivery process represents the way that any locality is going to manage and develop the investment in its area. Some local authorities establish a specific infrastructure delivery group, consisting of all infrastructure providers and, in some cases, stakeholders. This group can provide shared information on committed and expected projects, support integrated working and align delivery programmes. If there is a separation between those setting the vision and responsible for its delivery and the infrastructure delivery group then this may be problematic and potentially divisive.

Infrastructure delivery planning groups can operate at all scales. In the UK, national infrastructure is led by Infrastructure UK and the nations each have their own strategies and delivery mechanisms. The development of subregions and FEAs means that there is now an active approach to engagement at this scale (Centre for Cities, 2015). Within urban subregions, the focus may be on physical infrastructure compared with environmental infrastructure in rural areas. Local authorities will encompass green and physical infrastructure and may have more focus on social infrastructure (DCN, 2012). This will be highlighted at the neighbourhood or parish level.

Different spatial scales need to work together in an integrated way. Communities and business do not distinguish between administrative boundaries and expect public bodies to work together to support them. Governance institutions at each scale have to be engaged with the others as all infrastructure provision and projects will potentially be serving wider areas (Stead and Meijers, 2009; Woltjer et al, 2015). This cross-boundary approach will be adopted by providers, albeit for their own infrastructure interests. Without understanding how providers operate across scales and engaging them in debates about the local position on provision and impact of future projects the result is likely to be fragmentation (Haughton et al, 2010).

When establishing an infrastructure group, all existing infrastructure providers will need to be identified. This may be through existing contact and working arrangements or in discussion with other departments in the local authority. There may also be some value at looking at other local authority infrastructure delivery plans or working group arrangements in order to identify potential providers that might otherwise be overlooked. The list of infrastructure providers may also depend on the range of services and provision in the area. If there is a university, for example, these can be considered as major providers of social and community infrastructure. However if there is no such provision, the local authority may still need to engage with nearby universities to consider whether any specific provision or outreach services need to be provided.

Once the infrastructure providers have been identified, the next step is to understand their capital investment priorities and decision-making procedures.

It is also necessary to identify the projects in their capital programmes. This will be an important list and in most local authority areas, is greater than initially anticipated. Even where there may be no facilities being planned, investment in maintenance and repair of existing facilities may also be associated with their remodelling and changing methods of service delivery. In some cases, projects may run over several years and there will be requirements for interim service delivery arrangements that may involve temporary buildings or traffic rerouting.

As individual infrastructure projects are identified, they can be included within a single schedule. This schedule can be organised in different ways to suit local preferences. Some local authorities have organised projects by type of infrastructure − in broad categories such as green infrastructure or by specific types like roads. Other local authorities have organised their schedules by localities so that it is possible to identify which projects are being delivered where and how they might fit together on the ground. In some cases, local authorities have grouped their projects by delivery date so that the programme can be considered each year. If these infrastructure schedules are kept within XML then they can be reconfigured using different categories.

Existing infrastructure may already be identified within geographical information systems (GIS) with associated informational and data layers. This allows interactive use by all interests − the community, institutions and organisations (Carsjens and Ligtenberg, 2007; McCall and Dunn, 2012). Establishing an infrastructure base line position is important in understanding existing provision and capacity for localities. This can be used as a basis for planning infrastructure and other investment (Williams, 2014). The geographical representation of infrastructure also helps when applying access criteria for different services and their current distribution. It may also assist in identifying where sustainable efficiencies can be created by examining and assessing the existing distribution of facilities and their potential clustering. The GIS will also assist in identifying all similar types of infrastructure such as sports facilities, swimming pools and community meetings places regardless of their ownership and management regimes.

This GIS representation will also assist in the consideration of any proposed schemes or the effect of applying different access standards. It will help to identify whether there is likely to be capacity when used with other evidence. It will also help to demonstrate the effect of demographic change or the introduction of new facilities into specific areas. By applying a risk assessment overlay to this process, it will also be possible to identify when infrastructure is likely to need maintenance or to be replaced. A similar risk assessment, using a red/amber/green designation, can help to identify facilities that will need some investment and show this visually. Such an approach can also identify areas likely to be undergoing the greatest demographic change − for example where age profiling existing households suggests that larger number of children may be expected in the future from the housing stock base as older households move to smaller accommodation.

In addition to the vision and policy framework, these GIS approaches can support decision making by democratic leaders and the communities that they serve. They can be a focus of discussion about potential change in an informed way and may serve to challenge institutional hoarding of infrastructure within communities under pressure for specific facilities. They also help to support the business case for new facilities and can create a platform for advocacy and investment prioritisation.

Much of this approach will also be informed by the engagement with infrastructure providers (Holt and Baker, 2014). While their formal plans for change and investment will indicate their programme, more informal discussions or workshops of multiple infrastructure providers may reveal advanced thinking on forthcoming capacity or supply challenges. This can build on the tacit knowledge used by all infrastructure delivery providers. These workshops may be held regularly if much change is envisaged. At a minimum, an annual event, where updates on programmes and more informal workshopping on specific localities will enable the retention and currency of this knowledge exchange. These workshops will also assist in understanding the ways that institutions make their decisions including those about the prioritisation of one scheme over another. Workshops also provide a more neutral discussion about infrastructure requirements than the more pressurised debates that are undertaken when there are specific development priorities and these discussions are translated into negotiations.

Evidence gathering

The evidence for any infrastructure delivery planning process needs to be current and also be able to take into account changes expected in the future. These changes may be reflections of policy or institutional priorities, or wider development or demographic change in the territory under consideration. The collection, integration and examination of this evidence, with the possible use of scenarios to plan for alternative outcomes are an important part of the process. Without this, schemes may falter or it may be difficult to make a case for investment either from providers or to be funded through other means including developer or private sector funding.

It is also important that the evidence is in a form that can be shared with providers and users and on national open data standards. This allows alternative scenarios and solutions to be considered and assessed and may assist in supporting the achievement of the vision in ways that were not initially envisaged. The population estimates should be common to all bodies. A practical approach to evidence gathering is set out in Box 2.2.

Box 2.2: Infrastructure requirements: approaches to evidence collection

- Create an infrastructure categories list for the area.
- Establish a baseline of existing facilities from all sectors on a GIS base.
- Review the condition, capacity and use of each of the public facilities.
- Review existing and expected changes in household occupation, employment and growth.
- Establish a GIS database of all publicly owned land and buildings in the area.
- Identify all infrastructure schemes in build and committed to add to the baseline.
- Identify standards to be applied for each infrastructure type, apply them and identify gaps.
- Collate a database of all funding streams that can contribute to the mainstream delivery programme.
- Collate a database of all other known sources of funding or work with those who have this information.
- Identify potential opportunities for public sector co-location with organisations.
- Identify opportunities for asset release from public sector property and service reviews.
- Consider any relocations that might contribute to reductions in climate change.
- Identify facilities that should be capable of dual use such as swimming pools in schools and universities or the private sector.

Standards and deficits

The objectives for the territorial vision for any area will incorporate a range of thematic objectives derived from local priorities, government and the EU (CEC, 2013d). These will include access to facilities, their capacity and quality. In order to assess priorities for investment and aspirational and development changes, new investment or regeneration will be considered as well as the distribution, quality and capacity of existing infrastructure.

In order to make assessments of existing infrastructure and identify any deficits, it is necessary to apply service standards (DCLG, 2012). In the UK, many of these service standards were set nationally including access to school or libraries, response times for the emergency services and access to open space and playing fields. These national standards were abolished between 2000 and 2010 and local standards should be identified, adopted and applied in spatial plans at all scales. The standards will need evidential underpinning as they will be used to promote the case for investment or development contributions to support the requirements of new development. Different standards may be adopted for rural and urban locations in the same local authority or FEA.

The process starts with an identification of all standards that are required. In some cases standards may need to change to comply with new environmental legislation or respond to changing service delivery models. Once the standards have been identified they are applied to the baseline infrastructure and these resulting assessments can be recorded through GIS layers. When applying access standards it is important to take into account barriers such as waterways, railway tracks or roads. Isochrones by travel mode including walking, cycling and public transport might be more appropriate (CEC, 2009).

Standards should be reviewed annually and formally adopted by the governance body that will be responsible for their application. This process of formal adoption will give the standards more credibility and will have a greater influence on other service providers.

An infrastructure delivery plan

An infrastructure delivery plan (IDP) is the place where the aspirations, objectives, requirements for upgrading and new development and the priorities identified for specific projects come together. It is a means of delivering the strategy and its spatial expression for any territory. The IDP will explain about how it has been derived, its role in prioritising projects and the ways it will be updated. Each project will be identified by its owner, location, funding and phasing and any dependencies between it and other projects.

IDP presentation will depend on local preferences. One option is to group projects geographically so that any resident, community, business or investor can identify what is committed and identified for the future in their area. Users can assess future development proposals, identify gaps and to understand the effects of implementation in their area. This territorial presentation can also assist potential investors to identify gaps or supporting projects.

Another way of presenting an IDP is thematically (London Borough of Croydon, 2014). This approach aligns the projects with their role in delivery and directly supports the strategy for the area. In this form, the role of each project in achieving an integrated whole is identified. It also allows the IDP to demonstrate how these priorities are being delivered across the governance area.

A third way of setting out an IDP is by type of infrastructure – physical, environmental/green and social and community. Within these categories, infrastructure might be grouped by type, for example in health or education, and this will also demonstrate where there may be service gaps. This approach aligns the plan to infrastructure providers and may make it easier for them to be engaged in the process but it may be less usable for residents and other investors. If the IDP is GIS based or constructed using XML, then it will be possible to create community and thematic versions of the IDP in addition to provider-based versions. Using this method may also be useful for checking purposes. It is also important that the providers understand the role of their projects as part of the whole IDP. Another way of presenting the IDP is in time tranches – for example in annual or five-year bands. This provides a focus on delivery and may be important where there is a concern about dependencies between projects and budget cycles.

However the IDP is presented there may be a need to include it within sustainability appraisals that are undertaken for the overall territorial strategies and spatial plan. Once the IDP has been assembled it should be kept up to date with project developments and progress. It should also be reviewed on a regular basis and to take into account new infrastructure projects and developments.

Delivery

The delivery of the IDP is an essential component of spatial planning. This requires proactive engagement by the governance body responsible for the strategy and spatial plan. It should also engage those responsible for the delivery and management of services within this body. Their role in engaging in the delivery process for their own services and working with other institutions to deliver the IDP is essential for its success.

The delivery can be assisted by the use of project management techniques such as PRINCE2, which includes the appointment of a senior responsible owner (SRO) for each project, a project board and project manager (Morphet, 2015). Project boards may be grouped into programme boards that combine projects of the same type, locality or development site. It is the responsibility of the SRO to manage the interface between the project and the organisations supporting its delivery including that responsible for its subsequent operation.

A strategic monitoring and progress group that will be able to report on the progress of projects across the whole IDP and arrange for additional resources or changes in the priorities should be established. This group will also be responsible for identifying any perceived gaps and reporting them to the board managing the territorial strategy.

These reporting arrangements are the same in all types of organisation and are essential for successful progress in delivery. There may be a separation between groups concerned with the delivery of the projects and identifying priority schemes but it is important that these come together at board level.

Finance for infrastructure delivery

The sources of funding that are brought together through the process of delivery of the IDP include all main sources of funding available for capital investment. The main sources of funding are shown in Box 2.3 and discussed further below.

Box 2.3: Sources of funding for infrastructure
- government funds for schools, health, transport, regeneration
- private sector investment
- community and voluntary sector investment
- competitive schemes, for example Heritage Lottery Funds
- charitable investment
- hybrid body funding, for example utilities, Housing Associations
- specific purpose vehicles set up to promote local investment
- developers' contributions.

Principles of capital funding

The creation of infrastructure results in capital assets with their own value. These assets are identified in the financial accounts of the organisation that owns them and are treated in a specific way. The valuation of the asset is set at a cautious resale value. The costs of investing in an asset will be recognised for taxation purposes and receive special allowances. Once complete, the maintenance and repair of this asset may also attract tax benefits. Capital assets that are expected to have a life of 30 years or more can be used as security against which loans can be raised to undertake more capital investment.

The amount of capital available to undertake new development or maintenance in any organisation will be limited by financial standards and accounting practices. Until 2014, the accounting practices of the public sector and private sector were different, particularly in the ways they accounted for capital expenditure. However, between 2013 and 2017 there has been a convergence between the two sets of practices towards the use of the International Financial Reporting Standards (IFRS) that will be completed within the UK by 2017 (Audit Commission, 2010). IFRS will have little effect on the private sector, on which it is based, whereas it will allow the public sector to use their assets in different ways. IFRS will also account for planned maintenance through establishing longer-term allocations or set aside funds for replacement rather than funding repairs and maintenance for some assets from annual revenue income. The introduction of IFRS is a major benefit for all sectors as it should enable joint ventures and comparative assessments.

Funding for capital investment can be obtained from banks through loans. It can be also be funded through organisational financial reserves or raised through bonds on the markets. For public sector capital funding, the Public Works Loan Board (PWLB) has provided funding at lower interest rates than the market and this has encouraged public authorities to use its services. This means that the government's loans book is supported by highly secure debtors that have good credit ratings. Public sector debtors are also attractive to the private sector for the same reason and groups of local authorities are now coming together to attempt to raise bonds on the open market to benefit from the quality of their financial ratings.

Capital investment can also be funded through pension funds and insurance companies. Here the managers of the funds are seeking longer-term safe investment schemes where they can lend the pensioners' or insureds' funds in order to be able to achieve a return over the longer period. Pension funds and insurance companies seek mixed investment strategies and hold a range of loans in their portfolios. However, as they are funding capital assets they also have the security of being able to obtain some value from the assets should there be a default by the borrower. Some capital investment for infrastructure is funded through the EU and the European Investment Bank (EIB). This may be through financial contributions and loans to some schemes including TEN-T.

In some local authorities, the pension fund has been used to invest directly in asset purchase. In Greater Manchester, the pension fund has been used to purchase a series of regional airports and is now moving to invest directly in house-building. The EU Directive on pensions (CEC, 2003) means that individuals will be able to remove some of their funds from their pension pots, using it as a personal bank. This may mean that there will be smaller funds available for capital investment from these sources but could also mean more individual investment in infrastructure projects such as buy-to-let housing.

In some cases the pension funds of other countries have purchased infrastructure assets in the UK. The most active of these have been the pension funds in Canada and Australia. The way these funds operate is influenced by their own domestic infrastructure markets (Inderst and Della Croce, 2013). In Canada, much of the infrastructure is still owned by the public sector. There is a strong bond market and a culture of public–private partnerships (PPP) to fund investment. The pension funds are larger and are able to keep a high proportion of their assets in investment with less focus on their liquidity. In Australia, more infrastructure is owned by the private sector and there is a less active bond market. In Canada all major pension funds have purchased infrastructure across the globe and the assets owned in the UK include 'High Speed One, the railway line that connects London to the Channel Tunnel; Scotia, Scotland's biggest gas network; the ports of Southampton and Grimsby; Birmingham and Bristol airports' (Blackden, 2012).

Regulated markets

Some infrastructure is operated within regulated markets and these are primarily services of general economic interest (SGEI) defined by the EU and also subject to World Trade Organization (WTO) competition agreements (Meunier, 2005). In this case there is a hybrid approach to investment in new assets. The state regulates the provision and market while infrastructure providers are from all sectors. In the private sector, funding for infrastructure will primarily be generated from fees and charges for services. The companies provide regular investment programmes to the regulator and use these to make pricing proposals. Infrastructure projects needs are then assessed. Regulators will consider the investment proposed together with the consequent effects on consumer prices. Some regulated markets are not subject to price caps, including telephony and digital services. Here the companies purchase licences from the government and then use their income to invest in infrastructure to meet customer need. The price to the consumer is not regulated.

Some services have moved between types of regulated market. The provision of networks of rail services in the UK has been in the private sector and then transferred to a publicly owned company. In this case, the nationally owned company still has to make requests for funding for maintenance but as rail investment costs are unlikely to be returned through revenue then investment is funded from taxation. Decisions on price rises are made by politicians although the rail regulator does have a role in this process.

Unregulated markets

Some infrastructure investment is through unregulated markets and entirely from income or returns from investment. The most typical examples here are retail, leisure facilities such as sports and leisure centres, cinemas, cafes, restaurants and some social care facilities for children and care services for older people. These services can be provided where the operator considers they will provide a return on investment. In some cases the operator will fund the development of a building such as a multiplex cinema or leisure club, but in others they may lease space to operate their services from other asset owners. This may be more typical of shops where retailers take fixed-term leases and are subject to rent reviews during the period of the lease. Although the lease is not an asset in the same way as a building, it still enables the leaseholder to assign that lease to another user and generate some income if the assignee is willing to pay more. Similarly if a retailer goes out of business, any leases may be taken into account in meeting their debts through reassignment.

While the providers of these services raise funds for their infrastructure, they are also the beneficiaries of the planning system that identifies optimal locations for investment. In some cases, planning may restrict the volume of similar infrastructure providers within a specific area. Planning policies include defined retail areas. The planning system supports these centres through investment in transport and other facilities. The planning application process can also require that privately operated social and community infrastructure is provided as part of larger development schemes in town centres or in housing development. These provide opportunities for businesses to operate within a secure environment with wider policy support. Finally, the planning system can restrict the location and operation of businesses where concentration might cause harm. This includes the clustering of hot food takeaway shops around school gates and the proliferation of betting shops in a high street.

Publicly funded infrastructure

Public sector infrastructure funding will be derived from taxation and other government income. The public sector can also raise funds from the private sector through bonds and loans against assets. Finally, as in the period following the financial crisis in 2007, the government can print more money through policies of quantitative easing.

The government will allocate funding for infrastructure investment through periodic spending reviews that may last between five and seven years, will span the life of a parliamentary term and may frequently use the EU programme periods. In the UK the spending review periods have been 2007-14 and 2015-20 compared with the EU programme periods of 2006-13 and 2014-20. In Ireland these periods relate directly to EU programmes. The annual budget cycles also reflect the EU cycle for the public sector in the autumn statement and pre-budget report in late November and the domestic budget in spring.

At national level, the application of these funds generated through taxation, fees and charges will be determined by a policy-led approach. This may be through agreements (with the EU), external commentary (from the OECD and IMF) through evidence or through political choices (Short and Kopp, 2005a, 2005b; Helm, 2013). One example is through assessments of policy-led investment is in airports in the south-east ranging from the Roskill Commission (1971) to the reviews by Eddington (2006), Davies (2015) and the Mayor of London (2015). Airport capacity investment may be undertaken by the private or public sectors but the decision on where the capacity is to be located is a national question and this is therefore policy lead planning.

The OECD found investment levels of 1% of GDP in transport in those countries that are regarded as good infrastructure providers (Short and Kopp, 2005b). This sets an input benchmark measure for states. However, these figures reflect neither the state of existing infrastructure nor any assessment of return on this investment against such criteria of improved economic outputs, improved mobility or reductions in worklessness.

The political component of policy-led infrastructure planning can also lead to policy capture by specific interests close to or advising government. In some cases this can be translated into optimism bias for schemes and their outcomes may lead officials to consistently underestimate the costs of the proposals (Flyvbjerg et al, 2008). Alternatively there can be attempts to ensure that projects can enter the budget programme at an underestimated cost and then attract the full funding costs later in the project as no politician will want to see a scheme left half-completed.

A policy-based approach might also suggest more focus on evidence-based policy making or 'what works' (Cabinet Office, 2013). In this, policy planning is informed by earlier decision-making and project performance. However, this approach may use political horizons that are short with more pressure on announcements than delivery. Further, civil servants have less experience in delivery and, unlike in local government, their career advancement does not rest on completing successful projects but rather initiating new ones.

A further criticism of evidence-based policy making is that the senior civil servants advising ministers consider relying on a research-based approach may be too prescriptive not least as they argue that circumstances vary and no two decision-making moments are the same (Parsons, 2002). However, governments have been criticised for their expenditure on major projects that can go wrong through short-termism and switching budget priorities so that problems then emerge as unintended consequents in other infrastructure (Margetts and Hood, 2012).

For local authorities, funds for infrastructure investment will be provided through income derived from council tax, from government, fees and charges and existing assets. Local authorities can borrow funds from the government, EIB or the private sector. They may also make loans to each other or raise funds together through bond issues (Jenkins and Pickard, 2015). Central government controls the distribution of council tax and business rate income to local authorities and retains some controls on housing investment (Wilson, 2013). However, the introduction of the IFRS and the Localism Act 2011 has had an influence on the way these funds can be invested. Further, the application of the EU principle of subsidiarity in the Lisbon Treaty has also required the decentralisation of funding (CEC, 2013b).

Local authorities have land and property assets that have been managed through their service responsibilities rather than as an asset portfolio as in the private sector (Audit Commission, 2009). There have been a range of UK initiatives to review this approach and also to combine information and asset management for all public services within the same location (HMT and DCLG, 2010). As well as pressures to combine assets, public bodies have been encouraged to join up or at least share services and accommodation at the local level. This may be through local authority mergers, combining staff teams or operating public sector single access points. These approaches all have the benefit of benefit of reducing the need for accommodation and releasing assets for other uses that can generate income or capital for further investment (DCLG, 2011a; Thomson and Wilkes, 2014). Some of these initiatives have been through the generation of joint working between different scales of government through community budgets for health and social care. These again are concerned with reducing back office costs of staff and buildings and transferring these funds to service delivery (Keeling, 2013).

Government has also pioneered other ways of generating funds for infrastructure using PPP schemes through the Private Finance Initiative (PFI). Through these the private sector will put forward the funds and then it will take an additional fee for taking on the risk of managing the infrastructure (Roumboutsos and Pantelias, 2014). There are many ways of constructing PPPs and these may be culturally related within different state systems (Albalate et al, 2015; van den Hurk et al, 2015).

Other public sector organisations such as housing associations will also receive central and local government funding; income from rents; bank loans; and may raise funds on the bond markets individually or jointly (Pickard et al, 2012).

When public sector bodies are engaged in the delivery of projects, including contributing their own assets, then there is a requirement to work within the EU state aid rules. These are in support of competition in the single market (Almunia, 2011) and any project can be contested by the EC (European Commission) or member states. In the UK, the project for the nuclear power station at Hinkley Point, was referred to the EC in 2014 for investigation and the financial agreements were subsequently amended.

Publicly generated infrastructure funds

While the public sector can directly invest in infrastructure it can also support the generation of investment. First, this may be through the planning system where it can identify priorities, gaps and preferred locations that will be supported (Adams and Watkins, 2014). Second, the public sector can provide loans to support specific types of investment and these will be within the regulations agreed within the EU. In the past, grant aid has been provided to organisations but since 2014 this has been shifted to loans that have to be repaid (CEC, 2013b).

Another way that the public sector can generate infrastructure investment is through the funds that are associated with planning applications (Taylor, 2011). Here the regulating authorities can seek funds for the amelioration of the development through s106 of the 1991 Planning Act or they can adopt a CIL within the Planning Act 2008. While s106 funds are applied directly to the consequences of the development, CIL may be used for investment in any location within the local authority area (DCLG, 2011b; Qualtrough, 2011). In neither case is there any specific link to the IDP in the negotiation process although this may be done in practice as the IDP can demonstrate the need for specific infrastructure investment in the locality.

The ability of any local authority to generate these development funds will depend on a number of factors including the viability of the scheme within the market, market considerations in any location, and the type of scheme. The market will also be affected by the overall economic climate (HCA, 2009).

Conclusions

Spatial planning is concerned with delivery. Infrastructure delivery planning is central to that delivery process in direct role of identifying visions, locations and policies but also in the way that it can frame the future for places and investment. In this chapter effective methods for infrastructure delivery planning have been discussed together with mechanisms for funding.

Notes

[1] CIL is a policy introduced in England and Wales by government in 2008 to help to generate income to support local authorities for the provision of infrastructure in their area through predetermined levels of financial contributions related to its size, type and location.

[2] Should the UK vote to leave the EU, all trade with EU member states will have to be undertaken within the policy and legislation in these policy areas. Some policy areas such as trade and the environment also incorporate international agreements which the UK will be obliged to maintain in these circumstances.

THREE

Physical infrastructure delivery planning

Introduction

Physical infrastructure is primarily fixed and delivered through networks and nodes. It is focused on transport, water, waste, energy and telecommunications. One of the defining features of physical infrastructure is its interoperability within each mode although not necessarily between modes. Physical infrastructure has primarily an economic role but also makes contributions to social and environmental well-being.

Governments take a strong interest in infrastructure provision, investment and the coordination of agencies to reduce and manage risks (Gordon and Dion, 2008). Physical infrastructure is defined as critical by states when considering national security and resilience (McDaniels et al, 2008; Schmitt et al, 2013). This role defines the investment in and management of networks, and their use, as well as climate change (Corfee-Morlot et al, 2012) and security of energy supply. The main approach to effective infrastructure delivery is integration. It is important to understand how this integration works in practice through implementation timescales and delivery mechanisms before considering how networks, modes and nodes can be brought together at different spatial scales.

Transport

Transport can be considered as a single integrated set of infrastructure that supports economic and social activities and the achievement of environmental objectives. However, in practice, planning and programming of transport infrastructure is undertaken within different sectoral organisations, on different timelines and spatial scales (Akerman et al, 2000; Marshall and Banister, 2007). The planning approaches for the provision of transport infrastructure are managed by the state although each state may vary the extent they coordinate and incentivise particular types of investment.

Transport planning integrates transport modes and land uses. This integration is the basis for assessing transport investment schemes and their modelling undertaken through cost–benefit analysis (Mishan and Quah, 2007). These assessments are based on rational models that examine the effects of different types of transport investment on communities, individuals and businesses. Modelling methods can be vulnerable to challenges in their development and application. First, specific interests may be promoted through the model. This may favour one mode over another, for example roads over rail, cars over cyclists. Models may also give weight to some transport users by applying economic benefits to schemes on travel time saved using salary levels. This is problematic as women earn less than men (Ganser, 2009). Third, there may be a preference towards business users over social equity.

The focus on integration of transport infrastructure with land use is at the heart of the planning system and its role in the delivery of efficient, effective and sustainable places. The distribution and changes in land uses can have significant effects on costs to individuals, communities and business. It will also confer value in some locations over others. Investment in infrastructure can be made to alleviate congestion or as a means to encourage development (Oc and Tiesdell, 1991; Mejia-Dorantes and Lucas, 2014; Williams and Redmond, 2014).

Roads

The provision of roads is primarily by the public sector and funded from taxation or associated with private sector development. Roads can also be funded through private sector investment loans to the public sector or recouped through road user charging or tolls (Pagano and Perry, 2008). A central consideration for all road investment and management will be road enhancement and new routes that may be defined as addressing 'missing links' and 'bottle necks' (CEC, 2013a, 2013b).

A consideration in investment decision-making processes is what outcomes are privileged over others. While a focus on place and the economic contribution of roads to society may be an overriding determinant, decisions taken on road investment may be subject to other assessment processes such as improvements for existing road users over others (CEC, 2012b). This may favour private car commuters rather than freight or public transport users of road space (Gray, 2002; Jenson and Richardson, 2004; Ganser, 2009). Roads can be used in ways that encourage and implement a sustainable transport policy, combining fixed highway capacity containment, fiscal policies for fuels and other traffic management measures such as multipassenger lanes and bus priority measures (Banister, 2008; CEC, 2013g).

The methods used for the development and enhancement of roads may be based on technical planning models that seek to ascribe costs and benefits to investment (Mishan and Quah, 2007). However, in some countries, the financial methods of appraisal undertaken are not always used to make decisions (Odeck, 1996). A second method assesses the disbenefits of poor accessibility using specific criteria. These may be based on social and sustainability factors rather than economic criteria.

Travel by road is a political concern. It is a preferred travel method for much of the population that has access to a car, as they are convenient to customise travel times and destinations (Anable, 2005; van Exel and Rietveld, 2010). The full costs of car travel are also hidden through sunk costs of vehicle purchase and insurance, intermittent fuel costs rather than payment at the point of use, and transferred costs to the community for road provision. Deliveries of goods and materials by road are favoured by business. Road transport also has associated costs that are not borne by the user but by society as a whole. These include the costs of initial investment in the road and its subsequent upkeep, which can be higher when lorry sizes increase. There are also spillover costs on air quality from the use of fuel and economic costs transfer to non-optimal use of public transport (Wallis et al, 2012).

An important question when planning for roads is 'peak car'. This considers whether car use has reached its maximum levels in Western countries and whether there will be lower car use in the future. Disincentives for car-commuting through fuel taxes and additional parking levies, fewer parking places and improved access through public transport can be generated through public policy (Metz, 2013). A number of indicators suggest car use may be in decline in the future (Goodwin, 2012). These include fewer young people with driving licences and a weakening in the link between affluence and personal mobility. There are also cultural shifts in favour of sustainability and health that are associated with public transport. The implications of peak car and its effects on investment and land use in the future have yet to be really understood (Headicar, 2013) but this is important to consider as part of infrastructure delivery planning.

Providing for roads through infrastructure delivery planning may require approaches that are horizontally and vertically integrated. National roads form the network and all localities are connected to it. This suggests that strategic road planning needs to be undertaken at least at the level of the FEA (functional economic area). More significant roads that form part of the TEN-T (Trans-European Network – Transport) (CEC, 2013a) corridors may be developed and improved within EU member states and delivered as local projects but it is also important to understand their role within the wider context.

Delivery by road may be the only option over shorter distances and in rural areas but when delivering across longer distances there may be other modes to consider such as short sea shipping, canals or railways. Goods can be delivered to an inland port or break-bulk centre that repackages the goods for distribution in mixed content/single destination loads, for example to a supermarket or fast food restaurant or geographically targeted deliveries. The rise in internet shopping has also increased the demand for urban distribution centres. In some cases roads may be used to improve the economy through increasing accessibility although this may also work in both directions, tempting more to travel out of the area. In areas that are primarily rural, road provision may be important for access for good to markets or to encourage tourism.

Infrastructure delivery planning will also be concerned with local road provision. This may include bypasses for specific towns and villages where historic core or river crossings mean that it is difficult to improve roads within the settlement. The development of bypasses can also widen the boundaries of settlements, zoning more development land within them. These processes can also be used to generate development value and contributions to the funding of the bypass (Carbonell and Yaro, 2005). Within built-up areas, road improvements may be required to access specific sites or to deal with problems such as road safety. These smaller schemes may be funded either through development or by the public authorities through budgets to support safety improvements. In some cases road carriage width may be reduced to enhance a walking environment by reducing traffic speeds.

Roads can be built to last for different periods of time. Using whole life costing (Boussabaine and Kirkham, 2008), more sustainable approaches to design on the initial investment will mean less funding is required for regular maintenance, although it will cost more at the outset.

The process for undertaking infrastructure delivery planning for roads is set out in Box 3.1.

Box 3.1: Infrastructure delivery planning for roads

- identify the role of transport in achieving spatial strategy
- identify the transport needs in the area under consideration
- assess the options to meet the transport needs by different modes or multimode solutions
- if a road is the best option, identify the main provider of the road at this scale in the network
- identify the investment and programming criteria of the likely provider
- identify the role of corridors and roads within this
- apply accessibility criteria to baseline and projected changes
- undertake gap analysis
- identify where road capacity can be improved through management including junctions, lane restrictions, bus priority measures
- prioritise projects against the strategy within stakeholders and community
- develop business cases for roads projects as part of integrated transport strategy
- use business case to support funding bids
- undertake design, obtain consents and acquire land
- implement.

Rail

The provision of rail services has varied in different EU states. In France and Belgium there was a strong state leadership as the private sector was unwilling to fund railways, unlike in the UK, although there was some private investment in specific railway companies that operated on a regional basis (Dobbin, 2001). In Germany, the state was not unified until later and comprised a series of individual administrations. The unification that was promoted through the customs union supported the growth of railways to transfer goods and passengers and also acted as a means of generating economic advantage in competition between cities. In the UK there was a strong private sector railway industry with lines and stations being developed in direct competition with each other. These legacies have had a strong influence on the subsequent application of competition into these rail systems (Lodge, 2003).

The way competition has been implemented has varied within each EU member state. The UK was the only member state to separate the rail network from the rail service providers in applying competition and the network was passed into the management of the private sector (Shaw, 2000). However, subsequent failures in maintenance led to the network company being returned to government management with EU permission in 2002. The rail service providers are operated as route franchises and these have changed over time. Some franchises have closed and the government has taken back responsibility before refranchising. The periods of the rail franchises vary and make it difficult for more centralised planning to be undertaken between routes and other transport modes.

The main interests of governments are in the provision of high-speed train services (HST), regulating the services and investment. HST networks were defined within the EU TEN-T networks (CEC, 1996b; Butcher, 2013) and have subsequently been revised (CEC, 2013c). HST routes in the EU are defined as having one of these three infrastructure characteristics:

* specially built high-speed lines equipped for speeds generally equal to or greater than 250 km/h
* specially upgraded high-speed lines equipped for speeds of the order of 200 km/h
* specially upgraded high-speed lines that have special features as a result of topographical, relief or town-planning constraints, on which the speed must be adapted to each case.
* (CEC, 1996c)

Within EU TEN-T policy, rail networks have been set within wider transport corridors with at least two other modes such as canals and roads (CEC, 2011a). HST lines have a territorial, economic and environmental purpose. They divert long-distance travel from roads and reduce carbon consumption. While HST routes are planned to extend across the EU's territory, they are also the subject of local opposition in their implementation. This is manifested in the UK, the Netherlands (Feinstein, 2008) France and Italy (Porta and Andretta, 2002; Zuchetti, 2013).

While rail companies operate commercially, the investment in rail is primarily through the public sector. Rail companies operate within a regulated structure. In the UK, services are in competition. This makes integrated services difficult, not least through differential fare structures and application of integrated ticketing across modes (Schumann, 1997; Blythe, 2004; Aberdeen City Council, 2015).

Infrastructure delivery planning for rail will depend on the existing network, its scale and integrated transport policy. Where there are investment priorities set out in national infrastructure or spatial plans these programmes and their relationship to local access to services and transport interchanges will be important. There may also be the potential for other development near the improved interchange through transport oriented development (TOD) (Ang and Marchal, 2013).

Where the rail services are supporting access within an FEA and access to national and international lines then infrastructure planning may depend on the funding available and the priorities placed on specific routes and interchanges. This may be supported through links to the core EU TEN-T access to the comprehensive network is critical in focusing future investment (CEC, 2013a). In these cases, it may be possible to support the development of new stations or the improvement of existing interchange facilities. However improvements in the FEA will depend on the current use of the networks and the extent they are used for freight or national routes. Within FEAs, rail will also be part of Sustainable Urban Mobility Plans (SUMP) (CEC, 2013g) and there will be pressures to localise and integrate rail management into an FEA-wide transport system with identified routes, integrated ticketing and a common livery.

Box 3.2: Infrastructure delivery planning for rail

Most infrastructure delivery planning for rail is likely to focus on improvements to existing services and include:

* the quality of the rolling stock
* capacity
* improving frequency and reliability of service through signalling, minor track improvements, platform and train lengths
* rail freight, improvements to ports – both inland and marine. In some cases there may a case for new rail stations on existing lines and less frequently new lines
* service and station improvements may also be a focus of regenerations in city centres or through
* parkway stations
* improved access into the rail system by improved means of approach and interchanges
* timetabling so that a multimode trip can be attractive
* integrated and smart ticketing
* integrated real-time data systems for passengers
* make stations destinations through the services that they provide including extended hours of opening, their architecture and immediate settings.

Metro systems

France, Germany and the Netherlands have heavily invested in light rail systems for metro areas while the UK has invested in some cities including Nottingham, Edinburgh, Sheffield, Manchester and Birmingham. The metro system can be located partly or wholly underground in the city centre such as in London, Glasgow, Newcastle or Brussels (Flyvbjerg et al, 2008). Metro systems are designed for rapid transit for longer distances than bus networks although some express bus priority services provide a complementary service. In some cities, metro systems have been developed as they are a more attractive alternative to car users and also provide a modern appearance to a city (Pagliara and Papa, 2011). They are also a statement of public sector investment and a commitment to sustainability.

Light rail systems may need to share road space with cars and their scale can be intimidating for pedestrians. The selection of routes can also be highly politicised (Taylor et al, 2009) as the introduction of a station or stop may increase residential and commercial property values (Du and Mulley, 2007; Hess and Almeida, 2007). Route investment criteria may vary between supporting movement within highly populated areas, reducing reliance on car use or improving access for the socially excluded. Also there are opportunities for light rail systems to be implemented in advance of development and for the system to be funded in part through the uplift in value. This approach can be supported by tax increment financing (TIF) systems (Greenhalgh et al, 2012; Squires and Lord, 2012). A major challenge in all metro systems is the effectiveness of the interchanges between modes and interoperability of tickets (Currie et al, 2011) that provide much quicker and efficient use particularly at peak times and also encourages passengers to switch routes at times of congestion or delay.

Light rail metro systems are expensive (Flyvbjerg et al, 2008) and their potential depends on the size of the city and the level of existing rail infrastructure that can be reused. In smaller or historic cities, congestion or heritage considerations may mean that a metro or similar system such as a guided busway may provides the only means of improving the system around the core, for example Bologna. Other options include the introduction of bus priority measures together with limited stop routes using high quality buses with Wi-Fi that provide a more flexible and less costly alternative and can be implemented quickly without any fixed network infrastructure. The likely effectiveness of other policy measures such as car restraint (Crampton, 2002) will also be an important consideration. The development of light rail systems as part of an infrastructure delivery programme will depend on the way a business case can be established for the investment shown in Box 3.3.

Box 3.3: Infrastructure delivery planning: light rail systems

The development of light rail systems as part of an infrastructure delivery programme will depend on:

- the way a business case can be established for the investment
- the configuration of the urban area and its inner core and the ways it is supported by other policy measures including buses and car restraint
- introducing a light rail system may also use routes that were formerly used by tramways – that have been used by fixed link routes and have road junctions designed to carry light rail systems
- in some cities, heavy rail lines may be converted to light rail use to become the bones of the system that can be developed with supporting investment
- metro systems require long-term planning and will need to demonstrate significant economic returns to attract investment
- revenue costs are unlikely to repay investment not least as routes will be travelling through the most expensive land uses in the city

- prior to considering metro system investment, alternative means such as express buses or dedicated busways may demonstrate that there is a ridership and these can be provided as a lower costs
- one of the main reasons for promoting metro systems has been to encourage modal switch by car commuters, primarily men (Matas, 2004; Abrate et al, 2009)
- metro systems support a modal shift is that associated with higher status than bus systems (Redman et al, 2013). However, experience in London has demonstrated that a greater switch can be encouraged through a variety of measures including integrated ticketing, real-time information and cashless payments.

Waterways

Maritime transport

Maritime transport can be safer and more efficient than other forms of transport, particularly for goods and materials. Through the TEN–T policies (CEC, 2013a) the EU adopted the motorways of the sea policy in 2001 and this has identified four EU routes that are designed to support traffic volume through investment in ports and other facilities. The wider EU Maritime Strategy 2018 was adopted in 2009 (CEC, 2009). The efficiency of maritime transport is related to the quality of port infrastructure and this discussion has now extended into marine spatial planning (Meiner, 2010; CEC, 2014c). This is an integrated approach to all maritime activity and intended to reduce conflicts between sectors and create different activities. Its integrated approach is also there to support investment and protect the environment.

Inland waterways

Inland waterways are canals, navigable rivers and lakes and their associated land facilities including docks, transfer stations and inland ports. Inland waterways are a safe and reliable means for transporting goods with low environmental impact. They also have the capacity for increased use and this can be encouraged through the development of inland ports. Inland waterways infrastructure was constructed in the 18th and 19th centuries so that much of the primary investment in the networks has been made. However, some may need improvements to make them navigable again. There may also be a need to invest in additional facilities. Inland waterways are also part of subregional, national and international systems and their management and any associated improvements need to be considered in an integrated way.

Within the EU, inland waterways are promoted as part of the EU's integrated transport policy (CEC, 2010). This runs to 2020 and includes support for improvements together with the strategy for the Danube within one of the macro regional strategies supported through the Cohesion programme. They also form part of the TEN–T networks (CEC, 2013a) and may be included within SUMPs within urban transport systems (CEC, 2013g). Waterways are used for specific activities such as transporting waste and aggregates with transfer stations built on the waterway edges. They can also support tourism and leisure activities.

Ports

The majority of coastal ports are situated on major river estuaries but can also be located inland. Ports are transport hubs and depend on access by specific vehicles or vessels and their interconnections with other locations by multiple transport modes. Within the EU, ports are an essential feature of external trade with 74% of goods leaving the EU by water (CEC, 2014c). However, there have been increasing concerns about bottlenecks and accessibility between the ports and their hinterlands that have now become a focus of EU policy. In 2013, the EC (European Commission) identified 327 sea ports as part of its TEN-T core and comprehensive network (CEC, 2013a, 2013d).

Ports are usually managed by separate port authorities and Verhoeven (2010) identifies three overriding models of ownership and management within the EU. These are a national body, a regional body and a private sector company that may own one or more ports. The governance of individual ports is identified as a factor in the exercise of their role and also their freedom to levy fees and charges and ownership of land assets. Verhoeven found that only 50% of port organisations own the land that they manage. While all port governance bodies had ambitions for growth, land use management practices were causing the most obstacles.

Policies and infrastructure development for ports, has to be considered at FEA, state, EU and international scales. In some locations in the UK, specific Citydeals between the government and the local authority have been agreed to support port development such as that in Plymouth and the South West Peninsula (HMG, 2015). Ports can also implement sustainable practices through their management and functions (Lam and Notteboom, 2014).

Inland ports are included in EU TEN-T policy where there is a priority for improving their infrastructure within the Regulation (article 14) although not all states have an inland port designated, as shown on the TEN-T map (CEC, 2013f Annexe 1 vol 1). Inland ports can be regarded as break-bulk centres and freight interchanges but they can have wider roles. Rodrigue et al (2010) identified three features of an inland port – its scale, containerisation and a fixed link with a sea port. Through case studies that included the inland ports of Lyon and Zaragoza, they concluded that, like maritime ports, the ownership and governance of the inland port can have a significant role in its success. They also found that where governance was extended to other bodies such as those responsible for local economic governance, this was a factor in the port's growth and job generation. They also identified the role of the private sector using inland port development as part of their property strategies and concluded that finding a balance between public policy and private interests will provide the most likely successful outcome.

Thus in coastal and inland ports, spatial planning, land ownerships and aspirations are central to success. Inland ports also need to be integrated within their FEAs, not least as the development of the land side of sea ports is becoming more important in their economies and this may mean that inland port development is favoured over that at the sea port (Witte et al, 2014).

Box 3.4: Planning for ports through infrastructure delivery planning

Where a port has been identified as a key node or hub within the TEN-T (CEC, 2013e) policy is likely to be improved through:

- streamlined planning and improvement processes at the national level
- corridor studies.
- Where a port is not part of the TEN-T core networks, then:
- promotion of its inclusion in the TEN-T policy through designation as part of the comprehensive network to be agreed by 2030
- associated land use and planning policies need to be adopted as part of the subregional growth programme or integrated territorial investment strategies
- linkages to rail and road networks and to other ports will develop the capacity and attractiveness of the network.

Energy

Energy planning is undertaken within sectors based on the generation of energy from a variety of locations that is fed into networks to act as supply for wider populations. In the case of gas and electricity this is done through major facilities. For renewables, such as wind power, waste, biomass or solar energy, these can be provided for commercial or local use with any surplus being fed into the energy grid.

Within the EU, energy is a pooled policy within the Single Market. Energy Europe is an initiative in the period 2014–20 including a range of specific actions such as the completion of an EU energy grid. The EU policy focuses on renewables although there has been a move away from policies for specific types to treating the sector as a whole. This leaves each member state to determine how the renewables contribution will be achieved. There are also other EU energy policies including carbon reduction and air quality. The targets adopted by Energy Europe for 2030 are:

- a 40% cut in greenhouse gas emissions compared to 1990 levels
- at least a 27% share of renewable energy consumption
- a 30% improvement in energy efficiency (compared to projection) (CEC, 2014a).

This plan also includes a reformed EU emissions trading scheme (ETS) and new indicators for the competitiveness and security of the energy system, such as price differences with major trading partners, diversification of supply, and interconnection capacity between EU countries. Finally, there is a focus on a new governance system based on national plans for competitive, secure and sustainable energy. These plans will follow a common EU approach. They are designed to ensure stronger investor certainty, greater transparency, enhanced policy coherence and improved coordination across the EU. The 2050 strategy is a roadmap (CEC, 2011b) focusing on reducing greenhouse gas emissions by 80%–95% when compared with 1990 levels by 2050. The roadmap also prioritised the replacement of energy infrastructure and new technologies.

Two further initiatives are shaping EU energy policy. The first is a focus on energy security. This was a priority in Europe 2020 (Monti, 2010) and is an underpinning approach to all energy policy not least as the EU imports 50% of the energy that it uses. In some countries the reliance on imported energy is much higher. It also varies between types of energy supply with over 90% crude oil and over 60% of natural gas being imported. Russia is the main supplier. Where there is dependence on an external supplier this may be prone to disputes, political tension and infrastructure problems. In 2014, the EU developed an energy security strategy (CEC, 2014b) that has a main focus on increasing energy efficiency and energy supply within the EU. There is also a renewed impetus to complete the internal energy market within the EU. This approach to energy policy gives the EU more soft power within its members and in the world (Goldthau and Sitter, 2014). The second strand of EU energy policy is the creation of the Energy Union. This initiative has five priorities as shown in Box 3.5.

Box 3.5: EU Energy Union: the five objectives

*   ensuring security of supply for Europe
*   deeper integration of EU national energy markets
*   reducing EU energy demand
*   reducing carbon emissions from the energy sector
*   promoting research and development in energy.

Source: CEC, 2015a

The implementation of these policies in member states will require a hybrid approach to regulation of markets and competition in supply. In order to achieve the appropriate level then there is a need to progress and support renewable energy. The focus on energy security may mean that there is a move towards state control of energy networks either through ownership or stricter regulation with supply being generated through distributed means to manage overdependence on specific suppliers and reduce energy risk.

The UK is in a particularly difficult position as many of its power stations are being decommissioned as they do not meet EU environmental operating standards set out in the large combustion plant directive (CEC, 2001a). Through this, plants built earlier than 2003 could either opt to comply with the emissions limits or 'opt out'. Plant that opted out has been limited to a maximum of 20,000 hours of further operation, and must close completely by the end of 2015. Across Europe, 205 plants have opted out, with Britain having the largest proportion of its overall supply.

Within the EU there has been an initiative to mobilise local energy investment (MLEI) using financial assistance to develop projects including refurbishment of buildings, district heating/cooling, energy efficient street-lighting, and clean urban transport. This is now funded from Horizon 2020, the EU's research and development programme.

Renewable energy can be provided in urban and rural areas. In rural areas, individual farms and businesses may have wind turbines or anaerobic digesters that can generate energy with any surplus being put back into the national grid. In urban areas, combined heat and power schemes are more likely to be fuelled by waste and these schemes are particularly common in some EU countries such as Denmark (Lund and Mathieson, 2009) and the Netherlands (Hoppe et al, 2015). These facilities might be associated with particular development such as a large housing area or a single area development, such as the Olympic Park in London (Davies, 2012).

Within urban areas, infrastructure networks for energy have been provided as town and cities have been developed. Where urban sites are redeveloped these can be supplied with energy through the existing network. However, when greenfield sites are developed then these energy networks and connections to the grids need to be installed. In the UK, the costs of these installations and extensions are not attributed to the developer of the land but are spread across all energy users through the regulated pricing mechanisms. Greenfield developments are a cost on the system, unlike the provision on development in existing built-up areas where the cost of networks are sunk in historic development costs.

Planning for energy infrastructure provision may primarily be concerned with the generation of the energy rather than shortage of supply to any particular property. One exception to this may be the provision for new manufacturing or service industries where there may be heavy energy consumption or an assured supply is required at all times. In these cases, the resilience of the infrastructure provision may be critical and secondary sources of supply will need to be provided, such as generators owned by individual companies. Where there are major users or medical activities continuity of supply is essential at the local level. Local authorities may also address energy resilience in emergency planning operations including support for more vulnerable individuals if there is a loss of supply in the winter.

The planning requirements for any specific energy provision will depend on its scale. Larger planning applications will be managed through national processes such as in France (Marshall, 2009e) or the NSIP (Nationally Significant Infrastructure Project) process in the UK where national policy will establish the case for the further development of energy supply and then specific applications to provide supply will be made by energy institutions or companies. For other energy provision, the approach taken will depend on the proximity to other development and scale of the proposals. In areas where there have been major energy plants, there are subsequent problems of land contamination and remediation before reuse. The polluter pays for this remediation (CEC, 2004). However for older power stations this remediation cost is transferred to the state or to the private sector. On the sites of some former town-gas holders, the value of the site means that the costs of remediation are economically viable and can be included in development. However, in areas where there is a lower level of economic activity, these former power stations may stand unused for some time.

While sources of gas and oil have been depleting, the discovery and use of shale gas in the US has transformed the energy market (Stevens, 2012). It has provided the US with supply that supports their energy security and also reduced prices for consumers. This has made production costs lower and exports more attractive. The International Gas Union has identified that shale gas available across the world can potentially contribute 32% of the energy available (IGU, 2014). This has meant that there are energy security and economic pressures to access shale gas and put this into regular energy supply.

In the EU shale gas is regarded as an unconventional source of energy and there are public concerns about health and safety. In 2014, the EC adopted a recommendation communicated to all member states that identified minimum standards to be adopted in domestic legislation including environmental impact assessments. All member states were expected to adopt this recommendation by 2015. The EC is committed to undertaking more work on the legal framework for regulating shale gas. At present there are no statements on the role of shale gas in the EU's wider energy supply policy. Public concern to reduce carbon emissions and reduce the use of energy resources has led to the creation of the 'keep in the ground campaign' that is particularly focused on the investment in energy by pension and investment funds including those owned by universities and other public bodies.

Approaches to infrastructure delivery planning for energy are shown in Box 3.6.

Box 3.6: Approaches to infrastructure delivery planning for energy
- consider energy system as a whole for each governance scale;
- monitor existing consumption;
- identify how energy consumption can be reduced through retrofitting changing working practices, increasing public transport provision and use through integrated ticketing and other measures;
- introduce measures to reduce car use;
- identify potential for increase in renewable energy supplies;
- establish a local energy scheme;
- assess energy supply in all new developments;
- reduce air conditioning.

Water and drainage

Water management is operated through a number of systems. The first is water supply for drinking and other input uses into industrial and commercial processes. The second is the management of waste water, in a domestic or industrial setting and will include foul water and rainfall runoff. There will also be separate systems for managing water in urban areas through drainage into networks or now increasingly through sustainable urban drainage systems (SUDS) (Fryd et al, 2010). In urban and rural areas management for run-off if there is heavy rainfall or high tides or surges in rivers is needed.

The provision of drinking water is through a publicly regulated system. In the UK this is provided by commercial companies operating within a regulated market. The processes are the same for water as other utilities – that is, through individual companies making a case to the regulator about their relative costs of supply, maintenance and new provision. Much of the cost will be in improving networks as much water is lost through existing systems. These processes will vary in different parts of the country depending on the ease of supply. Much of the water for urban areas is brought by pipelines from rural areas.

Foul water may be managed by the same company as drinking water provision or separately. The management of foul water is through another network and it is passed through the sewers to the water treatments works usually at the edge of cities. As urban areas grow these works may require additional capacity and new water treatments facilities may be required.

Surface water drainage in urban areas had traditionally been designed to run off into sewers through street drainage and gullies that need to be maintained. Where this is not the case, heavy rainfall or river overflows can lead to serious urban flooding. In urban areas there is now a move to install SUDS so that rainfall can soak back into the ground and replenish the water table. SUDS operate in a number of countries and apply to all new development including hard standings in domestic properties and gardens (Environment Agency, 2008).

In rural areas, surface water runs off into fields and meadows that are part of the flood management system. However, recent severe floods in the UK have led to re-examination of their potential causes and method of management (HoC, 2015). In some cases, river maintenance including dredging has been stopped due to cost-cutting, reducing the capacity of the rivers to manage the flows. Second, the agricultural management of the uplands has changed (Pitt, 2007) meaning that it has been less able to cope with absorbing the scale of water that might fall or come from melted snow. The third reason is thought to be climate change where changing levels of rainfall have led to higher ground water levels and reducing the ability to cope with these increases.

Where flooding has occurred then new management and planning tools are required. These may include no development in flood plains although this practice has largely been abandoned in the UK as the pressure for additional housing grows. A second approach is to require new planning design controls so that ground floors in developments are used only for non-residential use such as garages and storage thus reducing the threats to life and property when floods occur. Past floods have also led to the establishment of new institutional management regimes. First-time flooding has increased since 2013 and is a major potential risk over the whole country.

There may also be coastal flooding and erosion that is caused by the weather. In 2013, there was a tidal surge in the east of the UK and in 2014 there was a weather bomb that affected the west of the country. As an island, the UK is prey to a number of different weather systems and, in some cases, the outcomes when they meet. In mainland Europe there has been a rise in river flooding caused by a combination of rainfall and melting glaciers increasing the water released into river systems. In some areas, such as the south of France, there have been increased land slips and flooding inland as smaller river systems fail to cope with the changing circumstances.

Planning for water supply and flooding are part of the planning process. The capacity of water systems in all of these different ways has to be managed and taken into account when identifying sites for all types of development as shown in Box 3.7.

Box 3.7: Approaches to infrastructure delivery planning for water supply
- Identify capacity of existing systems and networks.
- Identify existing and expected demand on current usage.
- Identify means of reducing pressure on capacity including water reuse and SUDS.
- Identify projects that are already committed by providers.
- Identify potential projects for reductions in network use.
- Identify locations where additional capacity is required.

Waste

The management of waste is undertaken in a number of ways. In domestic premises there is a focus on recycling and waste minimisation through EU directives on packaging and the landfill taxes that serve to encourage local authorities to support recycling (CEC, 2008). As recycling practices grow, this may have design implications for new development, including separated bins and storage areas for waste and recycling. There may also need to be more strategic spaces at depots or where recyclables can be stored and sorted.

Waste that cannot be recycled is sent into landfill and is subject to a landfill tax (CEC, 1996a). Landfill occurs where minerals have been extracted but there are concerns about toxic water leaching into the river and water systems and the product of previous landfill creating volatile methane gas. In some European states, energy supply is generated through incineration of waste and with increased recycling there may not be enough waste within that state to supply incineration plants. This means that waste from some countries, such as the UK, is being extracted from landfill sites and transported to countries such as Denmark and the Netherlands for use in energy creation (Hogland et al, 2010).

Planning for waste is the responsibility of local authorities (Davoudi, 2000) and includes design for storage, waste to energy, recyclables, landfill sites and reducing packaging. Approaches to infrastructure delivery planning for waste and recycling are shown in Box 3.8.

> **Box 3.8: Approaches to infrastructure delivery planning for waste and recycling**
> - Assess current recycling and waste levels at present.
> - Assess future levels of waste and recycling.
> - Identify ways of reducing waste stream and increasing recycling.
> - Identify ways of using waste for energy.
> - Consider policies for design of housing and other buildings to increase capacity for recyclable storage before collection.

Telecommunications

The provision of telecommunications to all properties in any country is now defined as an essential utility (Graham and Marvin, 2001). The speed and provision of broadband is said to affect the nation's economy and its level of entrepreneurship (Hodson and Marvin, 2010). Within the EU there has been a particular focus on rural broadband to support the rural economy (Preston et al, 2007) and in the UK this has been developed in Cornwall and Scotland. Not only is there a concern with provision but also with speed and scale of capacity that will affect connection and download times. There is further pressure on the services through online entertainment systems for films and TV and the use of multiple devices to view TV or undertake any interactions in one household.

Conclusions

Physical infrastructure requires long-term planning and is challenged by the silo structures of providers within and between sectors. Much spatial planning is concerned with the delivery of new infrastructure but this needs to be set within the context of existing capacity, reuse and repurposing in order to maximise its use before investment is made in new provision. More active engagement in retrofitting and design will also assist in maximising the use of existing provision. Where new infrastructure is required, considering longer-term trends and the potential for flexible operation in and between networks including infrastructure channels and access chambers will also be more efficient and effective.

FOUR

Environmental and green infrastructure

Introduction

Green infrastructure is used as a generic term to identify practices and investment that support the environment (CEC, 2013i). Green infrastructure ranges in scale and type from major flood alleviation schemes to small open spaces. In this chapter, rural and larger scale green land uses are discussed as environmental infrastructure while the term green infrastructure is used for urban settings. Tzoulas et al (2007) define green infrastructure as comprising 'of all natural, semi–natural and artificial networks of multifunctional ecological systems within, around and between urban areas, at all spatial scales' (p 169) and can include all types of formal and informal spaces including gardens (Cameron et al, 2012).

Linkages between environmental and green infrastructure are an important consideration in their provision and the associated value that they generate. Together they are a major contributor to the resilience of any locality, its people and economy as well as its environment. Environmental and green infrastructure also support biodiversity and contribute to the visual impact of places acting as an important component of health and well–being.

Roles of environmental and green infrastructure

Biodiversity

Environmental and green infrastructure has a core role in the protection and support of biodiversity as it operates vertically and horizontally through ecosystems (Duffy et al, 2007). While biodiversity is important in specific locations, this is within the construct of wider governance and regulatory systems. The EU has had a long-standing interest in biodiversity although this has primarily been through legislation on specific aspects (Jordan, 2008) until 2012 when a more integrated approach was introduced (CEC, 2012c). The delivery of biodiversity through infrastructure is part of the EU's strategy as set out in *Biodiversity 2020* (CEC, 2011e) and is applied through all public projects. This strategy has six targets. Target 2, that there will 'Better protection for ecosystems, and more use of green infrastructure' (CEC, 2011c) is shown in Box 4.1 and is supported by a range of actions as set out in Box 4.2.

The role of green and environmental infrastructure in delivering Target 2 of the EU's 2020 Biodiversity Strategy is set out in a technical report by EC (European Commission) staff (CEC, 2013i). The components of green infrastructure have

Box 4.1: Biodiversity Strategy 2020 Target 2: Green infrastructure

This target is based on the EU view that:

> many ecosystems and their services have been degraded, largely as a result of land fragmentation. Nearly 30 % of the EU territory is moderately to very highly fragmented[...]. Target 2 focuses on maintaining and enhancing ecosystem services and restoring degraded ecosystems by incorporating green infrastructure in spatial planning. This will contribute to the EU's sustainable growth objectives and to mitigating and adapting to climate change, while promoting economic, territorial and social cohesion and safeguarding the EU's cultural heritage. It will also ensure better functional connectivity between ecosystems within and between Natura 2000 areas and in the wider countryside. Target 2 incorporates the global target agreed by EU Member States and the EU in Nagoya to restore 15% of degraded ecosystems by 2020. (CEC, 2011c, para 3.2)

Box 4.2: EU Biodiversity strategy 2020 Target 2: Green Infrastructure actions

By 2020, ecosystems and their services are maintained and enhanced by establishing green infrastructure and restoring at least 15% of degraded ecosystems.

Action 5: Improve knowledge of ecosystems and their services in the EU

(5) Member States, with the assistance of the Commission, will map and assess the state of ecosystems and their services in their national territory by 2014, assess the economic value of such services, and promote the integration of these values into accounting and reporting systems at EU and national level by 2020.

Action 6: Set priorities to restore and promote the use of green infrastructure

(6a) By 2014, Member States, with the assistance of the Commission, will develop a strategic framework to set priorities for ecosystem restoration at sub-national, national and EU level.

(6b) The Commission will develop a Green Infrastructure Strategy by 2012 to promote the deployment of green infrastructure in the EU in urban and rural areas, including through incentives to encourage up-front investments in green infrastructure projects and the maintenance of ecosystem services, for example through better targeted use of EU funding streams and Public Private Partnerships.

Action 7: Ensure no net loss of biodiversity and ecosystem services

(7a) In collaboration with the Member States, the Commission will develop a methodology for assessing the impact of EU funded projects, plans and programmes on biodiversity by 2014.

(7b) The Commission will carry out further work with a view to proposing by 2015 an initiative to ensure there is no net loss of ecosystems and their services (e.g. through compensation or offsetting schemes). (CEC, 2011c, Annexe) been identified, as shown in Box 4.3, and the ways actions can be progressed are identified through the range of EC competencies and legislation and the activities undertaken at different scales of governance within the EU.

Box 4.3: Components of green infrastructure for biodiversity

- **Physical building blocks** – the network of green spaces in, which and through natural functions and processes are sustained;

- **Projects** – interventions designed to conserve, improve or restore nature, natural functions and processes to secure multiple ecosystem services for human society;

- **Planning** – integrating the conservation, improvement and restoration of nature, natural functions and processes into spatial planning and territorial development and sustainably delivering the associated benefits of human society;

- **Tools** – methodologies and techniques that help us understand the value of the benefits nature provides to human society and mobilise the investments necessary to sustain and enhance these benefits (CEC, 2013c, ')

The EC technical report also identifies the main contributions that such infrastructure makes in supporting biodiversity and the ways this can be achieved as set out in Table 4.1. It illustrates the economic benefits of this investment through the use of case studies from across the EU and Switzerland including green roof-building regulations in Basel, restoration of canals in England, flood plains in Germany and a river garden in France.

Within the EU an action plan to deliver the strategy includes biodiversity proofing of the EU budgets and Cohesion funds (CEC, 2013b). In order to monitor the progress towards achieving these objectives in each member state and across the EU as a whole, the European Environment Agency has adopted a set of streamlined biodiversity indicators so that comparison of progress can be made across the EU's territory (European Environment Agency, 2012). Assessments of the role of environmental and green infrastructure need to consider the integration of biodiversity into wider systems including within EU territorial Cohesion policy. This may take longer to assess including developing ways of measuring the effects and benefits of integration.

Each member state is responsible for preparing a strategy to implement the 2020 Biodiversity Strategy. In the UK, this response was published by each nation. For example, in England this was as *Biodiversity 2020: A strategy for England's wildlife*

Table 4.1: Overview of green and environmental infrastructure benefits

Benefit group	Specific green infrastructure benefits
Enhanced efficiency of natural resources	Maintenance of soil fertility Biological control Pollination Storage of freshwater resources
Climate change mitigation and adaptation	Carbon storage and sequestration Temperature control Storm damage control
Disaster prevention	Erosion control Reduction of the risk of forest fires Flood hazard reduction
Water management	Regulation of water flows Water purification Water provisioning
Land and soil management	Reduction of soil erosion Maintaining/enhancing soil's organic matter Increasing soil fertility and productivity Mitigating land take, fragmentation and soil sealing Improving land quality and making land more attractive Higher property values
Conservation benefits	Existence value of habitat, species and genetic diversity Bequest and altruist value of habitat, species and genetic diversity for future generations
Agriculture and forestry	Multifunctional resilient agriculture and forestry Enhancing pollination Enhancing pest control
Low-carbon transport and energy	Better integrated, less fragmented transport solutions Innovative energy solutions
Investment and employment	Better image More investment More employment Labour productivity
Health and well-being	Air quality and noise regulation Accessibility for exercise and amenity Better health and social conditions
Tourism and recreation	Destinations made more attractive Range and capacity of recreational opportunities
Education	Teaching resource and 'natural laboratory'
Resilience	Resilience of ecosystem services

Source: CEC, 2013c pp 4–5 adapted from: http://ec.europa.eu/environment/nature/ecosystems/studies. htm#implementation

and ecosystem services (Defra, 2011b) that covered the period to 2020. The success of the *Biodiversity Strategy 2020* is based on the progress in earlier programmes although evidence shows this has been mixed, as there have been trade-offs in competing priorities between land uses. The use of a common frame of indicators can simplify the approach to achieving biodiversity and improve the effectiveness of the strategy's targets. Further, rather than focusing on all the EU's territory, there would be benefits in focusing on locations where biodiversity, habitat conservation and ecosystem services are concentrated (Maes et al, 2012).

Mitigating and adapting for climate change

The role of green infrastructure is central to mitigating climate change (OECD, 2008) while infrastructure planning and delivery is central to adaptation and the changes required for the future. Policies for dealing with the threats of climate change are set within the UN Framework Convention on Climate Change through the 1997 Kyoto protocol and subsequent discussions including those in Paris in 2015. The protocol is concerned with carbon reduction measures. Much of this will be implemented through energy management in manufacturing and transport. Other contributions include management of emissions from landfill sites and the role of forestry in rural areas (Canadell and Raupach, 2008; Lindner et al, 2008), landscape management (Pielke et al, 2002) and tree planting in urban areas (Gill et al, 2007).

Heat island effects occur in urban areas (Steeneveld et al, 2011) and green space can have a significant role in influencing and cooling the micro-climate (Santamouris, 2007). When urban areas heat up, there can be a danger to life particularly for older and vulnerable people. The role of green infrastructure in helping to reduce urban temperatures through increasing street trees, and small open spaces can contribute to summer temperature reductions not least in areas where it is not possible to create major new open spaces (Gill et al, 2009). Other contributions to reducing urban heat islands include green roofs (Susca et al, 2011) and a reduction in paved surfaces (Golden and Kaloush, 2006).

While the contribution of green and environmental infrastructure in helping to manage climate change is understood, there are still challenges in implementation. Green space can be in fragmented ownership and management. In some cases its role is accidental rather than purposeful. In a review of case studies, where green infrastructure had been used to help manage climate change, Kazmierczak and Carter (2010) found that there were a range of practices. These are shown in Box 4.4 and can be applied in the processes of infrastructure delivery planning.

Barriers to the implementation of green infrastructure to mitigate climate change can be associated with attempts to quantify the degree of benefits compared with costs of implementation or the opportunity costs. Across Europe, the Covenant of Mayors has committed to prepare sustainable energy action plans for their localities including target for CO_2 reductions. By 2015, nearly 5,000 plans had been prepared. However, as Reckien et al (2014) have shown, 35% European cities do not have a dedicated climate change mitigation plan and 72% have no adaptation plan so this is a policy area that may receive more attention in the future.

Box 4.4: Climate change adaptation in green spaces: challenges

- collaboration with external stakeholders;
- strong leadership or championship;
- access to funding;
- awareness levels within the organisation;
- outsourcing research and other actions;
- human resources and skills;
- public awareness and engagement;
- quality and availability of information and data;
- position of adaptation on the list of priorities;
- development of local regulations and policies.

Source: Kazmierczak and Carter, 2010, p iii

Resilience

Environmental and green infrastructure are components in the resilience of land systems – that is, to manage disturbances and absorb them before any major changes are experienced in that system (Gunderson, 2001: 4; Walker et al, 2006). This resilience is a measure of how much disturbance (like storms, fire or pollutants) an ecosystem can handle without shifting into a qualitatively different state. It is the capacity of a system to 'withstand shocks and surprises and to rebuild itself if damaged' (Stockholm Resilience Centre, 2015).

Green infrastructure is a component of urban resilience (Foster et al, 2011) and assessments need to be systematic and incorporate costs of inactivity compared with the damage that can occur including loss of life, damage to property and business disruption (Leichenko, 2011). The methods that are applied to undertake assessments of potential shocks are variable and the dependencies between elements of the ecosystems are not well understood, particularly in urban areas (Sellberg et al, 2015). The management of natural resources is frequently undertaken separately and in compartmentalised ways (Berkes and Folke, 2000).

Planning for resilience also has a major role in managing climate change, particularly through adaptation in urban areas. By using these measures it may be possible to 'predict and prevent' but these approaches have also been criticised as being partial and not including shocks or unexpected events (Tyler and Moench, 2012). At the same time, taking measures to support adaptation may also have their own unintended consequences (6, 2010).

The provision of resilience is through institutions and agencies. These may be those concerned with environmental regulation or management. Where there is new development, this will be provided by planning. The practices of review and adaptation in all of these include cultural dimensions (Davoudi et al, 2013) and an assessment of relative priorities that is then translated into funded programmes. In the case of the floods in Somerset in 2014, the change in agency responsibility was identified as a contributor (HoC, 2015).

Planning for infrastructure delivery resilience uses evidence of past events together with future scenarios based on risk and emergency planning. Resilience and prevention can be incorporated into development locations and design codes (Cruz and Okada, 2008; Kibert, 2012). More relational approaches may be required with individual land managers in ecosystems areas (Wilkins, 2008; de Groot et al, 2010). This includes risk management and the application of resilience policies within the response preparation of individual agencies and institutions (Carina and Keskitalo, 2010). The potential use of emergency planning measures including using scenario tests may provide opportunities to consider not just the known but unknown unknowns (Palomo et al, 2011).

Resilience practices are being implemented with European cities. In the UK, preparation is said to be slow although there are examples where integrated (for example, Greater Manchester, 2015) and standalone (such as Mayor of London, 2011) reviews and actions plans have been prepared (Carter, 2011). In Zurich, a climate protection unit has responsibility across the whole organisation for the preparation and implementation of strategies, plans and projects (Alber and Kern, 2008).

Economic value

Infrastructure provision creates value for all land. Environmental infrastructure includes the provision of services that are used outside the source area (Stern, 2007). In rural areas, environmental infrastructure is critical in drainage systems, provision of adequate water and protection against flooding (Benedict and McMahon, 2012). Environmental infrastructure also plays a central role in maintaining resilience and protecting urban areas through links to green infrastructure systems (Foster et al, 2011). This infrastructure provides value to land in ways that may be less visible and understood than through other types. The absence of environmental infrastructure may only be apparent when the system is overwhelmed, such as by a flood (Ellis, 2013), and is effective investment practice (Jaffe, 2011).

The value of environmental and green infrastructure to land, buildings and places is provided, in part, through the planning system that assesses the resilience and potential remedial measures required to protect development land. In the exercise of planning regulation, there may be contested priorities between the provision of green infrastructure and other development including housing, particularly where this is an economic need in a locality (Roe and Mell, 2013). In these cases, where potential development sites are located in flood plains, on estuaries and coasts or below sea level, specific mitigation measures are required. In areas that have been identified as potential flood risks then flood risk assessments are required (Ligtvoet et al, 2009; DCLG, 2014a) and the development will only be permitted if the form and design are able to mitigate any risk identified (RIBA, nd).

Planning also assesses the capacity of services for land proposed for development. In this case, any mitigation may be provided and funded by the developer. However, in all utility services, such as water, energy and telecommunications, the cost of provision is through the fees and charges made to all existing users through regulated pricing systems. The methods of funding new environmental measures for open space or wider resilience are more diffused and may be reliant on the state. The role of planning in creating value for land in this way can be overlooked and underestimated (Marvin and Guy, 1997; Adams and Watkins, 2014).

In addition to the role and contribution of specific infrastructure types, there is also a cumulative and networked effect of the ways infrastructure works together (Jay et al, 2007; Therivel and Ross, 2007) although this may be difficult to assess in practice (Wärnbäck and Hilding-Rydevik, 2009). The interdependency of environmental and green infrastructure may be within geographies or systems (Rosenberg and Carhart, 2013). While there are benefits of positive interdependencies there may also be challenges when they are not fully examined or understood and subsequent problems can occur. Much of this will be identified through risk assessment but there are also occasions when phenomena occur for the first time. As with all assessments that model effects, the values contained within the assessment system will identify whose interests are being privileged and this may give rise to contestation and disputes in the process. This may also involve assessments of human rights (Jensen et al, 2015).

Mental and physical health

There is a direct relationship between green infrastructure and health (Tzoulas et al, 2007; Abraham et al, 2010). The relationships between health and green infrastructure are for mental and physical well-being and also for safety. Environmental and green infrastructure also plays an important role in the provision of food as well as offering opportunities for personal recreation and the positive mental responses provided by landscape at all scales (Ulrich, 1979; Benedict and McMahon, 2012). While there is evidence of the contribution of landscape and green space to mental health, it is difficult to identify how this works in practice (Lee and Maheswaran, 2011). When considering the relationship with personal health, Nielsen and Hansen (2007) and Sugiyama et al (2008) found that physical and mental health was supported by access to green space.

An increasingly urbanised population will place more pressure on existing green space and it may need to be managed differently or more space may be required (Stigsdotter et al, 2010). When considering physical health, a common way of approaching the provision and protection of green spaces is for planning policy makers to adopt a standard or criteria-based approach (Van Herzele and Wiedemann, 2003; Barbosa et al, 2007). In the UK, the informal standard adopted for sport and recreation is that proposed by Fields in Trust (FIT) (formerly the National Playing Fields Association). These include playing fields, local play areas with and without equipment and neighbourhood play areas with equipment (FIT, 2012). These spaces might be informal or formal and in some cases access might be confined to specific age groups or those whose residences provide access to a private open space. Although these standards are indicative and have been widely used they have no legal basis in the UK. Where local authorities wish to impose space standards this should be based on evidence, using specific and local research on demography, accessibility and patterns of use.

Other standards are linked to access so that no member of an urban population should live more than x metres away from access to some kind of open space. Where these standards have not been met, then parks have been created in urban areas, for example La Villette in Paris and Mile End and Burgess Parks in London. Access standards can be extended across scales and types of open space.

The role of green spaces in mental health is also important. Here the green space may not be accessed but viewed from the outside. Green spaces can be places to meet and locations for social activity either planned or unplanned, such as dog-walking. A view of green space from an apartment enables people to cope better with stress, and lessens mental fatigue and aggression (Kuo, 2001; Kuo and Sullivan, 2001). Urban green space can also support place identification and differentiation and a connection with the seasons.

Access to open space and the ways it is managed also has an influence on residents' attachment to an area. The design of green spaces is also important to mental health and safety can be enhanced through designing out crime measures.

Community involvement

Environmental and green space can be important in community involvement and cohesion (Wates, 2014). The role of urban parks can be a feature of community governance and include events and specific activities. The sense of relationship to urban spaces can define community boundaries and be characteristic of 'home'. This is an attribute of open space that is associated with all age groups although the specific associations and benefits may change at different points in the life cycle (Sugiyama et al, 2008). Community management can be undertaken by open space groups specifically set up to undertake this task or can be more informal. In some cases there will be a 'friends' group that does not manage the open space directly but supports activities and fund raising.

Community engagement can also extend to citizen science (Irwin, 1995) and the ways local ecosystems are managed (Cooper et al, 2007). As Haughton et al (2015) have shown, the role of local expertise in the management of environmental infrastructure is critical. They further argue that where water services have been transferred to the private sector there has been a loss of this expertise in public authorities, traditionally the producers of some of these services. This use of local knowledge and priority setting in green infrastructure planning is also advocated by Kambites and Owen (2006).

Integration

The challenge of environmental and green infrastructure is also one of integration between systems and places. The role of ecosystems and their mutual dependency is central to an integrative approach. When these systems are seen separately then this may reduce resilience or give rise to other problems. As Jordan (2008) has shown, there are difficulties in integrating all the elements that comprise environmental and green infrastructure and also with social and economic infrastructure, but this challenge is one that is now the focus of policy.

Environmental infrastructure

One of the core roles of environmental infrastructure is in the provision of environmental protection through land management schemes. These are elements in the relationships between urban areas and their hinterlands and changes in environmental management practices can result in flooding in urban and rural areas. While much of the discussion about environmental infrastructure is concerned with its management and maintenance and the potential problems that it can cause, it is also important to remember that it has more positive roles in the creation of energy, food and natural resources and in mental and physical health. It is also a central component of any economy and has to be considered in this way.

Habitat management

The role of habitat management includes protection and enhancement and is achieved through conservation, contributing towards wider environmental infrastructure. Within the EU, the Habitats Directive is the cornerstone of environmental conservation. The Directive was adopted in 1992 and updated since with a consolidated version of the Directive published in 2007. In 2013 an interpretation manual for European habitat was published (CEC, 2013j, 2013k). The manual sets out each type of habitat and then the elements that need to be considered. These include coasts, scrub, grasslands, rocky areas and forests. The manual helps to classify and identify the types of habitat for which the Directive provides the legal framework for the ways they are to be managed and protected. The EU habitats legislation is undergoing a fitness check known as REFIT (CEC, 2015d) to assess whether the legislation is meeting the original purposes, the costs of implementation and methods of application in different member states.

Methods of habitat management included in infrastructure delivery plans will take into account any specific local features. These local features can be directly related to a biodiversity plan that identifies where habitat management can contribute to the wider environmental infrastructure system. Habitat management may be achieved through specific projects, particularly where these are of importance or are high risk. In other cases, there may be ways of implementing habitat protection and enhancement through schemes for development. In order to achieve these ends there will need to be widespread coordination between those that have formal responsibility for habitats and community groups.

Ecosystem management and eco-services

Ecosystem management is defined by the UN as 'an approach to natural resource management that focuses on sustaining ecosystems to meet ecological and human needs in the future'[1] and is one of the UN Environmental Programme (UNEP) priorities. The approach adopted by the UN is based on regulation and restoration and considers this work in different types of area – freshwater, marine and coastal, and territorial ecosystems. The methodology selected by the UNEP for achieving better ecosystem management is through its integration into mainstream activities rather than separately. This involves making the case for action within governance structures and society, gathering the evidence and undertaking the task (UNEP, nd).

Ecosystems are part of natural capital. Ecosystem services focus on developing institutional capacity to support ecosystems, extend beyond restoration and regulation and include disaster management and mitigation. They are also concerned with the benefits of ecosystems to society and how these might be measured in a uniform way (Boyd and Banzhaf, 2007; Fisher et al, 2009). This approach has also been used by the EU in its assessment of the implementation of its *Biodiversity Strategy 2020* (Maes et al, 2012). This is based on *The Economics of Eco-systems and Bio-diversity* (TEEB). The TEEB approach has been adopted by UNEP and has been considered within the EU (CEC, 2009) and is associated with the identification and use of financial instruments and evaluations.

Planning for environmental management

One of the major concerns in planning for environmental management is its governance framework. The management of environmental and green infrastructure systems is complex and still being understood in theoretical rather than practical terms (Jordan, 2008). However, the OECD has argued that there needs to be a more integrated approach within the management of environmental and green systems and, to achieve sustainability, these have to be mainstreamed as part of a governance agenda (OECD, 2002).

The integration of environmental and green policies within governance systems remains problematic. The EU has started to develop this approach in the Lisbon Treaty 2007 with the principle of policy integration focuses on territory and place and away from sectors. Before this, an attempt to integrate sustainable development principles into EU policy making was attempted through the Cardiff Process (Jordan and Schout, 2006) but this was not effective and has been overtaken by more recent integration approaches (Morphet, 2013a). Where jurisdictions have a fragmented approach to infrastructure delivery, focusing primarily on sectors, managed by different government departments and agencies, it is possible to plan for infrastructure delivery projects. However what may be achieved through one project may be detrimental to others (Therivel and Ross, 2007).

The role of governance, including policy objectives and outcomes is critical in achieving this more integrated approach (Jordan and Lenschow, 2010). In the EU this is reinforced by common objectives and the creation of added value rather than considering each project as an end in itself. This means of achieving integration is through a territorial focus rather than a concentration on the provider institutions. While infrastructure providers have to make assessments of capacity requirements, their methods may rely on internal criteria rather than the combined effects for the specific project within its wider locus.

The use of infrastructure delivery plans that are led and managed by each governance scale is a way to address this. Democratic bodies responsible for places can identify ways of working together and can broker different programmes and projects. They can also bring together the providers, particularly where there are risks to be managed or new development to be planned. Local authorities can support infrastructure through their planning and development processes. Where institutional providers are less willing to act or see priorities elsewhere then local authorities can act as advocates and pump–primers. They may also work in groups that can include a water catchment area, estuary or river basin and develop integrated plans for managing the whole system. These may then be delivered through projects in a combined programme.

Green infrastructure

Green infrastructure is a core component of supporting and creating urban sustainability. While creating environments that encourage walking and cycling and use of public transport, it also has a role in urban containment and compact cities. It also has a role in making links between urban areas and the countryside. This is undertaken through specific physical measures to support containment such as green belts (Hall, 1977; Elson, 1986) and urban forests (Nowak, 2006). The introduction of ecosystems services planning has been associated with land use planning systems as Niemelä et al (2010) demonstrate in Finland and Bateman et al (2013) in the UK. Some approaches also rely on policy that requires interpretation in specific cases when development is proposed.

Implementing green infrastructure to promote sustainability needs a systematic approach that can identify how urban areas are growing and changing. There also has to be some public and political will to implement these changes and these may be contested when there are other social or economic matters to consider such as poor or indifferent housing or the need for new employment locations. Some approaches put these together to create park settings for housing and employment but these will be at lower densities. While they may create better settings for living and new green corridors to the countryside, they do not necessarily meet other sustainable objectives such as travel by public transport and walkable social infrastructure.

Within cities, growth may be supported through densification, reusing land for new purposes and increasing the density at the same time. Former dockland, railway lands or wholesale market areas are land uses within the city that can be reutilised for other purposes. These sites may have roles in supporting biodiversity and 'meanwhile' vegetation and an important visual role in the streetscape. When densified, these spaces can contribute to the green infrastructure in new ways and reinforce urban resilience at the same time.

Compact cities can be contrasted with edge cites or urban sprawl where suburbanised, low density areas outside the city limits and administration have grown to support the city's economy functions. The political and administrative relationships between these areas are critical although they are frequently fragmented, particularly in relation to transport (Merk, 2014). Developing more sustainable approaches to functional economic areas by finding ways of aligning the administrative boundaries to the economic space or to support local administration working together in ways that create a common democratic decision–making space.

Where cities are densifying then the role of green infrastructure can be more important. If people are living in smaller homes or apartments, then they may not have access to gardens or personal green space. In this case public spaces can become more important and their quality and management will be a priority. The management of green space may also need to change to reflect this role within localities (Jim, 2004). There may be a need for more children's play area and spaces within commercial and employment area for lunchtime physical activity and walking. Compact cities also suggest a greater focus on street greening through trees and other vegetation, including the promotion of window boxes and planters.

Where green infrastructure has been provided as an essential component of development it can be used to maintain property values. Green space has a specific value and although it may have an informal appearance it will generally be set within bounded spaces and formally managed. There may be room for informal seating and events space for lunchtime activities such as winter skating rinks, hard court games, markets or performance. However, the green space may not be networked into other similar spaces and biodiversity may be a concern. These spaces might be privately owned and, though there may be public access, the owners may be able to restrict this unless secured by legal agreements. A feature of green infrastructure planning has been identified as the role of its connectivity and also some coherence in the way that it is being planned (Kambites and Owen, 2006) including spatial, social and ecological functions and administrative or organisational connectivity.

Some countries have developed specific policy tools for protecting, providing and promoting the role of green infrastructure. In Sweden for example, towns and cities are encouraged to prepare a green plan (Sansdtrom, 2002). Kambites and Owen (2006) argue that green infrastructure planning should be embedded as part of the overall planning process and not undertaken separately. However, the way green spaces are managed impacts on the policies. If they are managed primarily for recreation by specialists, then they may become repositories for more facilities and different types of recreation. In these cases, running, keep-fit equipment, tennis courts and play areas may also be located within a single green space and may create 'rooms' rather than a whole from the perspective of the user. These are more provider- than user-based approaches to green space (Morphet, 1994).

Green belts

Green belts have been used as a means of urban containment and a separation between urban and rural areas since they were first proposed in 1935 around London and then included within the 1947 Town and Country Planning Act to be used where urbanisation was to be restricted for the future. Green-belt land was expected to be used for agriculture, forestry and outside leisure (Elson, 1986). They have become particularly important within planning policy and practice within the UK and have attained a protected status that is similar to national parks. See Box 4.5.

Box 4.5: Role of the English greenbelt as defined by the government
- to check the unrestricted sprawl of large built-up areas;
- to prevent neighbouring towns from merging into one another;
- to assist in safeguarding the countryside from encroachment;
- to preserve the setting and special character of historic towns;
- to assist in urban regeneration, by encouraging the recycling of derelict and other urban land.

Source: DCLG, 2012

The stated opportunities and benefits once an area of land has been defined as green belt are as shown in Box 4.6.

Box 4.6: Planning benefits of the English green belt as defined by government
- providing opportunities for access to the open countryside for the urban population;
- providing opportunities for outdoor sport and outdoor recreation near urban areas;
- the retention of attractive landscapes and the enhancement of landscapes, near to where people live;
- improvement of damaged and derelict land around towns;
- the securing of nature conservation interests;
- the retention of land in agricultural, forestry and related uses.

Source DCLG, 2012

While green belts have become popular with communities they are not always so popular with land owners who may wish to see their sites sold and developed for housing. They may keep their land in poor condition, managing it so that it is unattractive to neighbours so that there can be community pressure to develop the land and remove their eyesore. In these cases, green–belt land use may be intensified through new business and horsieculture.

Parks

Parks are formally defined and most frequently owned and maintained by the public sector. Parks may be provided in different ways, through specific park creation, landscaping in development or handed down from previous generations, and are all considered as a part of the wider network of open space. Parks can be assessed by the quality and scale of provision. In the UK, most local plans prepared by local authorities will include an open space standard and identify areas that are in deficit against this standard. There may also be associated criteria for the number of play areas, informal and formal gardens and areas of healthy exercise including cycle tracks and outdoor equipment. In some parks there will be courts for games such as tennis and playing fields for football, hockey or rugby. The use of open spaces may depend on their attractiveness to potential users and they can add value to neighbouring residential areas.

Urban greening

Urban greening can take a variety of forms from parks and landscaped areas to gardens paths and cycleways. In some cases networks routes are created by joining green spaces together such as the High Line in New York or canal/former rail track paths that contribute to wider networks.

Urban farming and guerrilla gardening

In some areas, where urban land uses have been abandoned, there has been a return to 'meanwhile' and guerrilla gardening and the use of land for farming or allotments to grow food. 'Meanwhile' gardens have frequently emerged on spaces that are earmarked for development but where the market is not ready for the development. These can include long-standing examples such as the Mudchute Farm in the Canary Wharf area and the Camley Street gardens at Kings Cross in London. Formerly, these sites were low–value and underused. These areas are now development magnets and are going through a transition from meanwhile space to essential greening lungs within areas that are now more densely developed. The provision of public spaces has been made as part of the developments but they are public realm spaces than natural gardens and so these meanwhile gardens present an important opportunity to complement what is now being provided.

In other cities, such as Detroit, the urban flight has led to larger tracts of land being left vacant and these sites are used to develop crops for food, not least for a population that is workless and poor (Sugrue, 2014). As Choo (2011) shows, this approach is also being used in other cities that are changing their planning ordinances where land has been abandoned. In addition to promoting urban sustainability and contributing to food security, urban farming can also contribute to biodiversity and wider ecosystems (Colasanti et al, 2012).

A further approach is guerrilla gardening where residents or communities take over space and plant them as gardens. These may be vacant spaces or can be unused tree pits along public highways. This approach has been adopted in numerous cities, for example Kingston, Ontario (Crane et al, 2013) and Birmingham (Adams et al, 2014).

Infrastructure delivery planning for environmental and green infrastructure

The approach to infrastructure delivery planning for environmental and green infrastructure is shown in Boxes 4.7 and 4.8.

Box 4.7: Approaches to environmental infrastructure delivery planning
- define the resilience challenges that need to be addressed including flooding, air quality, erosion and habitat;
- establish governance group that is co-terminus with catchment and risk areas;
- establish stakeholder and community groups that can advise and hold governance group to account;
- identify existing capacity;
- prepare risk register and assess relative risk;
- identify potential mitigation of risks;
- identify projects that will contribute to mitigation;
- identify areas where mitigation can be addressed through locational and design policies in the spatial plan;
- devise and implement monitoring programme;
- review risk register annually or after any event.

Box 4.8: Approaches to green infrastructure delivery planning
- identify standards for each type of green infrastructure based on population, density, age groups, air quality, drainage, biodiversity and health;
- develop standards with stakeholders and the community;
- identify governance groups that should adopt these standards;
- identify existing capacity against these standards;
- identify sites and policies for the locations in deficit;
- identify projects to meet these deficits including new provision and widening access to existing provision;
- identify locations for street trees and other informal greening.

Conclusions

This chapter has discussed the economic, social and environmental role of green infrastructure and the ways it supports community resilience including both health and safety. It has emphasised the need to develop and adopt local standards and the importance of maximising the potential of existing capacity between institutional owners before providing new. There has also been an emphasis on the role of resilience in all locations and use of risk assessments to identify where policies and projects should be prioritised.

Note

[1] See http://www.unep.org/ecosystemmanagement/Introduction/tabid/293/language/en–US/Default.aspx

FIVE

Social and community infrastructure

Introduction

Social and community infrastructure is essential for the functioning of society, including the economy. It includes all aspects of caring for individuals and contributing towards community life. Unlike other forms of infrastructure, it is the most varied in scale and type of provider. While universities and hospitals can be defined as major infrastructure on a national or subregional scale, they are funded by a range of sources including the state, research funds, donations, their own commercial operations and other charitable fundraising. At the other end of the scale, coffee shops that provide essential networking and community meetings spaces are frequently provided by sole business proprietors but are also operated by larger multinational companies and charities. Sports and leisure facilities may be owned by their members or the private sector, and funded by government, sports associations' grants, fundraising or charitable donations. Many social and community facilities are run and managed by volunteers including personal support, sport and youth organisations.

Social and community infrastructure operates in an integrated way. Services funded by the state for health and education are supplemented by voluntary and community services and the location of this infrastructure within communities can do much to support social cohesion. This is a form of social capital that has been identified as being critical to societal well-being that is essential for social order and a growing economy (Putnam, 2001). Social and community infrastructure is associated with happiness and its contribution to GDP (Stiglitz et al, 2009; Layard, 2011) through quality of life bundles that can be measured and compared between states (OECD, 2013).

The absence of social capital could be a contributor to areas with lagging economic growth as found in French and Italian rural areas (Callois and Aubert, 2007; Magnani and Struffi, 2009). In rural areas, social isolation may be a major concern and social cohesion can be promoted through other types of activities including the use of technology to allow for social networking and access to services including education and health (Simpson, 2005). In rural development programmes in the EU, the provision of networks and opportunities for engagement using the internet is a priority (Shortall, 2008).

The social pressures placed on individuals through community values can also be an important by-product of the maturing of social infrastructure in any locality. When new communities or neighbourhoods are developed, new residents do not want to wait for social and community facilities to be provided (Taylor, 2011) and expect provision from the outset. The mechanisms and methods of providing new infrastructure sit alongside that of managing existing infrastructure to its optimum in a sustainable way.

Social and community infrastructure also benefits from community contributions through volunteering. Local leaders act as advocates within and between the community and outside bodies. This might be supported through formal governance mechanisms including parish and community councils and neighbourhood groups. In new settlements, community development can be enhanced through proactive injection of community leadership and the nurturing of organisations to support the community as it grows. This is a long-standing approach used in new towns (Stott et al, 2009).

Social infrastructure can be considered in different groups that are all planned separately within and between sectors. While all social infrastructure will have operating models and constraints, they are brought together in a spatial context by the planning system, which identifies optimal locations for community provision and manages change, growth and decline in the provision of services.

Role of social and community infrastructure

Public safety

One of the core purposes of social and community infrastructure is a concern for public safety and security. This includes the provision of the institutions of law and order, including the police, law courts, prisons and associated facilities, and fire and rescue services. Some of these facilities need a high-profile public presence that is reinforced by their monumental architecture such as law courts while others including prisons are more likely to be in locations that are less visible (Clifford and Tewdwr-Jones, 2013). For some services, such as police and fire and rescue, locations are chosen for operational reasons as well as visibility. There is some evidence that the locational requirements of these services may be changing. The police may be moving towards integration with other public services for the first point of contact while telephone services may be provided through call centres away from the front desk (Millie, 2012). In Cornwall the first combined police, fire and ambulance officer has been appointed (April 2015).

Social and community infrastructure for public safety are concerned with location and interoperability. The degree of integration that is required in customer-facing delivery and back-office services will have an important influence on location and change. Where services no longer need town or city centre facilities, then accommodation can be vacated and used for other purposes. Sales of property assets can also generate income. Some services may be less popular neighbours, such as prisons or offender release hostels. Where these are long established in the community they will be accepted and part of social and economic fabric; however, where new facilities are proposed these may bring public disquiet and community opposition (Varney, 2006).

Social cohesion

The role of social and community infrastructure in promoting social cohesion is through the fixed investment of buildings, public spaces and other facilities together with the social networks that support them. This combination of community facilities and organisations creates social capital that is a central component of social cohesion and a public good (Kawachi and Berkman, 2000). Social and community infrastructure also creates continuity and a sense of belonging to specific localities that persists (Forrest and Kearns, 2001), creating local identities associated with specific buildings as repositories for memories. The degree of engagement within institutions is a measure of community trust (Letki, 2008).

Social cohesion can also be identified through place and belonging. This might be through residence in a village or specific suburb that has a common transport or access system or is reliant on one set of infrastructure for its services, including education and health. This dependence can foster strong community bonds that may be a support mechanism but may be seen as being threatened when populations change.

In some cases the use of community facilities can be focused on specific groups. This can be a means of supporting in-coming migrant groups, where they are from a specific country or from one religion. This may also create a more divided approach. Religious affiliation in society may be more important than nationality or place of birth. The provision of community facilities and places of worship for some groups may engender hostility and opposition (Dwyer, 2013).

While Putnam (2001) argues that strong associations with social and community groups is more likely to bring individual conformity and greater trust between individuals, there are also cases where such membership will bring conformity to more malign or destructive outcomes such as through gang membership (Garcia and McDowell, 2010). Even groups that have a strong membership or team ethos, such as sports clubs, can have cultural value sets that promote exclusions based on race or gender (Levi, 1996). Also for groups that may be organised and aware of institutional frameworks and be part of these networks, access to funding for facilities may be easier than those that are more disparate. Here comparisons can be made between a male-dominated sports club and facilities for women to play sport. In all of these cases there can be more focus on gatekeeper roles – who is in or out, or how long does an individual wait for membership – than the wider role within the community.

Taking a more individuated approach to membership within an organisation can have effects on demands for infrastructure. If groups are excluded from the use of facilities through informal membership criteria, then they may seek the provision of their own. Where facilities are at their maximum use then this will be justified but frequently facilities that are provided through public funding and donation are not fully used and small communities may have an oversupply of facilities that are difficult to maintain and fund. For sports halls, community centres and schools, the focus of the management of the institution can be more important than the sustainable management of the facilities for the community.

The economy

Social and community infrastructure has an important role in the economy and can be significant in the relative success of the state (Hall and Jones, 1998). This is particularly in relation to the development, skills and health of the population including those in work and their dependents. The level of education and skills available within any society will be an important component in its GDP as will its ability to attract highly educated and skilled people from elsewhere. Health services primarily support the population but also make a major contribution to research and development and to the wider economy.

The understanding of social and community facilities as a support to the economy has been developed through a public health agenda and relationships between housing, social and community facilities and places of work. Some facilities support communities near homes including parks, play areas, primary health and school provision, retail and other services. Others are located in town and city centres in order to support their viability. These may include specialist sports facilities such as ice skating rinks, theatres and concert halls, and major hospitals and universities.

The role of central place theory, operating at multiple scales, has been an important determinant in the provision of social and communality infrastructure. Support by public transport has reinforced their predominance. Edge of town retailing and services have appeared and then been tempered by changes in sustainable lifestyles, and micro convenience stores in transport locations or in smaller centres (Dennis et al, 2002). The rise of internet services for banking, finance, retail and travel have led to a decline in shops in the high street whereas others have combined a high street and internet experience through Click and Collect.

Sustainable communities

The location of social and community infrastructure is an important feature of sustainable communities, carbon reduction and equity. The ability to access health, education and leisure facilities that are available and with sufficient capacity is an important feature of life and if these facilities are only accessible by car then this will filter users by age, income and gender. Younger people have less access to cars and may have to rely on adults to drive them to leisure activities. Similarly older people may not have cars or be willing to travel in the evening. The primary locations for social and community infrastructure will be in town centres or transport hubs, or on paths and cycle routes. Also communities need access to work locations that is available at times that support working lives and when selecting a home location, journey to work and access to childcare and other facilities will be important considerations.

Social infrastructure: education

Preschool and nursery

Preschool provision is most frequently located near to homes, workplaces or transport hubs and user choice may depend on whether the child attends all day or for shorter sessions. Preschool provision may be through various types of facilities including schools with older children and in workplace nurseries. This provision may be by the private sector, public sector or through charities.

Adequate preschool provision is important for the child and the economic activity levels of the parents and is important for all communities. Purpose-built facilities can be provided when schools are planned. In older residential areas, provision may be located in community centres. Where new residential development and communities are master-planned, it is important to consider the location of preschool facilities. It may be necessary to locate some larger houses within neighbourhoods or to build this kind of business into the viability model of any community facilities. Smaller childcare and preschool provision can use other spaces such as larger shops or space within retail complexes for shoppers and workers in the area.

It is important to assess current and future provision of preschool facilities. The life cycle of housing occupation in areas built at the same time will mean that the requirements for such facilities will change and more flexible approaches to provision may be the best option. The provision of preschool facilities may be important in regeneration schemes or those areas with higher levels of unemployment and provide training facilities in the area (Melhuish et al, 2004). Standards for preschool facilities should be adopted and a proactive approach taken with potential providers including extensions to existing facilities. As urban areas become more densified there will be more pressure for these facilities including provision near stations and transport hubs.

Schools

Planning for schools is a difficult and opaque activity that is seldom integrated into wider planning for any area. This lack of a joined-up approach makes it difficult to plan for school provision. The government funds the education of each child on a capitation basis and from this school buildings are funded. Demographic trends mean that the demands for provision in specific areas can change and decisions have to be made about school buildings and their life cycles. In these cases, it is possible to house more than one school in the same building and this may be an approach to maintain two schools that can be expanded again in future. Also schools for younger children can be located in vacant space in secondary schools if there is capacity. While most schools are located in purpose-built school buildings they are also now located in other types of development including vacant retail, office and health space.

There are pressures to build new schools for a number of reasons. The first may be demand or expectation of population growth through new development. In this case, housing expansion sites need to be assessed according to the capacity of existing infrastructure before being selected, to ensure a sustainable use of existing investment. There may be strong pressures to build new schools as part of new development not least as developers identify these community facilities as an aid to sales. There may be pressure to close schools that are failing or performing poorly. In this case it may be possible to close the school but to reuse the buildings for another school.

Planning for school places needs to be part of an integrated process for all infrastructure. Education and health services should use the same demographic evidence and projections to enable integrated planning for facilities. This may be difficult to achieve. There may also be pressure from the government to build new schools where this will mean a change in their management status away from local authority to centralised provision. Infrastructure delivery planning approaches for schools are shown in Box 5.1.

Box 5.1: Infrastructure planning for schools

- No national access for catchment standard so needs to be adopted locally.
- Local policies on siblings may have an effect on schools utilisation and capacity.
- Additionally provision may be required and can be made in temporary buildings within the school or using the post-war model of housing two schools in the same buildings on a temporary or permanent basis.
- School playing space is important for the community.
- Safeguarding playing fields and cross-utilisation of playing space may need to be negotiated.
- Further pressure to pair state and independent schools that may assist in facilities provision.
- Provision of school sports facilities need to be taken into account with other provision; that is, no need for multiple sports halls and swimming pools in settlements that cannot support them; individual ownership and use is not sustainable.
- If population decline is this a short-term event or is it symptomatic of a longer-term change be leading to school closures?
- On the event of a short-term demographic change, can schools' accommodation be used in meanwhile way until it is required again?
- What are the best uses for school accommodation outside school closure?
- Many former uses such as evening classes or use of leisure facilities have been lost. Should these be planning requirements in the provision of new schools?

Further and higher education

Education post-18 is undertaken by further education colleges (FE) and universities. FE colleges are funded directly by the state and also have to generate their own income. As well as providing some post-16 academic education they provide vocational training for trades and disciplines not served by universities although in some case FE colleges now provide the first year of a university course. Fees for FE college courses are funded by the state up to age 18 and after this either through the employer or specific government and/or EU funded schemes. Infrastructure delivery planning for FE is shown in Box 5.2.

Box 5.2: Infrastructure planning for further education

Planning for FE provision

- define catchment areas;
- usually multiple sites based on amalgamations of previous independent institutions – do these need to be rationalised?
- funding from government likely to be risky or stopped at short notice;
- management being passed to governance of functional economic areas;
- constant pressures to improve vocational education for skills;
- local planning requirements will depend on the mix between policy, demand, political lobbying and funding;
- site requirements: may be free-standing or more to consolidate several uses in one site funded by development on the released sites.

Universities are hybrid organisations that receive some funding from the state, as well as funding from students through fees, from the private sector for research sponsorship, and from the voluntary sector. They act as public bodies, companies and charities. The main concerns for universities will be the size and scale of expansion as they develop entrepreneurial and economic activities through smart specialisation policies as part of their contribution to the growth in the functional economic area (Foray, 2013; Morgan, 2013).

While universities are used all year round, many of their facilities for undergraduate students will be used for only up to 35 weeks per year. At other times there will be pressure to let student accommodation and other space for conferences or tourism. There may also be possibilities for dual-use of facilities, particularly for sport and leisure during the school holidays and outside term time. Many universities have developed science parks and other entrepreneurial activities (Phan et al, 2005; Rothaermel et al, 2007) while some are now opening academy schools. There is also potential for other types of land use being located on their campuses, including housing for older people (Burstow, 2014), where students can combine learning with a caring role.

University building and campus development will depend on location. In cities, university accommodation is at a premium and many universities have purchased former commercial buildings to house their expansion, such as the LSE in London and Liverpool John Moores University. Others are developing new campuses or satellites and some universities have restored historic buildings.

While most parts of the UK have universities, there has been a recent push to fill gaps as part of the economic growth strategy, through new university colleges (DIUS, 2008). Approaches to infrastructure delivery planning for universities are shown in Box 5.3.

Box 5.3: Infrastructure delivery planning for universities
- What is the university's 20 year plan?
- How does the university define its own campus or home location?
- Can the university expand in its current location? If not what other plans does it have?
- What are the university's smart specialisations and do they require new premises close to other activities within the functional economic area?
- Would development of the university's facilities make them more attractive for uses for conferences and tourism?
- Does the university have a city-centre presence?
- How accessible are the university's facilities by public transport?
- Is the university campus contributing to biodiversity?
- Which university facilities can be used by the community and are they available?
- What potential is there for the provision of other facilities including preschool nurseries, schools and older people's housing?

Social infrastructure: health

Public health

Public health is concerned with prevention through supporting healthy lifestyles including exercise, provision of clean air and housing. Public health policy depends on the planning system for the design and location of development, its setting within associated safe and secure walking and cycling areas and, where these are not present, through their retrofitted provision. In some cases housing has been demolished to create new parks in locations of low provision. The public health agenda also encompasses the management of dependencies, including gambling. Clusters of betting shops have been a challenge that has increasingly been addressed by planning control (DCMS, 2014). Similarly the fight against obesity is being addressed through the provisions of physical exercise opportunities but also the provision of fast food takeaway shops close to school gates (HUDU, 2013).

While public health is more infused into everyday life there are also requirements for clinics or places that can promote public health in easily accessible locations by schools, in shopping centres and with other facilities such as libraries. In some locations, health facilities are housed in the same building as leisure facilities that are used for social prescribing.

Public health services are also operated and funded by the voluntary sector. In some places, there are voluntary sector hubs where groups can share accommodation and costs. The accommodation required may depend on the services that are on offer, including meals on wheels or support to people with specific conditions or age–related activities. In some cases, the organisations will need a town–centre location such as advice services whereas in others they may need preparation space and room for vehicles.

The funding of primary health premises is channelled through GP practices that provide the services. The government provides funding as loans and GP practices may then either purchase or rent their premises. Some will also expand services within their buildings for use by allied health services including pharmacies.

Approaches to infrastructure delivery planning for public health is shown in Box 5.4.

Box 5.4: Approaches to infrastructure delivery planning for public health
- identification of public health targets for the population;
- identification of current public health of population;
- development of stakeholder, communities and governance groups;
- identification of the major concerns that need attention, such as mortality, obesity, dependencies and their locational distribution;
- identification of access standards to support public health;
- baseline assessment of facilities;
- gap analysis;
- identification of policies and existing infrastructure that can be used to address the gaps;
- identification of additional capacity and project development;
- monitoring and review.

Primary healthcare

Primary healthcare is the gateway in to other healthcare service and is an important part of the social facilities that are made available to communities by governments. The ways these primary health services are made available and used are important contributors to the health of the people of any state (Starfield et al, 2005). Most healthcare systems in Europe are funded at least in part from taxation as well as social insurance schemes, and vary in each state.

Convenient geographical access to primary health services is a central consideration in provision. With higher participation in the labour market, working age populations also want access at times that suit them, including in the evening and weekends. However, much of the use of primary healthcare is taken up by older people and children. For older people, access to other support services may be needed in the neighbourhood. In some localities, the provision of monitoring vital signs and use of medication is undertaken by pharmacists (NHS England, 2013).

The delivery of primary healthcare services is constantly changing with a greater proportion of procedures being undertaken in primary health clinics and fewer referrals to hospitals. There are considerable differences in life expectancy between communities and primary health services are focused on these communities rather than others where there is a greater degree of good health and longer life expectancy. The pressure for new and expanded primary health facilities can be made by the 'worried well' or those with greater access to the means of advocacy.

Some primary healthcare is provided within hospitals in more integrated approaches just as some primary health clinics are now undertaking procedures that were formerly only offered in hospitals. Primary healthcare facilities can be combined with other services that have aligned purpose including sports and leisure centres, libraries, housing and child care facilities (Jones et al, 2009). This may also be particularly important in rural areas where clusters of services may be located in multiservice outlets (Moseley et al, 2004). This approach may also be important for specific groups such as children where combining services may also lead to more integrated care and treatment (Mongon et al, 2010).

Approaches to infrastructure delivery planning for public health are shown in Box 5.5.

Box 5.5: Approaches to infrastructure delivery planning for primary health

- evidence and needs assessment of population including age profiles and accessibility;
- identification and liaison with provider groups, standards and committed programmes being applied for primary health provision including doctors, pharmacies and dentists;
- identification of stakeholders and community groups;
- baseline assessment of existing facilities including capacity;
- gap analysis between population needs and current facilities;
- identification of any policies and projects to meet gaps;
- monitoring and review system.

Secondary healthcare

Hospitals are provided for larger areas of population. Some hospitals provide a community role offering care close to residential areas and for easy access. Others provide national specialisms. Access and use of specific hospitals may depend on patient choice. Within the English health system there is competition between hospitals and any hospital's survival may depend on its success in attracting patients. In some cases hospitals join together in order to create a critical mass, introduce operational efficiencies and increase organisational resilience. There is also some evidence that competition between hospitals can lead to better patient outcomes (Cooper et al, 2011).

Hospital locations are important for patient and visitor accessibility. They are major employers and staff numbers are greater than might be expected for their floorspace given their 24-hour role. Hospitals employ a range of skilled and professional staff that have an impact on the housing market and contribute to the social and cultural life of the area. Hospitals may be attached to universities and undertake research that may lead to the creation of new companies or may encourage research firms to locate near them. Finally, the location of a major hospital may add to the quality of life and attractiveness of a place and give it some competitive edge in comparison with other locations.

Approaches to infrastructure delivery planning for secondary health are shown in Box 5.6.

Box 5.6: Approaches to infrastructure delivery planning for secondary health

- analysis of current secondary healthcare system including local and strategic health providers;
- analysis of access to existing facilities;
- identification and liaison with provider groups for secondary healthcare;
- analysis of local health market and commissioning practices and their likely implications for demand for services;
- assessment of existing capacity and estimates of future change including reducing, increasing and diversifying capacity;
- identification of policies and projects required to manage change;
- establishment of monitoring and review system.

Mental healthcare

The requirements of mental health services are frequently overlooked in the consideration of the provision of health infrastructure. Much of the provision of mental healthcare is undertaken within community settings and patients access their services through premises above shops in high streets and through health therapy centres. Some services are delivered in the home. Mental health residential facilities are also located in the community and range from residential units to community hospitals with a strong emphasis on the integration and coordination between the services provided (Saxena et al, 2007).

Much of the care of mental illness is undertaken in the family, particularly where it can be supported through drug treatment regimes. In some cases, mental health deterioration is associated with age, including dementia, and there may be the need for more residential care when families are no longer able to support individuals at home. With a population that is increasingly ageing these types of provision will be more important (Burstow, 2014).

Approaches to infrastructure delivery planning for mental health are shown in Box 5.7.

Box 5.7: Approaches to infrastructure delivery planning for mental health
- analysis of existing population and mental health;
- assessment of existing mental health providers, standards applied and any commitments for provision;
- identification of stakeholders and community groups;
- assessment of any gaps between population and facilities;
- identification of policies and projects to meet deficits;
- establishment of monitoring and review system.

Social care

Social care is provided for those who cannot care for themselves or who may not need constant medical care but who cannot live on their own or in a family setting. These include people with mental and physical disabilities including dementia. The provision of social care has several different levels within it depending on the support required by the individual. In some cases this will be through sheltered housing whereas in others it may require secure accommodation. Some providers offer the whole range whereas others specialise. Social care is provided by all three sectors and costs are charged to the individual or their family.

With a growing population of over-65-year-olds, the pressure on social care relating to ageing will continue and more provision is needed (Burstow, 2014). Care may be required in locations close to family and friends so that older people do not become isolated. The assessment of social care services is made by a government regulator who will inspect homes against a published standard. An assessment of the current provision in the area for any planning process needs to be considered and sites identified where social care provision can be made if there is a deficit. This may be part of wider schemes or through the repurposing of other accommodation such as that within hospital grounds. It may also be identified as a part of the housing land allocations.

While most focus is on residential care, an increasingly older population may require other support services such as day care on the same model as nurseries – that is, families bring their relatives to be cared for each day while they go to work. Other new business models may emerge and some places may choose to specialise in older people – their care, and research around their conditions and lives.

Approaches to infrastructure delivery planning for social care are shown in Box 5.8.

Box 5.8: Approaches to infrastructure delivery planning for social care
- demographic analysis of current population and estimates of needs for social care;
- identification of current provision;
- identification of providers and future plans for provision;
- identification of stakeholders and community groups;
- identification of gaps in provision;
- plans and policies for future provision;
- development of specific projects to meet any deficits;
- develop monitoring and review system.

Community infrastructure: libraries and the arts

Provision of facilities for libraries and the arts may be on a variety of scales and delivered by different providers. They are an essential feature of placemaking (Evans and Foord, 2008; Markusen and Gadwa, 2010) and can create a sense of identity and association with specific locations. They are also important elements of the quality of life associated with places. Within the EU, cultural policy and the promotion of place is a specific part of developing a local and an EU–wide identity (Sassatelli, 2002) and there has been a promotion of cultural industries as part of the smart growth agenda (Cooke and De Propris, 2011). This is supported through the European Agenda for Culture (CEC, 2007a) that has an associated set of work programmes to support accessible culture, heritage, the creative economy and cultural diversity. There is also a major focus on cultural tourism as to generate economic growth and urban regeneration policy (Cooke and Lazzeretti, 2008; OECD, 2009, 2014) as a means of improving places and the role that they can play in a national economy and cultural life. Improvements for visitors can also be used by residents and workers.

Some towns and cities have major arts and library facilities that are used in a national or sometimes international context. At the same time, many settlements will have local arts facilities including multipurpose halls where theatre and cinema are offered as well as other practical arts activities and are important in rural areas (Markusen, 2007). For all arts facilities, other than commercially provided cinemas, there are challenges about funding and many are reliant on grants and donations as well as income. Libraries have been funded by the public sector but are now frequently funded by the community and managed by volunteers.

The distribution and provision of libraries and arts facilities is based on a number of factors. For commercial facilities this will depend on viable markets for the use of the facility and other provision that is available. In some cases cities with a strategic or subregional role may be the locations of arts facilities as part of their economic growth strategy and cultural economy (Montgomery, 2003; Grodach and Loukaitou-Sideris, 2007). In the past, libraries have been provided using location and access standards although the provision of library infrastructure may be part of the historic infrastructure of communities (Dewe, 2012). The role of these buildings may change. Libraries are also coming under pressure from other forms of media and changing their role to be knowledge hubs and innovation centres.

Box 5.9: Planning for libraries and arts facilities

- identify current provision and roles performed;
- identify stakeholder groups for libraries and arts provision;
- identify a service standard;
- identify access to services and any gaps;
- identify delivery models including community and dual function services, for example with health;
- assess the current provision of arts facilities;
- identify any gaps in provision including potential to support economic role of town centres of functional economic areas;
- identify how these gaps might be filled.

Community infrastructure: emergency services

The emergency services – including fire, ambulance and police together with associated facilities such as prisons and courts – are essential social infrastructure that are funded by the state. For some of these facilities, such as prisons and courts, they may need to be in specific locations with prisons in accessible but not central locations unlike courts, which will usually be based in the town centres. Court buildings also have an important role in demonstrating that justice is being actively pursued and may be the most visible.

Police stations were formerly primarily located in town centres but there has been a more recent move in the UK to relocate them with other public services so that there is a common public access point. For other police services such as interview rooms and cells then these can be in edge of town locations that provide more space for vehicles. The reduction in stand-alone police stations and combining with other public services has freed up some of the public estate in cities and made these available for other development, including housing, providing income for the police services if these sites are sold. Police services are also combining some their back–office functions.

The location of fire stations was formerly in the heart of the city or in town centres as most of the fire incidents were in the built–up areas or where there were concentrations of manufacturing industry. Recently, more fire service time is spent on road traffic accidents and other emergency incidents such as flooding. Fire stations are now more frequently located on ring roads so that there can be access to motorways and other major roads and also to town centres if required. In smaller settlements, fire services may be provided by 'retained' fire staff that work in the area and can be called on if there is an incident in the area. Fire stations for fire appliances and training might still be located in the town centre to allow the part-time firefighters to access them easily.

The ambulance service has started to vary the way that it operates by segmenting its services into different vehicle types. In areas where traffic may be heavy or the streets narrow, such as in historic towns, ambulance staff may be on bicycles or motorcycles. They use cars for rapid response, particularly for heart attacks. Larger ambulance vehicle locations will be determined by geography and the distance from hospitals. Other emergency services might include rest centres that are used if there is a major incident and these are rarely purpose-built but are more likely to be housed in other buildings such as schools and community centres.

Courts and prisons are part of a national service and there may be little local control over their locations. Both are major employment generators, particularly prisons, having a 24-hour staff requirement. Access to prisons for visitors will be important. Assessing the current and future programmes for court and prison provision is a core element of any infrastructure delivery planning process.

Approaches to infrastructure delivery planning for emergency services are shown in Box 5.10.

Box 5.10: Approaches to infrastructure delivery planning for emergency services
- identification of providers of emergency services and standards;
- identification of baseline of current facilities;
- identification of longer-term vision for services, access and co-location requirements;
- identification of stakeholder and community groups;
- service planning process;
- identification of policies and projects that are required to implement changes to services or meet gaps in provision;
- establish monitoring and review.

Community infrastructure: leisure, recreation and sport

Leisure and recreation services are provided by all three sectors. Sports and leisure clubs may be owned by the private sector, local authorities, schools, trusts or the community and should be considered within a wider infrastructure framework, such as their access by public transport and locations in town centres. Leisure and recreation facilities can be important components of town–centre policy, drawing in users who will use other facilities. Where the community owns a sport or leisure club, then there will be pressure to maximise its use for other purposes in order to generate income for its maintenance and potential expansion.

Approaches to infrastructure delivery planning for leisure and sport are shown in Box 5.11.

Box 5.11: Approaches to infrastructure delivery planning for leisure and sport
- identification of standards for sports and leisure provision including access;
- baseline assessment of existing facilities across all institutional providers;
- identification of all providers;
- identification of stakeholders and community groups;
- make assessment of gaps between standards and supply;
- identify how gaps could be met through widening access to existing provision;
- identify policies and projects that may be required;
- establish monitor and review system.

Community infrastructure: networking and meeting

The role of informal meetings places in supporting social and community networking has developed over recent years. These include cafes, bars, public houses, restaurants and fast food outlets. They are associated with more informal working styles, particularly for sole traders. The availability of wireless networks define them as 'third places' (Rosenbaum, 2006) that offer neutral spaces to spend time, meet people and potentially seek social interaction as a means of combating loneliness or social isolation. Unlike bars and pubs, cafes are less gender stereotyped and are more associated with a working rather than a leisure environment. Also, meeting in a cafe is not construed as having a personal meaning but rather one of convenience.

In some types of industry, including high-tech, coffee shops are critical in an innovation culture. These coffee shops have also become know as places where job availability and new firm formation has been particularly prevalent. Also, coffee shops can be places to meet where there is no space within the home environment or when such meetings might be interrupted. Cafe culture is also identified as having a large role in the development of cultural quarters as a means of prompting regeneration (Montgomery, 2003) and can have an important role in place identification and branding (Evans, 2015) reinforcing the role of other types of social and community infrastructure.

Box 5.12: Approaches to infrastructure delivery planning for social and community services
- identify any standards for social and community services;
- identify baseline of existing capacity including use, access and quality;
- identify any policies required to support community provision;
- identify providers and any plans or requirements for facilities;
- identify gaps and any existing provision that could assist in meeting gaps;
- identify policies and projects required;
- establish a system of monitoring and review.

Community infrastructure: places of worship

Places of worship are important elements of community infrastructure. They act as community focal points and place identifiers particularly through architecture and positioning within the urban environment and rural landscape. The development of the infrastructure of places of worship may depend on the history of a locality and the complex mixture of buildings may represent a long history or in-migration and change. It also possible to see that a variety of buildings for worship have been reused by other faiths or shared by more than one faith. Places of worship may also play a role in the production of multicultural places (Gale and Naylor, 2002) and the articulation of the presence of groups within the community whether in the UK (Gale, 2008), the Netherlands (Maussen, 2004) or Germany (Kuppinger, 2011).

The provision of places of worship can be difficult in the planning process (Germain and Gagnon, 2003) and create tension, although the responses will vary between places (Dwyer, 2013, 2014). It is difficult to identify a way of setting standards for the provision of different types of places of worship. At the same time, places of worship are funded by the faith communities and not other organisations, although they may be accompanied by community meeting halls and centres that might have some wider funding contribution to their capital costs or their use through revenue funding from public and other institutions (McLoughlin, 2005).

Box 5.13: Approaches to infrastructure delivery planning for places of worship

- identify providers and places of worship and any future plans for new facilities;
- review baseline provision;
- identify any policies and projects.

Infrastructure delivery planning for social and community facilities

The provision of social and community infrastructure is based on a number of supply and demand factors as shown in Boxes 5.14 and 5.15.

Developing an infrastructure delivery plan for social and community infrastructure cannot be undertaken in isolation from consideration of other infrastructure questions such as the provision of transport. Also there will need to be policy considerations on the effectiveness of clustering and co-location of facilities in town centres or in public service hubs with the potential benefits that distributed facilities might bring to communities and supporting their economic and community life. These need to be considered within a wider planning framework or specific plan so that existing locations may be reinforced by new investment or a retraction on competing development elsewhere.

Box 5.14: Supply process
- identify providers, their standards and proposed projects;
- existing supply, location, capacity and use baseline;
- relationships with existing demographic profile;
- potential for expansion;
- potential for combining facilities;
- service reshaping;
- market reshaping.

Box 5.15: Demand process
- demography
- fashion
- changing social patterns
- changing economy.

Where new neighbourhoods or large housing developments are being considered it is also important to consider their location within an assessment of existing capacity and much of the requirements for new infrastructure may relate to the ways existing infrastructure can be used or repurposed. While social infrastructure may be planned for as part of wider public investment, the provision of community infrastructure may be more informal and any new settlements will need to design in the capacity for these changes over its life.

Conclusions

The provision of social and community infrastructure requires the definition of standards and a view of the baseline of existing facilities. The demographic profile of any area and the likely changes over time will have a significant influence on demand for facilities. However, provision models are dynamic and frequently change. This all suggests that close working relationships are required between those undertaking infrastructure delivery planning, providers and the communities they serve.

SIX

International context for infrastructure planning and investment

Introduction

The development of infrastructure policy and delivery is a matter of state policy and budgetary frameworks, set within an international policy context. This can include financial contributions, incentives or conditions that shape the delivery and management of infrastructure. Some international organisations, including the World Bank, the OECD, the IMF and the UN, set the contextual policy priorities and reinforce policy adoption through a variety of means. In this chapter, the role of the international bodies in framing infrastructure policy and legislation will be considered.

The World Trade Organization (WTO) forms treaties that determine competition between state and non-state providers. The European Union (EU) is a membership organisation, established through treaties between states that pool specific policy and compliance requirements. In this role, the EU regulates the implementation of WTO competition agreements and sets its own infrastructure policies that are agreed and implemented by member states as part of economic and social policy (Meunier, 2005; Woolcock, 2010; Morphet, 2013a).

International organisations each play a specific role and these may overlap or cause tensions. Environmental and equity principles are set within the policy leadership of the UN. The economic framework is influenced by the OECD (Mahon and McBride, 2009), a membership organisation that examines the performance of the economies of its members. The OECD advises on ways to improve components of national economies including transport, infrastructure, training, skills, education and working practices (Woodward, 2009; Martens and Jakobi, 2010). At times, economic, social and environmental objectives may be in competition and conflict particularly when there is a global economic downturn or an environmental disaster related to economic practices.

The funding context for infrastructure is provided by the World Bank, focusing on developing countries and the IMF for the developed world. These banks have a role in policy and direct funding that may be conditional on operational standards such as sustainability or to design infrastructure for public transport rather than private car or road investment as in South Africa (Todes, 2004; Harrison et al, 2008).

Infrastructure policies, as in other spheres, are developed and communicated between politicians, government officials and the private sector in a series of formal and informal processes. Infrastructure policies, including the origins of economic policies and practices are then adopted across the range of international bodies. Some policies are agreed formally between states but soft power networks such as the World Economic Forum (WEF) and other non–state actors including major management consulting companies such as McKinseys and Bain have a considerable influence on thought leadership and policy acceptance (Stone, 2004). The role of these institutions is considered and set within the context of policy transfer (Dolowitz and Marsh, 2000).

Funding

Infrastructure is funded from multiple sources including governments, sovereign wealth funds, pension funds, bonds and the private sector. The World Bank funds infrastructure in less developed countries through loans. Other funding sources are also now emerging including the BRICS (Brazil, Russia, India, China and South Africa) bank established in 2014. The European Investment Bank (EIB) provides loans for infrastructure, focusing on EU schemes, including Trans-European Networks (CEC, 2013a) and the Juncker programme (CEC, 2014d). The IMF also acts as an economic watchdog and can provide stabilising funding for economies that have specific and short-term difficulties.

There has also been an increase in public–private partnerships (PPP) for infrastructure funding where the risks are distributed between the partners and financial contributions from the private sector may be paid back over long periods of time (Grimsey and Lewis, 2007). These arrangements have been used by governments to fund investment in different types of infrastructure such as health, although the enthusiasm for this kind of financial arrangement may not always produce the most cost-effective methods of funding in the longer term (Hodge and Greve, 2007; Engel et al, 2013).

These international institutions have interests in the infrastructure investment and implementation policies of individual states. The WTO is concerned if excessive regulation is preventing open access to markets by foreign investors while the OECD and IMF monitor state levels of infrastructure investment and its role in economic competitiveness. The UN is concerned about the scale of sustainable solutions that are being used for infrastructure investment including competition between modes, use of renewable energy and sustainable cities.

International policy transfer in infrastructure policy

Infrastructure planning and delivery operates within this international context, set within parameters that are discussed and informally coordinated through global organisations. The communication and adoption of these policies use 'soft power' techniques where influence can be based on value and cultural systems, exchange of staff and informal alliances (Putnam and Bayne, 1987; Nye, 2004). These global organisations foster and encourage policy transfer between their members (Rose, 1993; Dolowitz and Marsh, 1996) through a variety of means that include comparative benchmarking, research, policy leadership and networks. Those engaged in policy transfer – politicians, civil servants, professionals – may all take some reassurance from adopting this approach and indeed some cover if there are subsequent problems and 'blame' for failure (Hood, 2012). However, reliance on the methods of policy transfer suggests further questions. What is the provenance of these policies and how are some privileged above others for adoption by global organisations? Another consideration is the potential over-reliance on external policy prescriptions by nations and a failure to consider the specific conditions for implementation in any country (Dolowitz and Marsh, 2000).

While policy transfer may be voluntary, it may also be reinforced through conditions associated with aid and loans although the policy may be changed to fit with specific local cultures or existing institutional arrangements. While most policy discussion may be on inputs, such as the application of policy framing or funding mechanisms, some organisations, including OECD, consider the effect of the outcomes of the policy application and their comparative effectiveness (Pollitt and Bouckaert, 2000). There can be negative effects if policy transfer is coercive, particularly where the policy is radically different from existing cultural norms (Morphet, 2013a). Here policies can be subverted or only partially implemented and the degree of pressure to adopt a specific model will be associated with political ideology and will.

This international context is critical to understanding the development and implementation of infrastructure policy and the role that it plays in wider economic policy making. It is also discussed in the language of 'what works' or 'learning from abroad' (Dolowitz and Marsh, 2000). This approach is regarded as being less risky by politicians and has the benefit of some understanding of risk even where this might be culturally bound. There is also some comfort in using policy packages based on experience elsewhere. This approach supports an international consultancy and advice business between states (Stone, 2004). Taking this approach can be more easily communicated to politicians and officials if a policy is already operating in other countries and is risk averse.

Policy transfer literature suggests that most policies are iterative, developing as they are passed between different state bureaucracies (Marsh and Sharman, 2009). However, policies can make a step change to include a new element or move in a different direction. One example of this is the rise in importance of infrastructure as part of economic growth. Infrastructure has always been an element of state investment policies but its importance has gradually increased. This may be related to the geopolitical changes since 1990 with the consequential need to connect with new markets and cheaper labour sources. Sustainability principles and climate change have grown in recognition in the operation of business since the UN Rio Earth Summit in 1992.

The development of endogenous growth theories have served to focus an increased attention of internal markets as well as those between states (Krugman, 1991, 2011). Finally the lack of investment in infrastructure has come to provide a secure haven for international funds since the economic crisis that started in

2007. Hence, a number of factors have promoted infrastructure investment and these have now reached the point where they are embedded in policy practice although delivery effectiveness may still be in development.

Why do these international trends and policies matter in understanding infrastructure delivery planning? For practitioners, the application and operation of policy, legislation and funding may appear to be the most important issues. However, these policies can influence the ways that they are applied and acceptable policy solutions framed. They will also help to identify policy priorities and assist those institutions seeking support and funding in the arguments that they make in business cases.

Roles of global policy institutions

Policy institutions are set by the roles that have been assigned to the organisations through legislative and cultural practice in international relations. In this section, each of the institutions considered is examined within its own purpose and objectives together with the type of policy influence it has on infrastructure policy and provision. The next section will consider how these operate together and serve to influence particular types and spatialities of projects.

United Nations

The UN has environmental, economic and social responsibilities, objectives and priorities that frame the delivery of infrastructure. The UN has taken a lead on the environment with the overarching philosophy of 'three pillars of sustainable development – the notion that you cannot, however successful economic indicators may be, progress unless you take the social and the environmental dimensions of sustainable development into account' (Steiner, 2014). The UN provides a forum for global discussions and in some cases negotiations on policy (Knill and Liefferink, 2007). While the UN is not a regulatory body, its agreed protocols and declarations create a policy framework adopted by other global organisations and states. The UN's environmental policies have a particular influence on infrastructure delivery planning including energy conservation, air quality and climate change,

Through the work of the Brundtland Commission (1987), the Rio Earth Summit (1992) and its recall meetings in 2013 and 2015, the UN has set a leadership agenda that creates a philosophical, moral and cultural framework for its members throughout the world. The environment is borderless and the UN has taken forward its work on climate change through the Kyoto Protocol (1997) and its subsequent renegotiation. The UN undertakes a role in global environmental monitoring and the environment programme extends to the use of fuels, pollution, demographic change and equity. One of the main objectives of the UN is to ensure that sustainable objectives and principles are enshrined within governmental decision-making at all scales. This may be translated into regulatory standards that frame the implementation of infrastructure and the relative priorities between transport modes or between types of investment – roads or flood defences.

There have also been critics of the UN approach. As a global organisation without specific powers, the UN can find it difficult to obtain agreement between states and then to reinforce implementation by its members. There are also concerns about the UN's global governance role and how effective this can be. As the role of the UN becomes stronger and more influential it becomes the target of specific interests and non-state actors to influence its views and shift its norms (Biermann and Pattberg, 2008). Even where policies are adopted they are reliant on local implementation and regulation and can also suffer from failures in horizontal and vertical integration.

The UN is focused on achieving world 2020 Millennium Development Goals for sustainable policies to be incorporated by governments and support to retain biodiversity. It has developed a programme and discussed it in Paris in 2015. This is focused on the relationship in contributions between developed and less developed countries particularly focusing on energy use and emissions.

Within the EU, the UN has had considerable influence on environmental policy and delivery mechanisms, including the development of specific policy instruments (Jordan et al, 2012). Knill and Liefferink (2007) directly linked specific UN meetings and debates on environmental policy with the EU's own environmental action programmes from 1972 onwards. Since then the relationship between the EU and the UN has been more symbiotic with the EU using the UN to promote its own policy agenda, including the Kyoto Protocol on climate change. This commits signatories to reductions in the emissions of six greenhouse gases and supported the introduction of an emissions trading regime. This has had a significant influence on a range of EU infrastructure policies and priorities from vehicle design to switches to public transport and journey reduction that have been delivered through a range of measures.

OECD

The OECD is a membership organisation founded, as the Organisation for European Economic Co-operation, in 1948 as part of the implementation of the post-Second World War Marshall Plan in Western Europe. Since then it has grown through widening membership and changing its role 'to promote policies that will improve the economic and social well-being of people around the world'. It operates through 'a forum (where) governments can work together to share experiences and seek solutions to common problems' (www.oecd.org/about/, 2014). The OECD encompasses all policies and actions that contribute towards economic and social well-being. These include assessments of the drivers of economic, social and environmental change, measurement of productivity and global flows of trade and investment, comparison of data, prediction of future trends and setting international standards in a range of areas including agriculture, tax and safety of chemicals.

The role of infrastructure in the OECD is developed through a range of policy areas including investment, local and regional development and governance. It also has specific programme areas for individual infrastructure types including energy and transport. The OECD has identified infrastructure as a major challenge for future development of economies and delivery of well-being through its study of strategic infrastructure needs to 2030 (Stevens et al, 2011) followed by studies on strategic transport infrastructure (OECD, 2012). This policy assessment was accompanied by case studies on particular locations drawn from its membership, primarily from the EU. The OECD research is predicated on the statement that 'Quality infrastructure is a pillar of international competitiveness. It is trade enhancing – especially for exports – and has positive impacts for economic growth' (Stevens et al, 2011, p 6) and is translated through assessments of infrastructure in each of its members.

The OECD works in three ways. First, it sets an economic agenda that is reinforced through assessments of its members' economic performance. Second, much of its research is focused on the 'what works' approach and the potential replication of policy solutions. Third, it identifies problems that impede the progress and implementation of 'what works' solutions and benchmarks all of its members to identify leaders and laggards.

The OECD has no power to compel its members to adopt policies or promote actions but it has a significant 'soft power' role (Nye, 1990, 2004), through comparing performance between members and associating this with the practices that have achieved these outcomes. However, Stone (2004) and Lal (2001) argue that the OECD can inculcate common economic norms and values that frame problem setting and the evaluation of any resolution. The OECD can also be invited by its members to consider specific problems or geographies by undertaking focused comparative reviews that are accompanied with specific recommendations, although these are not binding. In 1993, the OECD gave Norway a favourable review for its environmental policies (Hovden, 2004). This reinforced the approach to environmental policy and delivery that was being taken in Norway and in the other Scandinavian member states, thus providing them with a stronger voice in EU policy development.

The OECD is increasingly considering the relationships between infrastructure, institutions and governance that are involved with its provision and management. This has been a particular focus related to the adoption of new economic geography policies after Krugman (2004) and the subsequent development into an assessment framework that is being applied to all OECD members (Charbit, 2011). This creates a tension between central and local decision–making in governance models. The evidence suggests that local working can be more effective if managed in specific urban constructs such as FEAs. These are informing substate governance structures across the OECD (Brezzi and Veneri, 2014; Merk, 2014).

This approach is exemplified through studies undertaken by OECD of two types. The first is on specific areas, such as the relationship between metropolitan governance of transport and land use in Chicago (Merk, 2014). This study focused on the effects of governance fragmentation in the provision of transport and its consequential effects on economic performance of the FEA (functional economic area). In the Chicago tri-state region there are 784 special districts with transport responsibilities. Further, the ridership of public transport systems is low, as is the level of integration within the systems. While there are mechanisms for institutional cooperation, these are not vested with many powers and lack of leadership and vision of the transport system in Chicago is identified as costly and failing to generate investment.

The second type of study compares locations with similar spatial attributes and infrastructure. A study of the role of ports in local public policy and the relationship between the port's activities and the economy of its host city is an example. Merk and Dang (2012) argue that these are seldom considered together and economic growth synergies could be greater than generally understood. Where there are economic benefits to host cities these were primarily in activities associated with the port rather than as a consequence of any positive policies to promote ports, to generate business growth or specialisation. While R&D policies can assist in the interactions between the port and its host city, local economic growth was more likely to be engendered by wider improvements in transport interconnectivity, making the port a hub rather than a stub. Merk and Dang recommended to the OECD that port city packages should be designed as policy instruments and these approaches are operating within the EU policy sphere (CEC, 2013d).

The third OECD policy priority is cross-border working. This is also a priority within the EU where the single market is still hampered by differences in trading across borders and cultural non-tariff barriers to trade. The slow progress in dealing with problems of cross-border trade was identified as a priority in Europe 2020 (Monti, 2010). The OECD has undertaken some specific studies including in the island of Ireland (Nauwelaers et al, 2013b), across the Oresund between Denmark and Sweden (Nauwelaers et al, 2013a), between Finland and Estonia (Nauwelaers et al, 2013c) and Norway and Sweden (Nauwelaers et al, 2013d). These studies are focused on the way cross-border areas can operate as FEAs with a common economy, labour force and specialisation but are being held back by a lack of common governance and commitment from local and central government. This means that there are few strategies for these areas and they are not developed into combined investment programmes for infrastructure. This serves to undermine their success. While the EU is a driver in the development of cross-border projects, these initiatives are identified as being short-lived and not embedded in local culture.

In this example of policy agenda setting (Kingdon, 2003), the OECD and the EU have aligned approaches, with the OECD providing external and quasi-independent analysis of the challenges created by lack of commitment to working across borders in the EU and its potential economic effects. However, this approach is also underpinned by the EU's adoption of the OECD's preferred method for local economic development and analysis of FEAs. So these EU studies serve to reinforce the OECD's policy priorities and its ability to use these approaches in recommendations to other members where cross-border working is a practical reality. The OECD has also undertaken territorial reviews within Europe primarily within FEAs including Newcastle (2006), the Randstad (2007b) and Madrid (2007a). In each case, the reviews have taken an integrated approach.

The OECD has also considered specific concerns in relation to transport. In 1972, for example, it considered sulphur emissions from transport demonstrating that the effect of these pollutants was trans-boundary (McCormick, 2001). While it was agreed that the EU did not have the power to implement the recommendations of this study, it was taken up by the UN and then eventually agreed by 34 European states, wider than those in EU membership. Although Britain and Germany were against the proposed controls on emissions, and the resulting commitment was more general than had been anticipated, this process enabled the EU to take some action on emissions from vehicles. As McCormick argues, these steps did not represent a fully developed strategic policy on emissions or the environment but it demonstrated that the EU could implement an agreement that had developed through work undertaken initially by the OECD and then the UN.

The OECD also has a direct role in energy policy; membership of the International Energy Agency (IEA) is dependent on OECD membership. The IEA was founded by the United States and holds emergency stocks between members that may be shared in a crisis (Buchan, 2010). The OECD has located its energy policy interest in its green growth programme, focusing on business and technological innovations needed to implement a green growth policy. The OECD takes a proactive approach to developing the economy of green energy technology through its actions such as trawling the patents approved for new green technology products (OECD, 2012) and identifying where innovation is fastest, and associated with most economic efficiency in use. However, despite this progress, the OECD found that carbon emissions were not reducing so they recommended more focus on reductions in use and improving the reliability of renewable sources particularly for retention of supply within the energy grids.

The OECD has undertaken policy assessments across its membership including of budgetary processes, institutions and the effects that they may have on infrastructure investment (Boateng et al, 2014). Long-range social and economic forecasting for its members considers the challenges of the next 50 years (Braconier et al, 2014). These have been identified as slower economic growth and higher environmental costs for OECD members. These will frame future OECD assessments of their members and their resilience in being able to withstand or respond to these pressures. This makes institutional roles central in policy agenda setting and solution formation. These individual studies, usually published as OECD working papers, identify where states are falling behind others or neglecting challenges that have an influence on economic performance.

Working papers on the UK have identified poor infrastructure and inflexibilities in the housing market that have influenced labour migration (OECD, 2011a). In Belgium, which has a concentration of manufacturing industry and cheap non-renewable energy, the absence of a national policy to achieve lower emissions targets has been identified as a problem (Koźluk, 2011).

Thus the OECD exerts influence on its members in setting agenda priorities and then encouraging policy transfer through research and comparative studies as a means of initiating government policy change. The OECD's focus on infrastructure as an element of economic growth, together with its research on policy and delivery, have been included in country reports, and have identified priorities for different states to address. The OECD plays an important role in infrastructure policy and delivery although this is not much acknowledged by governments or wider research.

WTO

The WTO (and its predecessor GATT) is responsible for obtaining agreements between member nations about the ways trade is conducted between them. This had primarily been focused on trade for goods including electrical products and food. However, in 1976 an agreement was struck that committed members of the WTO to open services owned by public sector organisations to competition from the private sector (Meunier, 2005), through liberalisation of the markets. The agreement recognised the position in each state at the outset together with the political context in operation. In effect, each state identified how different sectors should be exposed to competition and how this would take place in a programme that would last for many years. In the UK, the priority was given to energy and transport in the 1980s and this was followed by some local authority contracting in the 1990s that had the greatest influence on waste management and back-office services. The remaining sectors of health and education were not tackled until the 2000s.

The WTO progresses by 'rounds' of talks that may extend over several years and, when concluded, they are agreed through a treaty implemented by its members. While each state that has signed the WTO treaty is responsible for implementation, the EU has become an intermediary in negotiation of these treaties and in reporting on their application and delivery. In some cases these agreements may be between all WTO members and on others agreements may be concluded between some members such as that on government procurement (GPA). Significant areas of EU economic activity are included in WTO agreements including agriculture and services, with particular attention on public services. The approach taken by the EU is 'rule based' or regulatory, although this style of negotiation has been less favoured by other members of the WTO since the beginning of the Doha Round in 1995 (Young, 2007; Adlung, 2009).

The approach to public sector contracting has been supported through policy and the procurement directives and is known as liberalisation within the EU's policy lexicon. The EC manages this process through different sectors and markets. These regulate the way public services can be exposed to competition including publication of notices in the *Official Journal of the European Union*. The EU public services approach includes three public procurement procedures – the open, the restricted and the negotiated. Once a method has been selected then this has to be followed through. Failure to abide by this legislation can result in legal proceedings, including criminal convictions. Any infringements are taken through the European Court of Justice (ECJ). Where there are specific economic concerns, states can request derogations in the implementation of these treaty obligations. However, despite these agreements it is clear that even within the EU there are many barriers to trade that are acting as protectors of state markets and reaching the potential for economic growth. In Europe 2020 (CEC, 2010), specific areas where trade is not open include those of services and also the ability of small firms to participate in the market.

In its wider interest in trade, the WTO is also concerned with the impact of infrastructure, particularly that of transport on the effectiveness of world trade and competitiveness of individual states (Nordås and Piermartini, 2004). This is seen to be a positive role that the WTO can take, particularly in countries with developing markets (Milner, 2009). The WTO also has to work with and incorporate other global agreements such as the Kyoto Protocol and apply pressure to use WTO agreements to deliver these protocols (Goh, 2004). The implications of this approach for infrastructure delivery planning have been that a hybrid system has been created whereby the providers of infrastructure may be from any sector but networks are all managed by regulators that operate at state level.

IMF

Like the OECD, the IMF was set up in 1945 as part of the reconstruction effort during and following the end of the Second World War. It is focused on economic stability and global growth. It has a more formal role on the surveillance of the economic health of individual countries and will support them if they have difficulties in meeting their balance of payments obligations. It also has a commitment to reducing poverty. As part of its remit it undertakes research on global financial health and also provides technical assistance to countries to help in the improvement of their economic performance.

The IMF has identified infrastructure as a core component of economic health and stability and economic growth. It has undertaken research to support this view and to demonstrate to its members the extent that infrastructure has an impact on spatial as well as national economic outcomes (Limao and Venables, 2001). It has also discussed the funding of infrastructure through different financial models and institutions such as public–private partnerships (Hammami et al, 2006) and a more recent interest in the role of investment in the public sector (Warner, 2014). The IMF considers these strategically across economies and in the longer run in comparisons with the OECD's shorter-term policy and delivery focus.

However, the major area where the IMF influences the provision of infrastructure investment and projects is through individual country reports that are prepared on its members. These may be general or focus on a particular concern such as poverty reduction or inequalities. These reports are important in setting economic policy and investment priorities. While the recommendations of the IMF may not be welcome, its influence in markets, setting rates and national credits scores that influence interest rates means that they cannot be ignored. Further if a country needs any specific help from the IMF, this is likely to tie them more closely to the economic policy prescriptions that have been set.

In the UK, as a part of its surveillance of economic health, the IMF has recommended that the government creates a greater economic stimulus through increased investment in infrastructure (IMF, 2012). The UK economic policies are regarded as different from those of the majority of other countries with its emphasis on the neo-liberal trade policies and curbing public expenditure. This is in comparison with the IMF that retains more welfarist values in the advice to its members. The IMF is also concerned with the development of trade with the BRICS economies and their role in proposing infrastructure within their own countries; and supporting investment in infrastructure in other countries, for example, the Chinese in Africa and in the UK. The IMF regards these relationships as important but also as having some risks that need to be considered.

World Bank

The World Bank was founded in 1944 and formerly known as the International Bank for Reconstruction and Development. The main focus of the World Bank is to reduce poverty for the world's poorest 40% of people. This means that its work is primarily geared towards developing countries and although initially based in Washington, DC it is now has a more distributed structure around the world. The policies of the World Bank are delivered through a range of measures that will improve economic growth to alleviate poverty and it works with states on joint projects where the World Bank is co-funder.

The World Bank is more similar to the OECD than the IMF and it focuses on detailed assessments and practical projects that promote change. The World Bank has a considerable interest in infrastructure investment, including for energy, transport and water. However, as a project partner in the development and delivery of schemes, including providing some of the funding, it has the ability to strongly influence the nature and type of solution such as sustainable transport or renewable energy. Like the OECD, the World Bank also considers the role of local governance and leadership and prompts policies associated with aligning governance with economic spaces, as also found in the OECD and EU.

In its approach to urban management, the World Bank is directly engaged with the political leadership of some state government and by using examples from other countries demonstrating that integrated approaches, to planning, transport and property assets, can attract private investors. This work considers transport pricing policies and training, that are also regarded as integral part of developing the economy capacity of urban areas.

Figure 6.1: Urbanisation policy framework

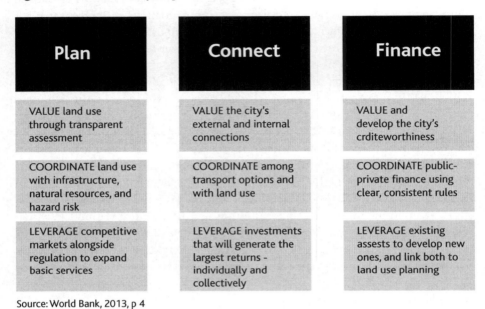

Plan	Connect	Finance
VALUE land use through transparent assessment	VALUE the city's external and internal connections	VALUE and develop the city's crditeworthiness
COORDINATE land use with infrastructure, natural resources, and hazard risk	COORDINATE among transport options and with land use	COORDINATE public-private finance using clear, consistent rules
LEVERAGE competitive markets alongside regulation to expand basic services	LEVERAGE investments that will generate the largest returns - individually and collectively	LEVERAGE existing assests to develop new ones, and link both to land use planning

Source: World Bank, 2013, p 4

BRICS Bank

The New Development or BRICS Bank is a multilateral development bank that has been established by the five founder BRICS nations at a meeting in Durban, South Africa in 2013. Its creation is an alternative to the World Bank and the dominant Western ideologies that are associated with it. The bank is located in Shanghai and it will create more competition and be primarily interested in supporting infrastructure investment projects, although as it was formally established in 2014 it will take a while for the project programmes to be agreed. This has been supplemented by the Asian infrastructure investment bank established in 2015.

World Economic Forum

The WEF is a think tank and lobby group for the interests of business. Its main annual event is in Davos where political and business leaders meet to discuss economies and ways business would like politicians to respond in their own countries. The WEF is a setting for informal ideas and influence. Most of its proceedings are in private, although it publishes policy and position papers, including those on infrastructure. It argues for greater investment in infrastructure to support business but recognises that this has to be in a way that meets 'green' objectives (WEF, 2013). Statements of policy like this from the WEF are important to politicians who might argue that investment in infrastructure is not a priority or that business's goals are for benefits such as lower taxation or less regulation. It also provides a means to engage in debate on infrastructure investment that has some wider policy anchorage within the business community worldwide. While infrastructure investment services business needs, the business community also sees this as an opportunity for investment and growth in the private sector and thus a means of business expansion.

The WEF had a focus on infrastructure development between 2014 and 2016 and has been encouraging governments and private capital markets to support investment. The WEF has identified the seven steps that governments can take in order to improve their potential for investment and these are set out in Box 6.1.

Box 6.1: Seven steps that governments can take in order to improve their investment potential

The seven steps are:

1. Understand the current infrastructure situation.
2. Formulate a long-term vision and medium-term goals.
3. Prepare a list of infrastructure deficiencies that need to be rectified and identify potential solutions to address these deficiencies.
4. Decide which potential solutions create the greatest impact in terms of economic growth, while considering social and environmental issues.
5. Decide who should pay for the infrastructure – users or taxpayers.
6. Finalize the prioritization of projects based on available cash resources (both government and private sector).
7. Move from planning to action. Publish and market the plan, ensure that the necessary policy changes are enacted and, for the selected projects, finalize the detailed preparation process so that 'bankable' projects can be tendered. (WEF, 2012, p 19)

For each project, the WEF recommends that specific information is published as shown in Box 6.2.

In 2014, the WEF produced a blueprint for infrastructure investment (WEF, 2014) for governments, advising on ways to attract investment from private capital. One of its main findings was that each government needs a strategic vision for infrastructure with an associated pipeline of visible projects. Within this, the WEF recommends that a clear role for investors is identified and that projects are set within a supportive regulatory framework and with long-term political support. In this blueprint, the WEF identifies the differences in the ways governments and investors view infrastructure with a clear statement of the interest of infrastructure to the private investor, as set out in Box 6.3.

Box 6.2: Infrastructure investment: setting out the project pipeline

Project-level details of a pipeline should include:

- description and current status
- regulatory model
- type of contract (e.g., concession, management and lease contract)
- estimated start date and duration of project
- estimated capital costs
- lead and involved government agencies and permit approval requirements
- key stakeholders (WEF, 2012, p 20)

Box 6.3: Infrastructure projects: attracting investment

A project's attractiveness is based on financial features that include:

- Stable returns, reliable cash flows and low volatility.
- Infrastructure projects are often a natural monopoly with high entry barriers. Once construction is completed and a demand pattern developed, project risks are low.
- Portfolio diversification. Returns show a lower correlation with other asset classes and the wider economy than other types of investments.
- Hedge against inflation. Concession agreements and regulatory models are frequently linked to changes in the inflation rate.
- Ability to put large amounts of money to work. For investors with deep pockets, the significant size of certain infrastructure projects can be very appealing (WEF, 2014, p 7).

The WEF points out that investment in brownfield infrastructure is less risky than greenfield investment as it will have a demand history.

The WEF produces an annual assessment and league table of state performance on infrastructure and although this has no formal role, it is a significant influence on state activity and investment and also on investment within states by business. The interaction and possible influence of the WEF on infrastructure delivery programmes can be noted through the actions of states including the UK (HMG, 2014) where although having the fifth largest economy in WEF tables, it comes 27th in the infrastructure table (WEF, 2014). These rankings are also used within the EU for FEA programmes (ESPON, 2013).

How do these institutional policies operate in practice?

One of the drivers of the joint working of the policies of international organisations is the prevailing economic orthodoxy. Since 1991, this has followed Krugman's notions of focusing on internal supply within FEAs – labour markets that are defined by commenting patterns of the labour force (Krugman, 1991). The effects of these theories can be seen through the development of city-focused policies within the OECD and EU and these are accompanied by assessments of the relative performance between FEAs in OECD countries. A similar approach is being used by the World Bank for their clients.

One of the major concerns of international policy makers is how far they have their own agendas (Shaffer, 2001) or are servants of their members; also, given their power, the extent they can be influenced by those who have commercial and state interests in the outcomes. Third, they may reinforce each other or work as 'good cop, bad cop' in any specific policy area.

Conclusions

The role of international institutions in infrastructure delivery planning at all state scales is significant although seldom recognised and discussed. Their importance is that between them these institutions can 'make the weather' at the international level and their identified emphases or priorities will be translated into local implementation. Understanding these issues and awareness of their research can provide more confidence in building business cases for funding from both the public and private sectors.

SEVEN

Infrastructure in the EU: policy, plans and practices

Introduction

Infrastructure policy has been a core priority within the EU from its creation (CEC, 1957). Since then, it has developed as a central component in the framework of institutional, geographical and economic development. Infrastructure forms an active policy arena at all spatial scales and across EU competencies. The EU framework for infrastructure policy includes managing the single market and its responsibilities for open competition in public services on behalf of the WTO. Infrastructure delivery planning in the EU encompasses social, economic and environmental dimensions that create frameworks for all member states. Infrastructure policies that are pooled within the EU include transport, energy, environment, water and digital networks. Through the single market, the EU is also concerned with cultural policy, including tourism and heritage. For practitioners, understanding the EU's policy trajectories and engaging with them particularly during their formulation can be critical in the consideration of strategic and local infrastructure delivery planning.

EU policy development and management

EU policies and programmes derive from treaties and are delivered through multi-annual programmes. The Lisbon Treaty was the last to be agreed, in 2007. Programmes range over six to seven years and deliver policy priorities, legislative programmes and targets for each member state. In the period 2010 onwards, these are set out for each state in Economic Convergence Agreements (2010 onwards) and the Partnership Agreements for Cohesion policy (CEC, 2013b). EU policy is implemented through legislation as Directives or Regulations. Directives indicate the objectives of specific policies and legal frameworks for member state interpretation with implementation deadlines. Regulations are implemented in the words as set out and without being approved by the member state's parliament. These programmes last longer than electoral terms and provide each member state with the potential for a general election and leadership change to accommodate shifts in policy direction (Goetz and Meyer-Sahling, 2009; Morphet, 2013a).

EU policy development and implementation will comprise the following elements:

Past policies/commitments

The EU is a continuing narrative with temporality of policies and a central component in their development and delivery (Goetz and Meyer-Sahling, 2009). The EU policy process is continuous (Morphet, 2013a) and while, in member states, policy narratives may change with the ideologies of different elected governments, in the EU there is a continued commitment to achieve ever closer union and stronger economic, social and territorial cohesion (Mendez, 2012). This approach sets the agenda and frameworks for policy and, while these may cause problems for individual member states, the process is enduring.

At the heart of the founding principles of the EU is the Single European Market (SEM) that has been further codified through the Single European Act (1985) and developed through Europe 2020 (Monti, 2010). The SEM has developed to include the social and cultural dimensions of difference between states set out in the principles of cohesion. Initially cohesion was defined in social and economic terms and from 2007 a third dimension – territory – was added. The cohesion principle is important in all EU programmes as it is a means of assessing the outcomes of policies and addressing lagging territories. Adding territorial cohesion has created a third lens for EU policy consideration that focuses on all policies coming together in specific locations (Barca, 2009; Sarmiento-Mirwaldt, 2015).

The EU's infrastructure policies have been developed in phases closely aligned to the contemporaneous dominant EU objectives. Transport was defined as a common policy sphere in article 3 of the Treaty of Rome 1957 that included powers to provide funding for transport where this supported better internal connections and applied to road, rail and inland waterways. Energy policy was developed through agreements on the European Atomic Energy Authority.

Between 1957 and 1972 the EU was primarily concerned with transport as a mechanism for the common market. The environmental dimension was strengthened in 1972 when Denmark and Sweden joined the EU (Morphet, 2013a). The dominant interest in the period 1985-92 was the development of the SEM when transport was recognised as a central component (Cockfield, 1994). Different environmental regulations in member states was construed as non-tariff barriers to trade, protecting domestic markets so the SEM also widened the scope of trade to include environmental and social dimensions in ways that were not always anticipated by member states (Haigh, 1987, 1996).

During the next phase of the EU's development between 1992 and 1999, the dominant focus of infrastructure was on its role on integrating the EU's territory. This was through the creation of Trans-European Networks (TEN) to connect major cities, including ports, economic centres and capitals. These networks include transport, energy and telecommunications. EU policies for each sector have been developed in parallel. In transport, the first wave of TEN-T (Trans-European Networks – Transport) policies followed the Maastricht Treaty in 1992, establishing the primary corridor networks as a response to Enlargement. Up to this point much of the Structural and Cohesion funds had been used for transport in the countries with lagging economies, for example Spain, but the economic challenges facing the accession states meant that there were wider economic and communications concerns to address. Following the adoption of the TEN-T Regulation (CEC, 1996b), there have been adjustments and refinements although the corridors remained unchanged.

The second wave of TEN-T policy was launched when territorial dimensions were added to the cohesion policy in the Lisbon Treaty (2007). There was a review of the functioning of the TEN-T policy and a new Regulation was adopted as part of the wider cohesion policy changes for the period 2014–20 in 2013 (CEC, 2013a). This second wave policy realigned some of the corridors and formalised integration between the TEN-T corridors and other infrastructure policies through the establishment of the core and comprehensive networks. The core networks are defined by the most important corridors and nodes – capitals, major cities and ports. The core network has an associated improvement programme that is expected to be completed by 2030. The comprehensive network is to be established by 2050 and includes linkages within the core network. Comprehensive networks are designed to link TEN-T with the transport networks within FEAs (functional economic areas) being developed through Sustainable Urban Management Plans (SUMPs) (CEC, 2007b, 2009). These programmes are supported through funding packages including *Connecting Europe* (CEC, 2011) and the Juncker plan (CEC, 2014d).

The policy for energy and the TEN-E (Trans–European Networks – Energy) network has developed in different ways and taken longer, using networks including the northern energy pipeline between Ireland, the UK and the Nordic and Mediterranean countries (CEC, 2006). These energy networks will eventually be connected into a single energy grid. The EU's energy policy is a priority for the period 2014–20 with a dominant concern for energy security. The single market in telecommunications has been developed to incorporate a digital agenda including interoperability, trust and security and an open market. There is also a focus on the use of digital means of communication by citizen and business. The digital agenda was developed as part of the Europe 2020 programme to improve the economy, including health and social care.

However, although there are dominant policies and initiatives during each multi-annual programme they are supplemented rather than replaced by additional policies for the following period. Hence the policy menu becomes more complex and interrelated over time (Stewart et al, 2012). The policies and programmes for energy were initially environmental, dominated by reductions in use and sustainable objectives to increase the provision of renewable energy sources and consumption. This was followed by the role of energy within the single market – the prices of different energy types and the competition between providers and between member states were all important to support the parity in the operation of the internal market. The most recent priorities have been for energy security.

Until 2007, cohesion policies have been concerned with relative social and economic inequalities in discrete localities. There has been no strategic plan for the EU's territories or analysis of the way sectoral policies have affected specific places. However, the EC (European Commission) has identified the need for a territorial strategy together with spatial planning policies since 1992. Spatial planning policies have developed through a number of different but allied initiatives, although these have not been identified by the EC as a single policy commitment. The changes from 1992 onwards shifted Cohesion policy away from lagging territories to economic and social linkages across borders through the INTERREG programme.

The European Spatial Development Perspective (ESDP) was evolved between 1992-99 (Faludi, 2004; Dühr et al, 2010), by an informal Ministerial Council. This informal approach was adopted as the UK challenged the EC's competences for planning. However, the EC also undertook two other initiatives. The first the preparation of *Europe 2000* (CEC, 1991) and *Europe 2000+* (CEC, 1994) led by the Commissioner for the Regions, who was British. Second, although the EC did not accept the UK view on their competences, it promoted the inclusion of territory into the next (Lisbon) Treaty so there would be no further challenges. The ESDP will be revived through the work on the European Territorial Vision 2050 (Mcrit, 2014) and will be presented at the beginning of the programming period 2021-28 when it will address spatial policy and infrastructure investment.

Another initiative was to reinforce and strengthen the role of substate governments in each member state. Although this may seem at odds with the development of a more strategic planning approach, the EC also recognised that the substate levels would support spatial policies and that their voices were not heard in these discussions. The Committee of the Regions (CoR) was established in the Maastricht Treaty and the principle of subsidiarity was enhanced in 1992 to provide a legal framework for distributing the roles and responsibilities within the state. The Lisbon Treaty gives the CoR responsibility for referring states to the European Court of Justice where subsidiarity is not being applied in governance (CoR, 2014).

Member state priorities and internal balance

Policy development implementation in the EU is also dependent on member state priorities and internal balancing. National interest in policy making can be presented in a variety of forms, including through appointed Commissioners in specific policy areas (Greenwood and Aspinwall, 2013).

Member states can also progress agendas through the rotating presidency. Given the number of member states, this opportunity presents itself once every 14 years and lasts for six months. However, this includes periods of influence before and after the presidency that lasts up to two years. The EC is aware of the presidency priorities of each member state, and they are mutually aligned. The highest presidency rewards come in the conclusion and naming of treaties or other EU conventions. Presidency periods are also assessed on the capability of the chairing role in ensuring other member states are in support of the agenda.

This will depend on the skills and diplomacy of each chair within the EC and other member states (Smeets and Vennix, 2014).

Success in the presidency role can be measured on a number of dimensions. Smeets and Vennix (2014) assess this primarily with an internal focus – whether the agenda was a success with the EC and members states and whether it delivered for the presidency. For the member state holding this role, success might be a specific agenda–setting process with some geospatial or policy ambitions. In some cases, a group of member states agree to develop some linked themes and initiatives through their presidency periods. This was the case in 2014–2016 when all the EU Presidencies (Italy, Latvia, Luxembourg and the Netherlands) focused on spatial planning at different scales – Italy at the urban level, Latvia at the small towns scale, Luxembourg at the pan–EU scale and the Netherlands on cities – culminating in the Pact of Amsterdam 2016.

The third way member states' priorities can be progressed through the EU is in the selection of implementation methods. If a member state has a preferred approach to delivering or managing a policy there is an advantage if it is adopted by the EC. In this case, the member state will have fewer transitional costs and first mover advantage for consultancy advice to other member states. Member states can also attempt to influence policy through the size and distribution of the budget. Member states can propose the use of informal methods between the Commission and the European Parliament where there are common interests.

External commitments and pressures

The role of the major global institutions in infrastructure policy and agenda setting are very closely entwined and at present represent neo–liberal hegemony, although, as noted earlier, the introduction of the BRICS Bank in 2014 may alter this weighting. The EU is strongly aligned to the overall economic policies of the UN, OECD, IMF and the World Bank and it also works with these organisations to promote common agendas through the World Economic Forum.

These agendas are now located in the new economic geography and sustainability narratives that encourage the development of FEAs as structuring units of economic activity and aligned governance (Gurria, 2014). These organisations prioritise strategic and sustainable infrastructure as a component in any global subregional economy. In the United States this is suggesting investment in heavy rail services. In the EU, one of the greatest considerations is the integration of the land area of the 28 member states and its partners in the European Economic Area (EEA) – Norway, Iceland and Lichtenstein – through TEN-T networks. These partnership states develop their own institutions and legislation to be in harmony with that of the EU. For EEA states this is automatic, whereas in Switzerland this is undertaken on a step–by–step basis and in 2000, over 85% of Swiss legislation was compliant (Kux and Sverdrup, 2000). Switzerland also has a special infrastructure relationship with the EU, set out in the EC-Swiss Transit Agreements (in 1992 and 2001) but remains outside any formal grouping.

The EU manages its competition role through the use and application of its legislation. Services must be tendered through a legislative framework, although this has been interpreted differently in each member state (Knill and Lenschow, 2005). Hence in the UK there has been a focus on tendering by the lowest price although a second method enables purchasers to assess potential bidders for the provision of goods and services by other means, including quality and a range of other criteria such as provision of training.

In each member state, public services have been exposed to competition, although in different groupings. In France, there has always been an open healthcare market between specialists and consultants while in Sweden many of the schools have been provided by the private sector. In all countries, open procurement in infrastructure has operated differently in each sector. The introduction of open procurement through deregulation in the UK services open to competition were primarily focused on infrastructure, commencing with coach travel (1980). Freight (1982), buses (1984), airlines (1984), airports (1985), docks (1989) and ports (1991) followed. The reform of air traffic control (1996) has been associated with later policies on integration of the service across the EU as part of the TEN-T programme to 2030.

Wider economic context of policy making

The wider EU economic context of policy making was particularly important at the time of economic downturn from 2007 and subsequent eurozone crisis that needed short- and longer-term action. However, the crisis has also enabled progress on EU economic and monetary policy, including greater regulation of the banks, policies for growth through investment and a new attack on the competition barriers in the SEM (Monti, 2010). This has been translated into the revised policy for TEN-T (2013), energy (2015), cohesion policy (CEC, 2013b) and matters that were formerly regarded as domestic responsibilities including housing, following the lead of the OECD. Thus the crisis has enabled the EU to progress its objectives rather than adopt new ones.

Barriers to EU infrastructure policy integration

While policy development within the EU is centralised through the development of treaties and multi-annual programmes, the delivery remains separated into the responsibility of different Commissioners, appointed by the member states and given specific roles by the President of the Council. Many Commissioners take the leadership responsibility for one DG (Directorate General). Each DG will have its own objectives and priorities. For infrastructure, these are divided between transport, energy, environment and telecommunications. Within the EU, these policy silos are increasingly identified as barriers to integration. There are three ways this is being tackled – institutional, economic and territorial and each of these is considered below.

Institutional barriers

Institutional policy silos within the EC have grown as the number of member states increased. Initially all member state Commissioners had a portfolio and as the spread of policy portfolios has grown then fragmentation has increased. Now that the EU has 28 member states other roles have been developed, including the introduction of overarching integrating policy coordinators who serve as EC vice presidents.

The EC has promoted integration between different DG priorities through a series of measures. This has included harmonising the timescales of different multi-annual programmes so that they can operate within the same time and policy framework, and develop cross-directorate initiatives. The third approach has been through direct coordination of policies and funding such as in the Cohesion programme 2014-20 (CEC, 2013b). Here, funding from different directorates operating to deliver the same objectives has been pooled into a single pot and accessed through member state Partnership Agreements and substate programmes. The programme now includes funding for FEA transport programmes, rural areas, training and the social fund, maritime, environment and regeneration. This is the first EU programme to integrate all programmes at the substate scales. The spatial dimension is an important means of offsetting institutional priorities and practices. It can also demonstrate the issues that this may bring (Liberatore, 1997).

Economic barriers to infrastructure integration

An assessment of the EU's economic future was undertaken in 2010 and set out in *Europe 2020* (Monti, 2010). Slow institutional progress on competitiveness and the single market were identified as holding back EU economic development and growth. Self-sufficient energy provision was identified as reducing reliance on unstable world markets. Finally, infrastructure investment in a multimodal corridor network to connect the EU's 300 major cities to encourage trade and movement of goods, services and people was recommended.

Territorial barriers to infrastructure integration

EU territorial policies have been focused on those locations with lagging economies and that operate across internal borders. Until 2014, funds to support these territories have been managed through different programmes that have different and sometimes conflicting objectives, differing timescales and complex reporting arrangements (Barca, 2009; CEC, 2013b).

EU Infrastructure policies by sector

Transport

EU policies for infrastructure are divided into different types of transport and are managed by different DGs although integrated approaches in transport have been increasing. The last policy review white paper proposed the creation of an integrated European Transport Area (CEC, 2011a) and this has set the context for all subsequent reviews and revisions of transport policies that range from TEN-T to local service accessibility. The white paper also recognised that transport provision and connections across the EU's territory needed improvement to support the internal market. It also recognised that transport is an important sector in the EU's economy and that there are some areas where the single market in transport has yet to be completed. All transport policy has to be sustainable.

The white paper emphasised the linkages between transport and other policies of the EU, including those for the environment, energy, economy and health. It also recognised the importance of longer-term spatial and strategic planning for transport, setting 2050 as its horizon with 2020/2030 as an intermediate deadline. The single European Transport Area has created a framework for policy integration for all modes, including sea and air. The white paper moves policy away from considering transport in sectors to territory, using economic corridor networks to support transport development and filling-in with inter- and intra-urban multimodal and sustainable transport systems.

Trans-European Networks

The development of the policy for TEN-T was a major outcome of the negotiations for the Treaty for the European Union in Maastricht in 1992. This was led by the then President of the Council, Jacques Delors, who had piloted the creation of the SEM in 1992. The fall of the Berlin Wall presented a major set of opportunities to enlarge the EU but also challenges about the ways existing member states, that had been receiving support for their lagging economies and regions, would respond. Within the EU, it would be financially impossible to provide accession states with the same level of support. The result was an approach that provided funding for existing recipients for a further period but then changed to a more strategic approach.

The introduction of TEN-T policy allowed the EC to develop a strategic approach to territory, and a more integrated approach to the EU as a whole, that was increasingly necessary given the uneven economies of existing and accession states. Across the EU, 300 cities were designated as nodes and the TEN-T corridors between them could be strengthened. Most of the new corridors were east–west in their orientation. The new corridors and nodes were agreed in a regulation (CEC, 1996b). Each corridor was made up of existing capacity and by strengthening specific links through schemes supported by member states and direct funding from the EU and loans from the European Investment Bank.

The extent to which the TEN-T network has been transparent in each member state has varied. In some, the EU support for routes and improvements has been made explicit whereas in others, such as the UK, this has not been discussed (Morphet, 2013a). This has given rise to particular problems as transport investment in the UK has long been subject to high levels of modelling and analysis but also considerable public debate about routes and priorities for funding. A failure to discuss the framing context of TEN-T policy has led to much wasted consideration of cost–benefit analysis on alternative routes and how nodes have been identified. The 1996 Regulation is clear about this and it cannot be challenged, but a lack of knowledge about its role has been detrimental to debate and further development of transport infrastructure policy within the UK.

TEN-T policy has been reviewed and a major reset was introduced following the inclusion of territory within the Commission's competencies as set out in the Lisbon Treaty (Alesina et al, 2005; Miller, 2010; Piris, 2010). The Barca Report (2009) set out both how these spatial competencies could be used and the approach to transport infrastructure. The result of this and subsequent reviews (CEC, 2011d) led to the development and agreement of a new TEN-T regulation (CEC, 2013a). This was adopted together with the new Cohesion regulation that extended EU policy to the whole of the EU's territory (CEC, 2013b). The revised TEN-T approach includes a new north–south orientation for the corridors recognising that the economic lag in the south of the EU has become more important after the financial crisis in 2007. TEN-T policies are also giving priority to sea transport as a more sustainable and reliable mode.

TEN-T networks and their adoption through the 2013 regulation provide policies and projects for inclusions within infrastructure delivery plans. They give policy certainty and parallel modes, as all corridors have three modes within them. They also provide further opportunities in the identification and development of the comprehensive network.

Sustainable Urban Mobility Plans

EU sustainable urban mobility policies (CEC, 2006, 2007b) identify the need for SUMPs that incorporate transport with the improvement of air quality (CEC, 2013b). SUMPS are for FEAs and complement the work being undertaken within the wider approach to cohesion policy. They have also been included within the Cohesion regulation (CEC, 2013b). The integration between modes is also reinforced by specific links to other programmes including that for TEN-T and the ESIF (European Structural and Investment Funds) funding programmes that have been prepared for the whole of the EU's area.

While the EC does not prescribe a specific method of preparing SUMP plans for each member state, it identifies the principles that should be use in the application of this policy and these are shown in Box 7.1. SUMPs should include a short-term delivery programme and allocate responsibilities for the delivery of each of project. The elements of urban transport that would typically be included are shown in Box 7.2 and the whole activity is expected to be integrated into the work of the local planning authority.

Box 7.1: Principles of Sustainable Urban Mobility Plans

A Sustainable Urban Mobility Plan seeks to contribute to development of an urban transport system which:

a. Is accessible and meets the basic mobility needs of all users;
b. Balances and responds to the diverse demands for mobility and transport services by citizens, businesses and industry;
c. Guides a balanced development and better integration of the different transport modes;
d. Meets the requirements of sustainability, balancing the need for economic viability, social equity, health and environmental quality;
e. Optimises efficiency and cost effectiveness;
f. Makes better use of urban space and of existing transport infrastructure and services;
g. Enhances the attractiveness of the urban environment, quality of life, and public health;
h. Improves traffic safety and security;
i. Reduces air and noise pollution, greenhouse gas emissions, and energy consumption; and
j. Contributes to a better overall performance of the trans-European transport network and the Europe's transport system as a whole. (adapted from CEC, 2013h, 2)

Box 7.2: Sustainable Urban Mobility Plans: transport modes

The following topics would typically be addressed in a SUMP:

a. Public transport
b. Non-motorised transport
c. Inter-modality
d. Urban road safety
e. Road transport (flowing and stationary)
f. Urban logistics
g. Mobility management
h. Intelligent Transport Systems (adapted from CEC, 2013h, 3-4)

Roads

The roads policy was updated in 2012 with *Road transport: A change of gear* (CEC, 2012b) and focused on the economic role of roads within the EU area but also the links with other parts of the market and across Switzerland to connect the north and the south. However road transport is also located in the context of other transport policies and sustainable principles. Roads are demand–led infrastructure that can be the easiest option for all transport users if there are no policy disincentives and alternative public transport provision. Roads are part of the TEN–T and SUMP networks, used within corridors and for public transport rather than private car use. Congested roads can lead to poor productivity in getting people, goods and materials to appropriate locations.

Rail

A white paper on the completion of the single market for rail in 1985 was instrumental in developing EU rail policy. This was followed by a white paper on railway policy in the EU (1990) and a directive in 1991 that established the principle that railway providers in the EU should be detached from their respective governments. Each member state chose their preferred approach and the UK was the only country to separate the rail network from the providers (Butcher, 2013).

Railway packages were implemented in 2001, 2004, 2007 and 2010 (Butcher, 2013) progressing legislation and operating through the selection of specific initiatives within the programme as a whole. Each member state then had a defined obligation to implement the legislation and initiatives. The priority objectives for EU rail policy are set out in Box 7.3.

Box 7.3: Objectives for EU rail policy
- opening rail markets
- promoting competition
- tackling barriers to market entry
- harmonisation of technical specifications (interoperability)
- harmonisation of safety standards and certification

Source: Office of Rail Regulator[1]

Interoperability policies accompanied high–speed services that came into force in 2002 (CEC, 1996b) as part of the TEN–T programme. This was extended to include other train services in the First Railway package (CEC, 1996b) and recast in 2011 to include a commitment to establish an investment framework and charging systems linked to wider objectives for the EU's territory as a whole. Subsequent rail packages progressed freight, pricing and transfer of funds for international passengers, and safety measures. The fourth railway package was focused on opening up railway provider markets to other companies and more competition (CEC, 2013c). In the UK, the application of EU rail legislation is through the Office of Rail Regulation (ORR) that has the responsibility for implementation.

Air

The development of EU air policy has been different from other transport sectors. In part this is because air services have been primarily by commercial carriers, although some countries have maintained support for national airlines. The main concern in planning the provision of air services are safety, the location of airports and the relative congestion of the EU skies that has reduced the potential for economic growth (CEC, 2015c). The policy for airports has focused on increasing capacity and by 2025 the demand will exceed supply of runway slots in a number of EU airports including London Gatwick, London Heathrow, Milan Linate, Paris Orly and Düsseldorf (CEC, 2011).

Although managing existing congestion will assist in these capacity pressures, the EU has also identified policies for further investment in airports within the context of TEN-T (CEC, 2013a) through the identification of core and comprehensive networks across the EU's territory. The EC identified more than 330 airports across the EU of which 82 are identified as core. The others as part of the comprehensive networks will support major cities and urban areas and provide feeder routes into the core network (CEC, 2011a).

Within this policy, airports require multimodal links including rail that are eligible for funding assistance and loan guarantees. These services can be supported by express buses but rail connections are regarded as preferable by the EC (CEC, 2011d). Airports can benefit from wider catchment areas if they can be connected to the rail network and supported by interoperable ticketing systems. The development of rail infrastructure at airports was identified as crucial from the outset (Costa, 2012) and important where airports are close to population agglomerations. While the core locations for airports have been confirmed in the TEN-T regulations (2013a) the process of identifying the other comprehensive network on supporting and regional airports is to be undertaken in the period to 2030.

Maritime

EU maritime infrastructure is a sustainable means of transporting goods for 90% of the EU's international exports. The EU's maritime strategy to 2018 was agreed in 2009. It included policies for identifying ports and communications to them and operations for maritime organisations and companies. Policies were set out in 2013 with linkages between ports and their hinterlands including the TEN-T networks being prioritised. As part of the TEN-T processes, the EC identified 329 ports across the EU's territory of which 104 were identified as core ports and identified as major nodes with Europe's defined transport corridors (CEC, 2013d, 2013e).

Inland waterways

Inland waterways are regarded as an important transport mode within the EU not least because they are a means of moving goods around and also they are regarded as having a low impact on the environment and as being sustainable. The EC also regards inland waterways as being good alternatives to road and rail and as having a strong level of reliability in comparison with other modes.

Other modes – walking, cycling

Within the EU, walking and cycling are regarded as part of the urban transport policy. Cycling is a mode that has been strongly supported through EC case studies and funding of projects and is a high priority for the development of transport infrastructure.

Energy

'The goals of energy policy – ensuring that energy is as cheap, secure and clean as possible – are the same at EU levels as at national level' (Buchan, 2010 p 359). The integration of energy supplies, particularly coal and nuclear energy, were part of the foundation of the EU including the Treaty of Paris 1951 that created the European Coal and Steel Community and the Treaty of Rome (1957) that created EURATOM, the European Atomic Energy Community. While these were seen to be dominant sources of energy, they were overtaken in importance by the use of oil. While energy has always been an EU central policy, there has never been an overarching approach or defined competence for energy although powers from the economic and environmental aspects of treaties and legislation have been used instead.

In 1992, the Maastricht Treaty established the TEN including that for energy, focusing on cross–border energy infrastructure and networks. These have been held by suppliers and not shared within individual member states. While much of the concern within the EU has been to deregulate the markets and encourage more competition this has been reverted into a more regulated market to ensure that networks are unbundled and markets remain open. The financial crisis and the growing fears about energy security have pushed energy forward as a priority for the period 2014–20.

The EU has a domestic and international interest in energy policy and supply. It has to look externally to the WTO to ensure compliance with the competition legislation within member states on the production and supply for energy. Further, much of the energy that is used in some countries, such as Germany and Poland, is provided from the Ukraine and Russia outside the EU. One of the EU's most important external relationships for energy supply is that with Norway, a member of the EEA and a quasi–member of the internal market. However, while the opening up of the energy market to competition is part of the WTO agreements, the operation of the energy market, including gas and oil, has not been included within the WTO arrangements as a whole (Goldthau and Sitter, 2014). While the EU has been developing external partnership and cooperation agreements for the supply of energy, there has also been a considerable focus on buffering the costs of energy when market prices move.

Energy infrastructure is an important consideration locally and nationally as well as across the EU. It can stretch in its reach from the construction of pipelines (Goldthau and Sitter, 2014) or grids and also to providing facilities for renewables – particularly wind and waste. It is also important as a consideration in standards in terms of buildings and their thermal capacity, the siting of development in towns, and the provision of more sustainable public transport rather than a dependency on private cars and petrol.

Gas and electricity

Gas was liberalised in the EU through a directive in 1998 and a single market for gas and electricity was finally implemented in 2014. This has been part of the energy package in *Europe 2020* where energy was prioritised. This included proposals for TEN-E infrastructure with interconnecting networks and storage facilities, and full integration of the whole market, including renewable energy sources and efficiency. This has been through specific transborder corridors, and a fund for implementing improvements and missing links from the Connecting Europe facility has been made available. The proposed TEN-E will be included within a regulation that, when agreed, will be adopted and be binding in the same ways as the regulations for Cohesion and TEN-T.

Considerations for infrastructure delivery planning can include improvements in networks and pipelines and energy supplies. These may all be major developments. With the scale of climate change targets, increased energy efficiency in housing and business through retrofitting and improved construction methods are also important.

Renewables – wind, wave, recyclables

The EU has a target of obtaining 20% of its energy consumption from renewables by 2020 (CEC, 2011b). Each member state has a target of 20% for renewables and prepared a national renewables policy and action plan. Subsequent progress reports show that the majority of member states have met their initial targets although progress is expected to slow in the subsequent period as investment in renewables can take long lead-in times.

Environment including water

The EU has been developing environmental policies since 1972 and these were significantly enhanced through the implementation of the SEM when environmental matters were seen to be important considerations in the regulation of member state markets. Since then subsequent directives have set targets and standards for waste and drinking water. In 2000 the EC proposed a single water framework directive so that the water system could be managed as whole. This included the role of river basin and surface water as a means of replenishing the system (Kallis and Butler, 2001).

In the Circular Economy package, a common EU target of 65% for recycling municipal waste was adopted (CEC, 2015) and higher air quality standards but, following press reports, these were initially proposed to be scrapped. However, subsequently there are reports that they have been substantially revised. The proposals were criticised as being difficult for businesses to meet in an economic climate where growth is a primary target.

Telecommunications

The Digital Agenda for Europe is part of the Europe 2020 package of measures to address the EU's economy (Monti, 2010). The twin concerns of this policy are the liberalisation of the market and to improve the service to consumers. A third strand is the importance of the digital environment for the European economy. The digital single market is seen to be an important factor for the e-commerce sector (CEC, 2000) and broadband provision is identified as being important in urban and rural areas.

The main considerations in infrastructure delivery planning are concerns with broadband speeds and 'not spots' where mobile phone communications are poor. These factors have a negative impact for users and businesses. Particular attention has been paid to rural areas and not least as business development and growth in rural areas can be significant and a major contributor to the economy.

The EU's social infrastructure

The EU's social infrastructure policies are primarily focused on education, skills and the free movement of labour. Other associated issues such as health and quality of life are also important elements of policy, particularly through the cultural agenda. Unlike physical and environmental/green infrastructure, social infrastructure in the EU is shared more with member states not least as much of this is personal and local. However, the role of the EU in the provision of social infrastructure is growing as this is also recognised as playing a greater role in economic growth and development (Stiglitz, 2015).

Engaging with EU policy making and delivery for infrastructure

The pooling of policies within the EU by member states and the responsibilities for the single market mean that it creates an important framework for all infrastructure policies. EU policy also has a developmental and long-term character and it is possible to consider the policies and principles in developing domestic policies or those for particular localities. While it might be possible to take a shorter-term view about this policy it is also important to recognise the priorities that have been set to 2050 in energy and transport and that these will shape domestic priorities within member states, including the UK, although they may not be linked in any kind of public discussion.

While most engagement with EU initiatives is at the point of their delivery, engagement at earlier stages can provide some opportunity for influence and also for an understanding of how policies are likely to be translated into legislation and initiatives. This understanding can be invaluable for longer-range infrastructure delivery planning. Even when engaged on the shorter-term delivery of projects, understanding the provenance of the policies and programmes that have provided these opportunities gives practitioners an edge in their advocacy and bidding processes. If schemes or projects can be identified as reducing bottlenecks or missing links – two major concepts in current EU transport policy – then they may stand a better chance of gaining funding even from within the member state, whose government will need to demonstrate compliance with their policy priorities to the EC.

A second element that can be demonstrated through programmes and projects may be a focus on integration and multilevel governance. In integration, it may be able to demonstrate how a particular project links more strategic and local networks through the creation of a hub or it may provide a better link between transport modes or environmental corridors. In demonstrating multilevel governance, then schemes that are being delivered through cooperation between scales of government, each exercising their appropriate role and providing a contribution towards funding, could also be a major focus in bid proposal.

In engaging with policy making then there are a number of ways this can be undertaken, as shown in Box 7.4.

Box 7.4: Ways of engaging in EU policy making processes
- through engagement with member state government – advising case studies
- through joining a trade association, professional body or representative group
- through belonging to an EU network, for example cities
- through being part of a spatial grouping through INTERREG
- through normal lobbying through MEPs and CoR
- direct relationships with the EC

Conclusions

In considering the role and operation of EU policy, it is important to consider the extent to which its policies are internally compatible or pulling against each other. While some institutional and operational reform such as that in the Cohesion programme has been able to align policies, priorities and programmes there are other tensions such as the role of competition in areas that are lagging (Colomb and Santinha, 2012).

The role of EU legislation in framing and strategically locating infrastructure is little understood and these are important considerations for practitioners. Engaging with the original policy and legislation can be challenging but joining in interested and locality groups can make the process of understanding and anticipation easier. Being alert to future directions of policy can also be helpful when major infrastructure projects are being developed, as understanding any role they may have within policies such as TEN-T, SUMPS or TEN-E may assist in their acceptance and delivery.

Note

[1] See http://orr.gov.uk/about-orr/what-we-do/the-law/eu-law

EIGHT

State infrastructure policy and planning

Introduction

Infrastructure planning is a core function of all states and nations. It is a central component of growth and efficiency in the economy and for resilience in coping with environmental shocks or disasters. States and nations are concerned with the quality of their infrastructure for their own purposes but also in international comparative evaluations undertaken by the OECD, the World Bank and the WEF (World Economic Forum) (OECD, 2011a; WEF, 2012; Sala-i-Martín et al, 2014). These include the state of infrastructure but also the institutional conditions that accompany its provision and improvement. These judgements may influence the evaluation of state economies and the propensity to invest by business and global capital.

National infrastructure planning to support the economy, sustainability and social activity within states is an essential feature of public planning and investment. States create the conditions and mechanisms for infrastructure planning and delivery. The state is responsible for regulation that will frame sustainable investment by different operators, identifying which locations, business sectors and communities will be privileged above others.

The majority of EU states prepare strategic spatial plans that indicate where future investment will be promoted, including infrastructure. All countries in the EU have such a plan, apart from the UK (Barca, 2009). The UK has a sectoral and aspatial national infrastructure planning regime established in 2008 and a National Infrastructure Plan that comprises sectoral pipeline projects (HMT and DCLG, 2010; HMT, 2011, 2014).

The legislation and priorities for infrastructure planning in the EU is a pooled responsibility that is implemented by member states, including the UK. The role of the member state is to agree and then implement policies for existing infrastructure and its management and interoperability. From 1972, EU priorities were for lagging regions but in 1996 this changed to major corridors and 300 city nodes (CEC, 1996b). The EU policies are now for the economy of the whole territory. In the UK, EU policy has focused on public transport and rail links to and between airports. Elsewhere, links across the Oresund between Denmark and Sweden and high-speed train (HST) services within and between countries such as France and Spain, or Germany, France, the Netherlands and the UK have been implemented (Givoni, 2006). This chapter discusses national infrastructure planning policies and implementation within this EU context.

State infrastructure delivery planning

What defines state infrastructure?

State interest in the provision of infrastructure is related to economic growth and resilience against environmental and market failures. This includes infrastructure maintenance for existing networks and providing for growth (Rhodes, 2014). Deficits in infrastructure are recognised by external bodies including the OECD and IMF. The WEF ranks all countries against each other on infrastructure provision. In the last survey by WEF (2014) for example, France was 10th, Germany was 11th and the UK was 27th, although ranked 5th in all economies.

The state has a role in all infrastructure provision, as shown in Box 8.1, not only where it has an implementation lead, such as in 'mega-projects', that are taken on by governments because their scale, complexity and importance.

Box 8.1: Government roles in infrastructure

Government roles in infrastructure are:

- to set the strategic framework including economic and sustainability objectives, spatial distribution, equity, access and longer-term planning;
- support and develop the interconnectivity between the state and other states;
- to interpret and deliver national commitments on climate change, competition;
- develop policy and legislation – within the EU this will primarily be undertaken at EU level;
- determine how this policy and legislation is going to be implemented within the institutional and legal frameworks including subsidiarity;
- determine the funding to be applied directly to provision;
- regulate the market for infrastructure subject to competition;
- plan for resilience and security of supply;
- ensure existing infrastructure is maintained and future proof provision;
- intervene in times of failure as last resort.

While infrastructure is considered within its mode or sector, there are also interdependencies between them. Transport modes work within corridors while suppliers are required to work together to ensure a complementary coverage and avoid 'not spots' in broadband or 'unbanked' settlements. Interoperability is important for resilience and infrastructure switching if there are problems or breakdowns. For civil society, this includes emergency planning in the case of energy failure, flooding or accidents and for the economic sectors this includes energy switching or alternative modes of transport and delivery. The resilience of national infrastructure is also important for national security policy and prevention of terrorism (Boin and McConnell, 2007).

The strategic context

While states assess infrastructure within their own borders, they are influenced by international organisations. The OECD has defined three core elements of state transport planning that its members should consider (OECD, 2011a). First moving away from financial and political short-termism. Second the OECD finds that state transport plans have the greatest economic impact when they are integrated into other national strategic plans rather than being standalone. Finally, planning infrastructure is not a technocratic process and but part of wider decision-making. The OECD argues that there should be engagement by stakeholders to increase the acceptability of schemes, particularly through multimodal rather than sectoral approaches.

Long-term infrastructure planning has to take into account economic growth. The OECD argues that state requirements for infrastructure to 2030 should be considered in a wider context to include energy, telecommunications and other services including water. It recommends that transport planning should define a framework of gateways and hubs linking inland transport systems with trading locations elsewhere in the world. In the EU, *Europe 2020* policy (CEC, 2014f) has a focus on external gateways to the United States and China.

Given the OECD's model (2011a), some convergence in the approaches adopted can be expected. In the US, the government has no infrastructure department and each type of infrastructure policy is led by different federal agencies. In the Department of Transportation for example, policy priorities include HST (USDOT, 2009) and drink driving. HST policy is focused on reducing road and air travel within the US to meet carbon targets. Like the EU, identified corridors receive funding for improvement projects including links to urban areas. Some corridors are designated for HST but not in others where major freight routes crossing rural areas already exist.

Infrastructure investment within the US is also concerned with its resilience against attack through the work of the Department of Homeland Security, set up after the 9/11 attacks in New York. The major concerns identified within the National Infrastructure Protection Plan (DHS, 2010) include sectoral plans for commerce, chemicals, communications and manufacturing that define the economic role of infrastructure, its interdependences and ways to make it more resilient.

The US has identified Megaregions, and the infrastructure required between and within them (Hagler, 2009; RPA, 2014). The Megaregions are major urban centres of national significance where population is increasing and densities are low. The five criteria that define US Megaregions are shown in Box 8.2. Although not all fulfil the criteria, the relationship between their economic role, infrastructure and density are critical. Identifying Megaregions creates certainty for investors and frameworks for federal infrastructure investment. In the US, where lack of skills in infrastructure planning and delivery has been identified as a major weakness, this fosters policy mobility and communities. Strategic plans within the Megaregions have used corridors and improving access to public transport through transport oriented development (TOD), significantly shaping future urban form.

Box 8.2: The criteria for defining US Megaregions

- environmental systems and topography
- infrastructure systems
- economic linkages
- settlement patterns and land use
- shared culture and history.

Source: adapted from Hagler, 2009

The OECD has recommended specific principles for state infrastructure frameworks, shown in Box 8.3.

Box 8.3: National Infrastructure policy frameworks: guidance on content

National policy frameworks must:

- set down how strategic infrastructure is to be planned, evaluated, developed and financed;
- provide a solid basis for communication with stakeholders and the public;
- highlight the importance of strategic infrastructure. (As the European Commission now recognises, there needs to be a focus on strategic, multimodal 'core networks' that can be funded and will be able to handle the major share of the future growth and transport tasks.);
- there needs to be a (new) 'strategic infrastructure' category that includes the major international gateways *and* their inland connections;
- the inclusion and linking of gateway and inland connection needs in national policy frameworks;
- national policy frameworks are also important for gateway structures and organisation;
- multi-year funding for *strategic/major projects*, supported by dedicated project-specific organisational and funding structures;
- fully funding an entire multimodal *programme of infrastructure projects* for ten years.

Source: adapted from OECD, 2011a

Working within the EU infrastructure policies

In the EU, states agree policy and then implement it (Morphet, 2013a). TEN-T (Trans-European Networks – Transport) supports corridors linking major EU cities (CEC, 1996b) and the corridors are not defined by cost–benefit evaluation methods. If the primary corridor linkage is based on the connection between two points rather than a needs-based approach then arguments for improvement within the corridor will be based on other factors, including achieving more sustainable modes of travel. Second, specific improvements in one country may be dealing with missing links or bottlenecks for the strategic route that crosses the whole of the EU and needs to be reflected in project evaluation.

EU policy application within member states does not have an easy engagement with traditional assessments of the need for mega-projects based on projections of future demand that will almost certainly be wrong (Hall, 1980; Flyvbjerg, 2014; Priemus and Zonneveld, 2003). However, the drivers for these projects are to create networks across the EU that support sustainable travel and energy.

The development and implementation of EU TEN (Trans-European Networks) corridors and the projects that support their implementation can be locally controversial. In the UK the corridor that has already been upgraded through the West Coast mainline is now being further developed through the implementation of the HS2 rail line and associated transport improvements within its corridor. In Italy, the east–west corridor connecting Kiev and Lisbon crosses the north of Italy. Like the HS2 scheme in the UK, the east–west corridor through Italy has also attracted local opposition and criticism of the methodology applied to undertake the assessment of the preferred transport modes, not least in their connections between the new and existing infrastructure (Fabbro and Dean, 2014).

Within states

Infrastructure planning within states is varied. In some, including the Netherlands, Ireland, Spain, Germany and France, there has been a long-standing approach to infrastructure planning at the national level and this is included within a multilevel governance approach to planning (Marshall, 2009a, 2009b, 2009c, 2009d). While infrastructure is managed by different government departments, a strategic plan incorporating economic and environmental objectives is a means of engaging in dialogue with the EC (European Commission). In countries with a strong strategic spatial planning culture, there is a sense that this is a national responsibility although there is no expectation that central government will be the major provider. Plans provide stability and security to investors. Where there are long-standing systems of strategic planning including infrastructure planning, these countries are ranked higher for infrastructure planning, delivery and capacity than those that do not, for example the UK.

In the Netherlands, infrastructure planning is included within the spatial planning system that operates at all levels including through National Plan and identifies the state's interests in infrastructure planning and delivery (Marshall, 2009a). This is undertaken within longer- and mid-term time horizons with shorter time-horizons plans which are then translated into projects. Within this infrastructure planning is undertaken sectorally such as for transport. While the Dutch system has formalised consultation there are concerns that the system may be too slow and has high levels of opposition to some schemes, particularly for roads (Stoelinga and Luikens, 2005).

In 2013, the Dutch government changed the planning system to reduce the level of national direction and devolved decision-making to the most appropriate levels of government. However, government retained the lead on infrastructure planning at international or interprovincial scales where there might be deadlock. The government adopted three national objectives that improved competitiveness, access and safety. The new policy statement is integrated, including networks below and above ground, and includes methods of delivery through frameworks, performance agreements, financial instruments and knowledge. Much of the concern about Dutch infrastructure planning remains that of integration between land use planning and transportation rather than between sectors (Arts et al, 2014). This moved the Dutch system from land use to spatial planning principles.

In Ireland a national spatial strategy was developed in 2002 for a period of 20 years, with a national development plan aligned to the EU Cohesion programme of 2006-07. As with the Regional Development Strategy (RDS) in Northern Ireland (DRD, 2001), the national spatial strategic plan in Ireland has a strong economic focus and has a strong focus on infrastructure including routes, networks, hubs and gateways. The national interest, conceptualised by Ireland's international approach, sets the national interest in this planning process.

Elsewhere such as in the UK and Italy, there has been a less centralised approach (Fabbro and Dean, 2014). In the UK, the position has changed over the period since devolution to the UK nations other than England started in 1999. Scotland, Wales and Northern Ireland have infrastructure delivery plans and while there is no national infrastructure plan for England there is a state plan prepared and published by the Treasury under the auspices of their organisation Infrastructure UK (HMT, 2014). In Italy and the UK the development and construction of infrastructure projects has been slower than in other countries and this is considered an urgent economic concern for the business organisations (CBI-URS, 2014).

This discussion suggests that a range of principles are used to develop infrastructure delivery planning at state level. These are shown in Box 8.4. The principles are important for those engaging in infrastructure delivery planning as they set criteria for assessment of the quality of infrastructure delivery in the

Box 8.4: State infrastructure delivery planning principles

States use the following principles in their infrastructure delivery planning:

- participation in the development of international frameworks and principles and linkages;
- application of those principles within the state in conjunction with national strategic plan;
- development of internal economic geography;
- support and preservations of the natural environment;
- application of equity and social access infrastructure criteria across the state;
- assessment of resilience requirements;
- institutional investment frameworks and programmes to address concerns raised in the application of these principles;
- declaration of political priorities;
- methods and institutions for implementation;
- assessment of effectiveness and resetting goals and principles.

locality or sector. They provide national standards that can be used to assess performance at all scales and provide the means to advocate particular schemes. There may also be the opportunity to make exception cases for infrastructure identified as being required but not prioritised through the application of national principles.

Institutional frameworks

The way in which states undertake their infrastructure planning and delivery will depend on their institutional structures. In those states with a federal structure, there is a clear demarcation of responsibilities for infrastructure planning and delivery between tiers of government. In the US where there is a strong federal structure, but also a more fragmented set of providers, the OECD has recently demonstrated that in Chicago there are over 780 different institutions and organisations responsible for some aspects of transport provision (Merk, 2014). In the EU, the application of subsidiarity has meant that all member states are moving towards defined responsibilities between tiers of government. In France there is a government department that applies subsidiarity tests for all government policy and expenditure.

Other institutional frameworks are important as infrastructure has an influence of quality of life and well-being characterised by access to services and peripherality (OECD, 2014b). While the geography of distance can be mitigated through the quality of broadband connections that have been a priority for EU rural areas, there can be poor access to direct medical care, education and social interaction. Institutions can also define infrastructure priorities in the state. In the UK, these are set out in a range of documents. The top 40 projects in the UK are set out in *National infrastructure plan* (HMT, 2014) and are organised within sectors. They are also primarily English schemes.

National infrastructure planning processes

The UK undertakes infrastructure delivery planning through sectoral silos that are characterised and reinforced by institutional arrangements through government departments and implementation of the World Trade Organization liberalisation agreements. This is reinforced through sectoral national market regulators appointed by government. Competition for supply has reduced investment in maintenance although many new schemes have received government support as part of EU policy commitments (Morphet, 2013a).

While spatial infrastructure planning for the whole of the UK has not been progressed, Scotland, Wales and Northern Ireland have identified a national context and the most important schemes are supported by the national parliament and assemblies since devolution. The first to develop this approach was Scotland through its National Planning Framework process. This has now been through three iterations – 2004, 2008 and 2012 – and in each the infrastructure priorities have been integral. These schemes have primarily been identified as priorities by the Scottish government but in the latest iteration, NPF 3, there was an open consultation for schemes that could be proposed (Scottish Government, 2014).

The Wales Spatial Plan (2004, 2011) identified subnational boards to progress infrastructure planning and delivery. The Wales Infrastructure Plan (Welsh Government, 2013, 2015) reinforced the contribution of infrastructure to the economy and continued to focus in subnational areas but these are now being supported through other state contractual mechanisms such as city deals. In Northern Ireland, infrastructure delivery planning has been set out in the RDS, identifying priorities and linked investment in infrastructure to wider objectives, including the economy of the island of Ireland and the wider peace process (Morphet, 2011c).

In England no national spatial planning processes exist for identifying infrastructure priorities. Strategic planning was undertaken by successive regional bodies that had a strong central government steer (Glasson and Marshall, 2007). These identified priorities but they have not been brought together and set within an England–wide strategic planning context (Wong et al, 2012). The UK government responded through the Planning Act 2008 (Bardens and Rhodes, 2013). where decisions about sectoral investment in infrastructure were removed from the local planning system and transferred to the UK Parliament using policies prepared for sectors by individual government departments.

One of the main criticisms of major infrastructure planning processes has been the length of time that the planning processes took (Eddington, 2007; Marshall, 2011). Since 2008, sectoral plans are set out in National Policy Statements (NPS) as shown in Table 8.1. These NPS are prepared within the constructs of public consultation, parliamentary scrutiny and environmental appraisal regimes (Owen and Walker, 2012). In some cases existing policy documents can be designated as NPS if they are complaint with these processes. The NPS define Nationally Significant Infrastructure Projects (NSIPs) within their ambit by scale or type of activity. Any promoters of an NSIP will need to build a case for it to be taken through this regime.

Table 8.1: UK National Infrastructure Policies by sector

NPS	Publication date
Energy	2011
Renewables	2011
Fossil fuel	2011
Electricity networks	2011
Oil and gas infrastructure	2011
Nuclear power	2011
Ports	2010

NPS	Publication date
National networks for transport	2014
Airports	awaited
Waste water	2011
Water supply	awaited
Hazardous waste	2011
Industrial and commercial	Not being published

The principle of an NSIP cannot be challenged once the NPS has been agreed. The examination of NSIP proposals is undertaken within defined procedural rules set out in the statutory instruments (2010, 102 and 103). Examination of the proposals is primarily administrative and decisions are given within a year from submission. This means considerable work before the submission of an application for a Development Consent Order (DCO) for the NSIP including the support from the local authority where the application is located. The applicant frames the DCO they require and all but one application submitted has been determined within the designated time scale. In 2010, the independent Infrastructure Planning Commission (IPC) set up in 2008 to undertake these examinations was transferred to the Planning Inspectorate sitting within government.

NSIPs comprise large-scale developments relating to energy, transport, water or waste, and extended to allow business and commercial projects to opt into this process in the Growth and Infrastructure Act 2013. Additionally, 'top 40 priority investment' projects in the UK infrastructure plan 2013 not included in other NSIP arrangements nor meeting the 2008 Act threshold would be classed as an NSIP and particularly relate to science and innovation schemes (Smith, 2014).

The NPS are in the management of individual government departments. They are not integrated in their spatial considerations or in the delivery of associated infrastructure. This aspatiality and lack of a territorial dimension is a continuing challenge. The publication of the NPS for networks (DfT, 2014) did not have any spatial dimensions nor did it relate to the new EU TEN-T regulation (CEC, 2013a).

The absence of a strategic infrastructure delivery planning process for the whole of the UK has been identified as an economic weakness in the EU's growth and stability pact agreement (CEC, 2010). In 2011, the OECD proposed some central reforms to the UK to support infrastructure delivery planning, suggesting a more strategic approach and integrating the national infrastructure project programme with the rest of the infrastructure delivery planning process. The OECD recommendations are set out in Box 8.5.

The UK infrastructure planning system introduced in 2008 suggests a number of questions for consideration. The first is the balance between local and national interests in these processes. This has been particularly illustrated in the application for additional nuclear energy power at Hinckley Point where not only the application for the new plant but also the associated planning applications for new housing and other development that will have a significant impact on the local area

> **Box 8.5: OECD Review of UK Infrastructure policy and delivery**
> - Make the planning system more flexible and predictable and provide incentives for local communities to release land for building, while continuing to protect the environment.
> - Improve public infrastructure, especially in transport.
> - Low investment in public infrastructure has contributed to congestion, especially in road transport and airports, hampering productivity.
> - **Actions taken:** Investment in infrastructure has been increased substantially in recent years, partly as a consequence of bringing forward investment during the recession. However, investment remains low compared with other OECD countries and current plans envisage a sharp fall in spending after 2010.
> - **Recommendations:** Free up more resources in other spending areas within current spending plans to mitigate cuts in infrastructure investment. Implement a national road pricing scheme to mitigate road congestion (Source: Economic policy reforms, 2011; Going for Growth OECD, 2011c, p 148)
>
> Source: OECD, 2011a

were deemed to be part of this process. Second, this is more of an administrative than planning process. While the planning concerns can be discussed when the NPS is published and consulted on, the principles of the development are accepted at the point when the proposal for an NSIP is accepted by the Planning Inspectorate. The information will be concerned with environmental impact and location, making the case for development.

A third concern is that the NPS are developed within silos and sponsored by different government departments. This lack of integration and loss of the potential for combined synergies is problematic while some sectors, for example airports, do not yet have an NPS. Further there is no specific requirement to establish need in the NSIP processes so that alternative sources or demand management are not considered as part of the examination process. This separation between sectors is a reflection of the Infrastructure UK plan. The only plans where there are integrated (horizontal and vertical) policies spanning sectors and scales is the infrastructure plans for Wales and Scotland and the integrated plan for Northern Ireland. There may be conflicts between different consultees as an outcome of this siloed process and the integration of national policy has not been examined before consideration (Glasson et al, 2013).

Is there any evidence that this new approach has made any significant improvement or has had any unintended consequences? Considering the marine sector, Boyes and Elliott (2015) demonstrate that the planning system has been overlain on existing complex subsystems to the point where there are major overlaps in responsibilities within the systems that have been established. This institutional pluralism may cause internal conflicts and competition. A positive outcome has been the ability to reflect on experience of its operation and make minor adjustments. These changes have been primarily procedural and minor but have generally been led by NIPA (National Infrastructure Planning Association), a cross-sectoral organisation set up by those working within the system.

The national infrastructure planning system remains a central process. While consultees and communities may be able to influence the detail of a scheme, the NPS system means that they are not able to challenge the principle of the development. Groves et al (2013) also argue that in some sectors such as energy, where a hybrid economic model prevails, private sector services are being returned to centralised decision-making. They conclude that 'possibility of effective engagement may be undermined by, first, the structures of governance that shape policy and, second, the planning system through infrastructure proposals pass' (p 352) and that:

> systems of governance where power is redistributed, to some degree, to private organisations with public duties, the accountability of these organisations in assessing need and managing risk must be included in the substantive issues of participation. We therefore concur with recent scholarship (Cotton and Devine-Wright, 2010a, 2010b, 2012; Cowell and Owens, 2006, 2011) which suggests that questions of national interest are likely to continue to prove their importance in shaping infrastructure siting conflicts (p 353)

There are no principles against which the proposals for the top 40 infrastructure projects can be assessed and they are grouped by sector. The National Infrastructure Plan has no explanation about of their provenance or the basis of their selection. Some projects included in this list reflect their position within TEN-T and TEN-E (Trans-European Networks – Energy) programmes. However, beyond this there is no territorial or spatial assessment of the relative priorities and expenditure between different parts of the country (Cox and Raikes, 2014).

Finally, the NPS system is national in that it applies to England (that is, as a nation) and not to the state (the UK). While some of the 2008 Planning Act and subsequent amendments apply in Wales, the acquisition of devolved planning powers to the Welsh Government in 2015 will separate these processes further.

Engaging in national infrastructure delivery planning

Engaging with the processes on state infrastructure delivery planning may be important as part of any local or FEA (functional economic area) strategic plan or programme. This section identifies the particular ways in which infrastructure delivery planning at state level can be influenced by subnational scales of government.

Have a strategic plan

When engaging with state processes of infrastructure planning it is important to have a strategic plan for the area. This needs to be wider than the administrative or economic boundaries of the area this creates a context that is important in making a case for investment that can clearly be identified and addressed. It will need to take into account prevailing policy and legislation, and that expected in coming years.

Within the EU this is relatively easy to identify as the existing policies and their antecedents are set out on the EC websites and the discussions about future policies are also clearly signalled through discussion papers and work programmes of the different EU institutions including the EC, the European Parliament and Committee of the Regions. Other ways in which EU policy directions can be understood include research and projects commissioned through EU-sponsored organisations including INTERREG, URBACT and ESPON. The groups have regular meetings when future strategy is discussed. There are also open events such as the Regions week where there are opportunities to discuss future policy.

All these approaches are important in framing the strategic plan and language that is used to describe the analysis and priorities. There are also model strategic plans that have been adopted by the EC and have been included as policy priorities for 2014–20. These include the plans for the Baltic Sea and Danube regions. These plans have been supported by the EC for a period of nearly 20 years and their support and development provides a model to consider other approaches.

The introduction of Integrated Territorial Investment (ITI) strategies and programmes as part of the EU's Cohesion programme 2014–20 (CEC, 2013b) provides a model although there are few examples available. Preparing a strategic plan enables engagement in discussion about the application of national and EU policies in specific places rather than through a sectoral approach. This shift from sectoral to spatial is an important policy redirection and it can be used to support specific arguments for locational choices.

Strategic planning for infrastructure is a political activity that supports locations, promotes improvements and identifies investment in new locations. Strategic policy is also based on political calculations. Resilience and security are also important components. These political dimensions are likely to have more influence than an evidence-based approach (Morphet, 2008) and the length of the political cycle is particularly important in strategic infrastructure planning (Coelho et al, 2014).

Understand EU context and priorities

All infrastructure schemes, at any scale, require understanding of the prevailing EU legislation, policies and objectives. These need to be understood in the preparation of any strategic plan and engagement with national priorities. The EC publishes regular updates of schemes that are being supported through EU programmes and other opportunities to contribute scheme proposals that sit within the EU's policy frameworks can be pitches directly to Brussels for informal feedback.

Demonstrate the economic benefit of any scheme in social, economic and environmental terms

While all proposed programmes and projects may be designed to have benefits across all Cohesion priorities – that is economic, social and environmental, it is also important to consider how to display these within the context of economic benefits. Since 2007 and the economic crisis, the economic dimension has taken precedence for all governments and while it is important to demonstrate the other elements of any project its economic significance is likely to be an overriding and determining factor.

Demonstrating the economic benefits of schemes that are primarily environmental or social will vary but can be identified. For example, an environmental scheme may provide the opportunity to develop new technology and support smaller enterprises or it may offer resilience for the local economy should there be any risk of environmental disaster. The environmental sector also offers the opportunity for business development and growth and in using schemes as a means of demonstrating how specific solutions can be applied in ways that may be replicated. The green economy is also taking an increasing proportion of the economic stricture so the ways any new schemes use energy and can provide energy into the grid system would be structuring features.

Demonstrating the economic benefits of social cohesion for infrastructure projects, maybe through access to services and to jobs, are important elements of the Cohesion programme objectives. They may provide social interaction and exercise for older people, can produce public health support, reduce costs of medical and social care, and illustrate new ways of achieving these ends. For those of working age, social cohesion may be demonstrated in any schemes through employment, recruitment and training practices, the opportunities for social enterprise, and through links with the university.

Identify where specific schemes may solve missing links and bottlenecks

One major concern for all infrastructure schemes in the EU is their ability to demonstrate that they are able to contribute to completing missing links or creating capacity where there are bottlenecks. This may be in all types of infrastructure where resilience may depend on solving these two challenges. Missing links may be addressed through fixed networks, through missing transport systems including roads or rail, or through competing links to energy networks and grids. Missing links may also be in terms of opportunities to promote economic growth such as the provision of a local university or bank; in the UK a number of areas have had no local university and the government has developed a programme for England to complete these gaps.

Where there are bottlenecks then there may be a range of ways of demonstrating how schemes can contribute to solving them, including demand management, alternative routes and other supply chains. Bottlenecks may also be dealt with through the provision of additional permanent or temporary, short-term capacity. Bottlenecks can occur at times when the economy is growing and may be in markets as well as in locations. The UK housing market and planning systems have been identified by the EU as bottlenecks that are reducing economic growth and the government has been required to address this (CEC, 2010). Following successive government reforms in 2010–15, this has led to the UK planning system moving closer to the prevailing approach within other member states, where the principle of development is established first and only then followed by a building permit.

Prioritise national network interchanges and hubs

Any infrastructure delivery plan may be able to demonstrate the value of individual projects if it can indicate how it reinforces the role of nationally or EU–defined hubs and interchanges. These may not be direct links but could be those that are created down the line and lead to shorter travel times or fewer changes. Supporting nodes may be important, particularly in rural areas. Social infrastructure hubs can help to reinforce specialisation and the development of further innovation. Expertise can be shared within business creating a tech hub or agglomeration.

Create projects that identify the ways an integrated approach using multilevel governance will provide a better outcome

Demonstrating how infrastructure projects are integrated within the scales of government and supported by multiple levels is central to gaining support for their implementation. This may be through contracts, as in France, or in cross–border formal partnerships, as in the Baltic Sea region. These multilevel agreements support projects through funding and agreements that reduce risks of partner withdrawal. Each scale of governance involved will also reinforce these projects through other strategic plans and projects to create horizontal and vertical integration.

Demonstrate how the project can be funded

While the investment in infrastructure and its operation is provided through all sectors, governments have a role in framing investment, the strategy and location for this infrastructure and how it will operate. The OECD identifies the role of public investment in infrastructure as critical to the economic and social well–being of all countries and further suggests that poor investment can erode economic growth opportunities (OECD, 2014b) although the decisions taken about locations for investment can have a considerable impact on the country even where there are choices between different growth poles. The OECD definition of public investment is shown in Box 8.6. While much of the main infrastructure investment framework and projects are set and undertaken by central governments and their agencies, the OECD also underlines the importance of subnational government in public investment.

Box 8.6: A definition of public investment

Generally, 'public investment' refers to capital expenditure on physical infrastructure (such as roads, government buildings, etc.) and soft infrastructure (for example, human capital development, innovation support, research and development, etc.) with a productive use that extends beyond a year. Public investment comprises direct and indirect investment. Direct investment is defined as gross capital formation and acquisitions, less disposals of non-financial non-produced assets during a given period. Indirect investment is defined as capital transfers i.e. investment grants and subsidies in cash or in kind made by sub-national governments to other institutional units. Information in this document focuses on direct public investment, unless otherwise specified.

The way public investment is measured across countries varies. Gross fixed capital formation is often used as the best available proxy for direct public investment. However, there are differences across countries. For example, in some countries private contributions to public investment are accounted for in national accounts, while in others this may not be the case. There is also some variation as to where expenditure on operations and maintenance is recorded.

Source: OECD, 2014b, p 4

The OECD also indicates potential weaknesses in the way public investment is managed in different countries. Sectoral investment within institutional silos or scalar layers is a major challenge in the coordination of investment horizontally and vertically. There may be policy and skills weaknesses in dealing with investment within different public institutions. Lastly, in some countries the centre may retain decision making and resources for investment and fail to decentralise these decisions through fiscal and governance means (OECD, 2014b).

Set up a budget and project team and start to identify how the project can be completed

One of the major risks in any national infrastructure programme is political influence in the process (CBI-URS, 2014). While the 2008 Planning Act promotes integration and guarantees a decision within a set period, this has been breached with ministerial approval. A second concern is that major infrastructure projects need support over a longer period than an election cycle and this makes larger, more politically charged projects more likely to be delayed until after the next general election. Some projects are undertaken quietly and contributions to more major schemes are broken up as individual improvements, and never shown as being part of a corridor improvement. This may mean less political debate but it also hides other major benefits being reached through strategic approaches.

A further risk is that the development and planning of new schemes can appear to be more attractive than spending funding on maintenance on existing routes. This lack of maintenance has had a detrimental effect on the provision of national rail and London Underground services that has left a legacy of work to be undertaken. While passengers and businesses like the benefits of the upgrades and smoother running, they are also very critical of the disruption that is caused during the works. In more recent years the methods of handling maintenance and upgrades of operational systems have been improved in a variety of ways and become more customer friendly, providing more information for forward planning. More care has been taken in simultaneous closure of alternative routes so that alternatives can be operated. Third, additional services on alternative lines have been offered to attempt to cope with any additional demand.

Concerns and particularly cost overruns on major projects may be inherent in their design and delivery and may need to be accepted as risks. Although there may be some expectation that lower costs are included within original estimates in order to gain acceptance of a project, the Omega Centre (2014) argues that although projects may go over budget this might be in order to enhance their flexibility and ability to respond to circumstances and change as the project develops. The Omega Centre also argued that major transport infrastructure projects may be framed too narrowly in terms of their costs and their potential benefits.

The National Audit Office (NAO, 2010) assessed the major risks in a national approach to planning for infrastructure and these are set out in Box 8.7.

Box 8.7: Key risks of value for money in infrastructure projects

- **Inaccurate identification of the need** for infrastructure. For example forecasters may overestimate demand, in which case benefits are lower than expected and poor value for money results.
- **Policy uncertainty.** This could result in project sponsors, lenders and contractors deferring or abandoning UK projects in favour of opportunities elsewhere. Financing charges for projects may rise as investors and lenders perceive policy uncertainty as a risk.
- **Failure to assess the cumulative impact** on consumers of funding infrastructure through user charges. This increases the risk of financial hardship for consumers, or the need for unplanned taxpayer support. This is a question which the National Audit Office will return to in examining how departments and regulators deploy their resources to secure consumer interests.
- **Taxpayer exposure to losses.** This will happen if the government guarantees to bear or share project risks – for example cost overruns – and that risk subsequently materialises.

- **Delivery costs are higher** than they should be. UK infrastructure costs have historically been higher than overseas. This could result in high costs for taxpayers and consumers and fewer projects going ahead than planned.

Source: Adapted from NAO, 2010

Develop a good communications plan and set of supporters

Finally, it is important for any project to have a good communications plan and a set of supporters who may be from different sectors and localities. These supporters may be stakeholders in the specific project and be beneficiaries of its proposed outcomes but they may also be representatives of wider society who might see that any specific project will recue social exclusion, improve access, develop the economy or improve intercommunications. These supporters can engage others who may be involved in decisions about the project and can create a platform of confidence for a scheme, which can reinforce its likelihood of success.

Conclusions

Infrastructure planning is a key function of the state to support the economy, resilience and access equity. While the state can provide leadership, in the EU this is undertaken within the constructs of pooled EU policy and legislation. The application of these policies can be used to create more integrated infrastructure planning. Alternatively, they can be managed as sectoral silos, with independent processes of decision making. The UK has adopted a silo approach that is aspatial. This is problematic in identifying priorities for new projects or improvements. It also means that engaging with these processes is difficult as selection criteria and locational determinants are not transparent.

NINE

Infrastructure delivery planning for functional economic areas and city regions

Introduction

Infrastructure is fundamental to all functional economic areas (FEAs) and sub/ city regions within their defined geographies and in relationship with their peripheries, hinterlands and markets. FEAs are of global policy interest (Krugman, 1991, 2011; Gurria, 2014) and the subnational geographic scale of choice for considering growth in national GDP, innovation, specialisation, sustainability and public service provision (Antikainen, 2005; Brezzi et al, 2011; Marsan and Maguire, 2011). FEAs promote policies for 'filling in', densification and the creation of compact cities based on public transport systems.

City subregions produce a high proportion of the world's GDP and also are more successful in attracting talent and investment than other places (Dobbs et al, 2011). While Europe has many cities, there are only three large cities or city areas that feature in world rankings – London, Paris and Rhein-Ruhr – although three cities in Norway in the European Economic Area – Oslo, Trondheim and Jönköping – all have the highest GDP per head (Dobbs et al, 2011). These findings suggest that the role of cities in the US and Europe will decline in their global role and economic contribution as they are outpaced by growing cities in the energising economies of China, India, Pakistan and some African nations.

FEAs have sustainable attributes through historic or sunk investment in infrastructure that now defines locations for businesses and people. The growth of governance institutions that align administrative and economic boundaries is apparent in cities across the world (Katz and Bradley, 2013; Bunker, 2014).

Infrastructure delivery planning is contextualised within wider state policy and institutional settings within FEAs. Transport is a primary consideration as the Journey to Work (JTW) area is used to define the boundaries of the FEA (DCLG, 2010; Dijkstra and Poelman, 2012). This may be between 40 minutes and an hour and the transport mode selected for the application of this definition may vary. In Europe, this will be set for public transport access but elsewhere it may be by car. The FEA may also be aligned to an environmental area including estuaries or coastal areas that link river systems or rural hinterlands and these may be an inherent feature of its resilience against flooding or other environmental risks.

The term 'subregional' will also be used to discuss FEAs. This is because the scale of FEAs is smaller than a region as commonly defined and yet they are larger than individual local authorities. In the UK, subregional planning has been practised in specific locations, such as Coventry/Warwick subregion (Coventry City Council, 1971), or the area between Reading and Basingstoke (Breheny, 1978). All local authorities in England have been able to pool their powers on a voluntary basis using s101 of the 1972 Local Government Act and this has been used for specific services such as waste, leisure and ICT. Democratic subregional authorities have been applied in parts of the UK, through metropolitan counties 1972–86 in England. Regional local authorities existed in Scotland 1973–96 (Wannop, 2013) and more recently Strategic Development Plan (SDP) areas in Scotland of Aberdeen, Dundee, Edinburgh and Glasgow were created through 2006 Planning etc Act (Clifford and Morphet, 2015).

The Sub-National Review of Economic Development and Regeneration in England (SNR) in 2007 started a policy focus towards FEAs (HMT, 2007). New approaches to democratic governance for FEAs in England followed within the 2009 Local Democracy, Economic Development and Construction Act in England that allows local authorities to create combined authorities that are confirmed through Parliamentary Orders. In 2010, Local Enterprise Partnerships (LEPs) were launched providing opportunities for local authorities to join together in voluntary FEA groupings that resulted in 39 LEPs for the whole of England (Morphet and Pemberton, 2013).

In other states, the economic character of subregions, particularly across borders, such as those across the Oresund between Copenhagen and Malmö (Lundquist and Trippl, 2009) and between France and Spain (Harguindéguy and Bray, 2009), have generated new ways of working (Jeffery, 2000). One the chief characteristics of these developments has been not only political and institutional reforms but also the focus on a brand or concept that can be used to promote the area that will support its economic development (Andersson, 2007).

The role of infrastructure delivery planning is a means of supporting and guiding investment in FEAs. It also assists in the sustainable optimisation of existing infrastructure. Infrastructure strategy is also a governance concern, including economic growth and well-being (RSA, 2014a; OECD, 2015). FEAs also fit within a national context and will be competing for public and private sector investment (OECD, 2014b). There are links between FEAs, as well as within them and, at times, groups of FEAs may work together on common energy, environment and transport systems (IPPR North, 2014). Larger social and community infrastructure, particularly for the arts, culture, higher education and major sporting and arena venues, operate within groups of FEAs.

While FEAs are frequently characterised as urban, they also include rural areas, such as national parks. Rural economies and resident populations may face challenges of overuse of landscapes by visitors or depopulation (ESPON, 2012). While rural FEAs have different configurations compared with cities, their infrastructure delivery is based on polycentric groupings of small and medium-sized towns (Brezzi and Veneri, 2014) that together provide the services, variety and efficiency of larger urban centres. Rural FEAs also need good network connections into the national transport systems.

Governance

One of the major issues for any FEA is its governance. Devolved governance has been identified as being critical for economic success (Ahrend et al, 2014) including arguments that city governance should be led by directly elected mayors (Barber, 2014) and aligned to the FEA as GDP is likely to be higher and grow faster (Ahrend and Schumann, 2014). Where governance is diffuse and fragmented this leads to inefficiencies and institutional sclerosis (Merk, 2014).

Implementing governance reforms that change from smaller administrative areas to ones that more fully reflect an FEA may be challenging, particularly where a new directly elected politician is responsible for making decisions for the whole area in comparison with more localised decisions in previous systems. There may also be concerns about party-political affiliations and the potential dominance of the cities over the suburban areas that have become part of this wider area. However, cities are dependent on the suburbs in a symbiotic relationship. FEAs can only function where the governance is balanced and represents more equal relationships between the city and its suburbs. Even where there have been governance reforms to align the economic and democratic governance boundaries, there will always be a need for strong relationships with areas that are peripheral or co-terminus. In some cases these may be adjacent cities and in others these will be rural areas (Brezzi and Veneri, 2014).

In the move to bring together FEAs and their administrative governance, new state spaces have emerged (Brenner, 2004). Some argue that these are fuzzy or soft spaces (Haughton et al, 2010) representing apolitical and non-democratic units that can be used by government but stand outside accountable government frameworks. In contrast, Pemberton and Morphet (2014) have argued that these are spaces of transitional territorialism and represent a shift in governance scales using soft-power methods to speed their implementation (Nye, 1990) without generating opposition from the local level. Using nudge (Thaler and Sunstein, 2009) and inducement theories, these new spaces are created and then the democratic governance is aligned to fit them. These approaches can also be encountered in Europe, the US (Carbonell and Yaro, 2005) and Australia, where joint planning panels that have a fundamental economic character and purpose differentiates them from what has gone before (Bishop, 2014).

Role of infrastructure delivery planning in FEAs and city regions

Infrastructure within cities together with their institutional capacity and regulatory frameworks are critical to their economic success (WEF, 2014). Hard networks in FEAs need to be supported by community and social infrastructure. FEAs and city regions need to demonstrate that there is a strategy for the area that can indicate where future priorities for growth and improvement will be located and that its associated infrastructure delivery programme is supported. This is a main feature to establish and maintain confidence from investors including those for infrastructure.

The economic role infrastructure

FEAs are defined by their economic character and contribution to the national and international economies (RTPI, 2014). Much of the economic infrastructure is represented by physical systems of energy, transport, water and waste implemented over longer periods of time. In the urban cores, that will be at the heart of most FEAs, a major consideration will be whether this infrastructure is adequate for current needs, its resilience and adaptability.

Economic infrastructure is provided through networks that are under, over and on the ground (Graham and Marvin, 2001). For most cities, telecommunications infrastructure will be problematic and a further consideration is the need for adaption to new technologies and systems as they become available. Commercial buildings may not be capable of adaptation to the demands of modern infrastructure. This might have an influence on the definition of the central area and suggest redevelopment or zoning redefining the city. The development of Canary Wharf in London is an example of this. Obsolete commercial buildings can be converted to hotels or housing. In rural areas, digital infrastructure may require different technical solutions and greater amounts of investment, while rural isolation may mean that there is stronger need for digital communications to support business, health, education and social relations (ESPON, 2012).

Energy consumption in FEAs might be increased through demands from equipment although initial building design or retrofitting can mitigate this (Fryd et al, 2010). Buildings can also be adapted to generate energy that can feed into the national network. Companies may work together on local energy schemes using biomass, waste or wind capacity and can use previously contaminated brownfield land that might otherwise have high restoration costs.

Repairing and replacing water infrastructure will have effects on city transport systems and can result in long working time delays and rerouting. Demand for water will increase as cities densify their populations and may require new approaches. Waste water in cities is a major concern in its potential relationships with urban flooding. All surface water is run off into drainage systems that can be inadequate to cope with sudden rainfall. The introduction of SUDS (sustainable urban draining systems) will have considerable effects in urban areas and may require redesign of landscaping and green space in more densely built-up areas. Many parks are located above underground car parks and other transport systems so providing SUDS will be difficult. This suggests a greater focus on the maintenance of the existing system and management of waste water to allow more capacity from existing provision. In London the capacity of the water system is critical, with major investment in new water pipelines and sewers.

The main economic infrastructure in all FEAs and city regions will be transport. As cities densify there is more focus on the reduction of car use through measures such as congestion charging and workplace parking levies, putting more pressure on public transport systems. The development of night–time economies and 24–hour working patterns means that transport systems are required to operate with greater frequency over longer periods of time (Montgomery, 2003). Maintenance of transport systems is a continuing challenge in the economic infrastructure management of any city and combined management of all transport systems is required in order to ensure that it functions effectively. This is reinforced by integrated ticketing across all modes of transport (Blythe, 2004) and the use of public information systems to alert and divert passengers where there are unexpected delays or incidents.

Investment in new economic infrastructure will be based on business cases to government that are primarily focused on their benefits to the FEA and national economy (EEDA, 2011; HMT, 2011). As cities are primary generators of carbon, investing in public transport can have a major impact on its reduction. Much of the debate about economic infrastructure may focus on the provision of new capacity through investment in fixed links such as roads or metro systems. Capacity can also be increased through updating existing infrastructure including signalling systems, train and platform lengths, internal design and seating capacity in buses and trains. Buses also provide flexible capacity. The use of integrated ticketing can also support specific pricing regimes that can manage demand by spreading journey times. Where transport companies own land, this can be used to promote development to support infrastructure investment within the city and on the periphery. Investment in transport can open areas to support the city through transport oriented development using new hubs, stations, bus routes and locations within integrated ticketing systems.

In rural areas the investment in economic infrastructure may be in its connections with national transport routes and corridors (CEC, 2013a), and ICT-supported transport provision. The management of bus times, hubs, coordinated links and the use of other more informal transport modes including car sharing all contribute to rural accessibility without investment in fixed infrastructure. The provision of new intermediate stations can make a contribution to areas to link them into national networks.

The environmental and green infrastructure

The strategic role of green spaces in FEAs is to provide resilience, biodiversity corridors and habitat, and healthy lifestyles. Green infrastructure is also an important element in climate–change adaptation offering the greatest opportunities for savings through transport planning and provision (Tzoulas et al, 2007; Carter, 2011). Within FEAs, green infrastructure contributes to mental and physical health (Nielsen and Hansen, 2007; Lee and Maheswaran, 2011). The design of non–obesogenic environments that encourage walking and cycling to work can provide significant opportunities for mode switching. The attractiveness and safety of walkways and parks will also influence healthier lifestyles. The quality of parks will influence choice of residential locations and may be an important factor in wider investments within FEAs. Green spaces contribute to supporting mental health, have calming effects, make people feel more attached to their location and give them a sense of belonging (Sugiyama et al, 2008). Green infrastructure in urban areas can also provide links to the rural periphery using former roads, railway lines and canal ways to act as links to and from and the city.

The role of an FEA in providing green infrastructure for its wider community is also an important consideration in its role in holding events such as concerts and major sporting meetings. In these cases the green infrastructure can provide significant economic and social benefits as well as its wider contributions to health and resilience.

The social and community infrastructure

Social and community infrastructure in FEAs and city regions is an essential component of quality of life and their economic role and will include the strategic and specialist facilities that will be used across the whole area. The quality and investment in these social facilities will be a main attractor to potential employees and investors. The provision of community facilities will also be important. Where there are higher employment activity rates, childcare will be required near workplaces, transport hubs and residential areas. Informal meeting places are part of the innovation and networking that is part of the economic role of the FEA and also the locations of arenas and major sporting venues that support tourism, the night-time economy and cultural industries.

Infrastructure delivery planning for social and community infrastructure will engage all public, private and voluntary sectors. The adequacy of current facilities for major hospital and universities and also the provision of specific facilities need to be assessed. The development of public transport may support co-location including the establishment of health quarters or allow universities to move into adjacent areas for potential smart specialisation (CEC, 2013b) or innovation facilities. Universities have also had a positive role in using listed and landmark buildings within cities that are protected but have outgrown their original use, and creating new knowledge hubs. Universities may require new accommodation and facilities. Some consideration of the public sector estate may be necessary to support this developing role. Universities can also use land and locations that may be less attractive to other users and create a night-time presence in areas that have had only a daytime role.

Other facilities such as arts, entertainment, sport and leisure will be located within FEAs while neighbourhood leisure facilities will be an important part of residential areas and add to their attractiveness. When developing new residential areas it is important to build in some flexibility to allow for changes in social and community infrastructure over time. Also sustainable principles mean that the extent of existing infrastructure should be assessed before creating new provision in any area. The management of infrastructure by specialist institutions such as schools or universities may lead to an overprovision if these are not made available on a wider basis. Other changes that can bring co-location between services including health and leisure, and universities and schools may also to reinforce local centres and assist in their maintenance.

Subregional theories and policy underpinning

The development of infrastructure delivery planning to underpin strategic policy and delivery in FEAs and city regions will be based on different models that may have economic and sustainable narratives. Strategic plans will use at least one of these models to characterise their areas and underpin infrastructure delivery planning. In summary, these models are:

Agglomerations and clusters

While urban areas may be functional and efficient, further success is derived from the agglomerations and clusters of types of synergistic business that locate in FEAs (RSA, 2014b). Agglomerations create self-reinforcing networks used by specialists for innovation and development that can stretch for a 100–200 km radius across state borders (Florida, 2003; Dobbs et al, 2011). The interconnections within agglomerations are important for their development and managed through local self-determination and metro governance (RSA, 2014a). It is possible to see how this is developing in a number of FEAs within Europe, following central government interventions as in Grenoble in France (Cremer-Schulte, 2014) or through the use of incentives and nudge as in the case of Switzerland (Kaiser, 2014) and the UK (Morphet and Pemberton, 2013).

Polycentricity

One of the devices that has been used to promote cross-boundary working in the EU is the use of economic geography and sustainability, focusing particularly on the role of polycentricity. This has promoted the interworking between multiple centres in FEAs to enhance the effectiveness and efficiency of urban agglomerations (Turok et al, 2004). The theory is based on the notions of complementarity and accessibility within the FEA to promote employment access for those currently excluded or marginalised in the labour market (Tochtermann and Clayton, 2011). Polycentricity first emerged as an approach to services allocation and functional spatial relationships in the European Spatial Development Perspective (CEC, 1999) and works particularly in Germany and the Netherlands and across land borders, for example on the island of Ireland. Like MLG (multilevel governance), polycentricity has been seen as normative rather than based on evidence, and promoted across the whole of the EU regardless of the differential success rates in its application (Davoudi and Strange, 2008; Faludi, 2010). The concept has also been used in peripheral regions of the EU such as the Atlantic Arc, where cities and large towns have complementary services and assets (Groth et al, 2011).

Sustainability

The application and organising principles of sustainable development suggest more compact connected urban areas that are defined by their scale, particularly through the public transport system (Arts et al, 2014). Sustainable approaches to development have environmental and efficiency benefits arising from renewable buildings which allow sunk investment to be reused. It is also a feature in defining their resilience (Berkes et al, 2000). Subregions benchmark their sustainable performance with each other (Tanguay et al, 2010; Brezzi et al, 2011). As climate-change policies become more challenging for states then the role of FEAs in helping to meet them will increase (Carter, 2011).

Subregional strategies: policy models

These policy narratives will have applications in strategic plans for investment and infrastructure delivery in the FEAs and city regions. However, they will also be combined with models of implementation that will prioritise delivery programmes. These include:

Reinforcing existing success

There is an assumption that focusing on success in FEAs will bring more success even when infrastructure and capacity might be overheated (Dijkstra and Poelman, 2012). In this approach, providing additional capacity is prioritised, such as airports and roads, and there may be less interest in regulating these areas if they are creating jobs and growth. This approach will follow the market and there will be less concern for sustainable growth and managing capacity more efficiently. Laissez-faire city growth may be less efficient in the longer run if it is car dependent (Goodwin, 2012). Where cities have been built in this way, there will be more focus on filling in and densifying developed areas to connect them to workplaces.

Replicating success – what works

In terms of developing policy models for government, an approach that has been adopted (Cabinet Office, 2013) in the UK is an approach of 'what works'. In 2013, the UK government established a series of what works centres based on specific topics, including one on local economic growth. This reviews all the research on the outcomes of specific policies and actions and identifies what has worked in practice. The question here is the definition of success and how actions are attributed to achieving this. Also it is important to consider whether the actions lie within specific geographies or points in the economic cycle. 'What works' is a soft version of policy transfer.

Redistributing success

Concern about economic and social imbalance in the UK was a driving political ideology for all governments from the 1930s to 2000. During this period, there was a focus on policies that shifted the population and economic growth to regions and areas that had less economic activity or were in decline after their primary industries had declined including the North–West, the North–East and parts of Scotland (Glasson and Marshall, 2007). Government policy was focused on the development of new and expanded towns, the movement of government offices to lagging regions and a variety of funding support measures, including grants to businesses willing to move to these areas. These policies were supported by economic planning councils and the NEDC (National Economic Development Council) when they were in operation. This approach was also transferred by the UK into the EU when it joined in 1972, implementing the structural funds and other associated Cohesion policies.

Within the UK, this focus on economic decline led to what was described as a 'race to the bottom' so that localities focused more on the factors that generated these grants and support rather than using them to support a recovery and economic growth. In 1992 this approach started to switch within the EU through the Maastricht Treaty and then in the UK it was changed in 2000 by the Labour government. However, debates about economic imbalances between parts of the country continue and there is a focus on developing regional 'powerhouses' to develop lower-performing economies within the UK. Spatial imbalances have been growing in the UK since the 1970s and a spatial strategy for England that rebalances economic and sustainable priorities and policy implementation may be required (Baker and Wong, 2013; Gardiner et al, 2014). The 'rebalancers' also argue for the same kind of integrated approach being developed at city region level as at national level using similar elements including integration and coordination of public sector investment and MLG.

While there are many supporters of evolution and subsidiarity, the transfer of the costs of underperformance to the locality's governance is a long-standing concern. Deas (2013) argues that this should be dealt with by the state through decisions on priorities for strategic investment. A lagging and underperforming FEA might be able to improve productivity and efficiency but this also needs to be contextualised in the wider state decisions on strategic infrastructure investment in transport for example and the location of strategic facilities and activities such as international sporting events will be supported. The RSA (2014b) argues that where a fiscal gap between FEA income (through taxation and other contributions) and expenditure in these areas (including unemployment benefits) develops, this underperformance should not be a charge on the state, as in more holistic welfarist policies, but should be placed as the responsibility of the FEA. The FEA's governance should be encouraged to undertake its own reforms and income generation to bring these costs and expenditure into balance.

Projections and models

Models are helpful in informing policy and other judgements within FEAs rather than 'predict and provide' tools. They have a role in strategic planning as they can assist in assessing capacity for environmental resilience and identify priorities for infrastructure investment. Demographic models are used to estimate capacity and demand for social and community facilities including schools, health and open space. Household formation and birth rates are also used but these need to be supplemented with other real-time data including registrations for health and school services. Within any FEA, institutions may use different demographic models and this practice may be problematic in service planning and delivery.

Sector-based

Sector-based approaches can be considered either as using systems to create the conditions for success, such as engaging and integrating the transport system, or through the application of broadband speed (RSA, 2014a, 2014b). A second approach can be through specialisation in one particular type of industry such as ICT in San Francisco and finance in London. However, even where these specialisms by sector occur, then there are also many other factors that support them such as higher education opportunities, attractive places to live and the culture that suits that particular sector (Wishlade, 2015).

Subregional strategies

While there are strong pressures to bring together local authorities to work together as a single unit within FEAs, there is also a need to consider the development of a plan or strategy that can be prepared that will indicate the objectives for the FEA, the gaps between the current and the desired position and the investment required to progress the objectives. New institutional structures are required to bring together autonomous administrative units of government. The strategy will be required for the FEA to engage with governments and the EU for specific projects. Projects will be identified from within the member local authorities, both those using their own assets and resources and also those using private or third sector funding. Strategic development with partners will enable institutions to align their own development proposals and derive added value from inclusion in the strategy as a whole. Demonstrating added value to any project can make funding easier to obtain for it and for others that may be linked to it.

Strategy development employs methods that create 'investor ready cities' (Siemens et al, 2014) through the identification of a vision that demonstrates how investors can contribute to its achievement. It will also be spatial and link with spatial plans at other scales (Healey, 2009). This suggests the application of business-planning processes including project planning, risk analysis and identification of dependencies between projects (CEC, 2014b; Morphet, 2015). The selection of projects will require specific economic methodologies and in the UK this will be based on the Treasury's *Green Book* (HMT, 2011) when some public sector funding is likely to be required. In Manchester, a specific methodology for determining priority projects has been developed based on the Green Book approach but also includes territorial and private sector components within its evaluation (Greater Manchester LEP, 2010).

The availability of funding through the application of assets to underpin loans, including bonds, may now be easier since the public and private sectors are working within the International Financial Reporting Standards, which is being implemented across OECD countries by 2017. This means that public–private partnerships and projects can be assessed using the same methodologies. This wider approach to the use of public sector funding can also open the potential for more local capital investment (Urbed, 2010; Symons, 2011).

The presentation of the FEA strategy will be important, with a vision lasting over 20 years although the specific programmes and projects will be grouped in shorter periods. The selection of the vision and its delivery programmes will be based in part on evidence and research as well as aspiration, and then assessed against the baseline. The delivery programme is located in the gap between the existing and the proposed positions and creates a coordinating framework across all governance scales (OECD, 2014b) from multiple investment sources (Della Croce and Yermo, 2013). The assessment of each project will identify how it will fulfil multiple strategic objectives (EEDA, 2011; HMT, 2011).

The success of the strategy depends on local priorities and can be changed flexibly by the FEA governance. A number of reviews of FEA governance approaches in the UK have stressed the importance of devolved decision-making and fiscal federalism (Lipton, 2011). Some FEAs are developing their own infrastructure delivery plans as part of their strategy. This includes London (Mayor of London, 2015) and other FEAs in England including the Solent, the Humber, West of England and Cumbria.

Delivery

Infrastructure delivery plans include the preparation of a strategic plan that incorporates existing investment and identifies FEA project priorities. However if this strategic plan is to be successful it has to include a delivery strategy and programme that is also owned by the strategy makers and not reliant on other institutions for programme management. A strategic spatial plan is a means to provide commitment and confidence to potential investors but it is also a clear indication to infrastructure providers of the impact on their own planning processes. This can also be more easily achieved where there is an alignment between the governance of the FEA and its boundary.

Coordinated investment

Integrated territorial investment (ITI) strategies form a basis of integrated infrastructure planning and delivery. This approach can enable new areas of the FEA to be opened up for housing or other activities and bring back to life existing areas through connecting them better into the infrastructure system. Integrated infrastructure investment will add value in comparison with sector–led programmes. However, in most countries sectoral infrastructure investment is the norm and it remains a challenge for any FEA to achieve an integrated programme and then to deliver it in ways that can add value. Selecting sites for housing and other development can then be undertaken, where there is existing infrastructure capacity. Where the scale of development justifies, there can be new investment. However, here the models to provide social and community infrastructure at the same time as the new housing can be used, as in the Netherlands (Falk and Hall, 2009).

Vertical and horizontal integration – MLG

Horizontal integration occurs where FEAs may work together to achieve specific ends such as in demonstrating a case for infrastructure investment. Where neighbouring FEAs might normally be in competition, cooperative working can be used to argue the case for national infrastructure investment. This is the basis of the 'powerhouse' narrative that is being used in the UK (Cox, 2014). This is also represented through the duty to cooperate in local plan–making in the UK.

Achieving vertical integration and subsidiarity between the scales of government in specific locations through MLG is difficult. Sharing powers and resources requires changes in culture from all scales of government, including devolving from the centre, which requires the application of the principle of subsidiarity. EU arguments for subsidiarity took a more formal character in the white paper on governance (CEC, 2001b) and were then included in the Lisbon Treaty (2007) focusing on territory and substate governance. This also gave power to the Committee of the Regions (CoR, 2014) to progress subsidiarity in member states and the Van den Brande report (2014) examined the ways that practical aspects of MLG and integration could be applied.

The opportunity to strengthen MLG and integration has been advanced through the Cohesion Regulation (CEC, 2013b) and the new requirements on each member state to set out how they will be working to deliver these principles in the period 2014–20. Each member state has set this out in their own Partnership Agreement (PA), framed within the construct on the Regulations but set within state governance scales and practices. These PAs were submitted in April 2014 with the promise that they would be signed off by the EC (European

Commission) by the end of that year. This was the case in general terms but more detailed approval of programmes and devolved powers followed. The UK for example, was the only member state to fail to devolve powers, responsibilities and programme responsibilities to local government in its PA submission (HMG, 2014b), although other states have also been less willing to adopt the new programmed approach at the local level. However, this was found to be outside the terms of the regulation and was subsequently revised in its final approved form (HMG, 2014c) with the inclusion of local authority freedom to use the operational constructs for programmes, ITI programmes and programmes for community-led local development (Miller, 2014; Morphet, 2015).

Across the EU, these new programmes, particularly ITI, are available to groups of local authorities in FEAs. Combining of a range of individual projects into a single programme has meant that it can address rural areas, ports, transport, the digital economy, training, sustainability and economic development (CEC, 2013b). In some cases, ITI strategies and programmes will be across state boundaries and be for larger areas. In the UK for example, the FEAs in England prepared ESIF (European Structural and Investment Funds) strategies as part of the process of the preparation of the PA, but their ownership by non-democratic LEPs were not eligible for consideration because they were not owned by local authorities. The UK government had to give way on this point.

In order to strengthen the commitment and working relationship between tiers of government, the Van den Brande report (2014) has suggested the use of Territorial Pacts (TPs) – MLG contracts for delivery that stretch from the EU to the locality and include the member state. In the UK, TPs are already being used through the establishment of city deals across a number of urban areas and, while starting as English initiatives, have been extended to Scotland and Wales.

While FEAs and subregions are determined by the boundaries defined by JTW isochrones they also have relationships with other FEAs and the other scales of government and these relationships may be critical for success. Within the FEA, this may depend on the willingness of the local authorities to work together or to deliver infrastructure projects that may serve the subregion as a whole (Parker and Mansfield, 2014). There may also be the opportunity to shift blame around within the FEA (Milio, 2014).

The location of infrastructure in one part of the FEA or just outside, in another FEA, may also cause political rivalry and competition. This is particularly where there is no tradition of working together (Dabrowski, 2014) or systems of governance vary in scales, for example between London and its periphery.

In some cases there may be a legal duty to cooperate with neighbouring local authorities in order to approximate an economic market area for specific land uses, such as transport or housing. This may be difficult if there is no overarching strategic plan as has been the case in England. However, the disconnect between the strategic LEP plans and those for individual local authorities remains a challenge (PAS, 2014). Given the power relations, it may also difficult for FEAs to work well with state governments. There is still an adult/child relationship rather than that of partners and this remains an enduring challenge. This is particularly the case when implementing projects that need to join up at the local level but may have some wider significance. The need to understand local as well as wider needs can be challenging with the state assuming the overarching and dominant role (Smith Institute, 2014a).

Challenges

Working within FEAs presents a number of challenges that have to be recognised and addressed in order to achieve effective working.

Establishing new governance arrangements

A challenge in the development of governance for FEAs is their formation and the determination of boundaries (DCLG, 2008). For some FEAs this may be clear but in others where there are polycentric patterns, concerns about inclusion and exclusion, scale and codependence are considerable. These will be framed by the political attraction of retained independence and separation but tempered with the benefits of operating at a more strategic scale and this is particularly important when considering the attraction of infrastructure projects. Larger FEAs may have more political influence and may be able to demonstrate that there is more experience in successful project delivery and less risk than in a smaller or more newly formed governance arrangements.

The approach to transition may also be difficult. While central government may wish for policy reasons to create alignment between FEAs and their governance there may be political or cultural barriers to achieving this easily. Governments have chosen other more neo–liberal fuzzy methods that have attempted to use competitions and incentives (Kaiser, 2014), particularly through successive policy transfers, in order to support this transition. This is especially the case in Ireland and England (Pemberton and Morphet, 2014; Adshead, 2014).

Consideration in dealing with these transitional challenges may relate to staged formations with some local authorities initially becoming members of more than one FEA group. Working together may become easier if there is confidence in the likely outcomes. If the working together provides more funding and investment then this will be attractive to politicians and communities, and may give more confidence to new institutions and working arrangements. Recognition by government, the EC or other bodies may also engender confidence in these new groups. Understanding what likely problems may emerge at the outset and how these are to be managed may also be part of any risk assessment.

The power distribution within any FEA will be important and ensuring that there is equality between all members may be significant to success. Where part of the FEA may be dominant, say including the city centre or the largest city if a polycentric cluster, then there may be a tendency to discriminate or overwhelm smaller authorities. This will reduce trust and cooperation, albeit their role is significant is meeting wider infrastructure or housing provision. Improved working relationships might be enhanced through widening the governance circle and using wider institutional representatives to maintain the balance between scales of local authorities (Rigg and O'Mahoney, 2013).

Partnership working can be challenging and may be improved by adopting a set of working principles as shown in Box 9.1.

Box 9.1: Principles for partnership working

1. Recognise and accept the need for partnership
2. Develop clarity and realism of purpose
3. Ensure commitment and ownership
4. Develop and maintain trust
5. Create clear and robust partnership arrangements
6. Monitor, measure and learn

Source: Lamie and Ball, 2010, p 115

Retention of central power

While FEAs benefit from an alignment between their economic and administrative boundaries, there are also questions of their remaining relationship with the centre, particularly in relation to project allocation and funding for infrastructure. While the FEAs can make business cases and demonstrate how any specific project will support the local and national economy, the power for approving nationally significant infrastructure projects remains with the centre. Also, the size of the budget allocated will be dependent on central government decisions. This distribution may be based on a variety of criteria including existing economic growth, that is, funding success by supporting growth to improve economic performance. There may also be an underlying political agenda (Mehiriz and Marceau, 2013). Even where there are developed systems of fiscal federalism (Oates, 2008) there will still be retributive mechanisms by the centre to different subregions. This is particularly relevant for intra-subregional transport systems where there is a strong public sector involvement in strategic provision and accessing funding through the European Investment Bank and private sector routes (Zegras et al, 2013) and may depend on the way the overriding priorities are framed and reflected in appraisal methods (Pettersson, 2013).

One of the major concerns here is the overriding culture of central government departments and how this is communicated to those engaged directly with the FEAs (Rigg and O'Mahoney, 2013). In England the establishment of Government Offices of the Regions (GORs) in 1992 was proposed as a single place-based, central government one-stop shop for local government. However, the civil servants in the GORs described these arrangements as co-location and took their policy briefs and held accountability to their home departments rather than to their regional director.

Future policy directions?

This is a very fertile area of policy development and one that is still evolving. It has an attraction within the EU because it can incorporate all of its territory and create potential contracts that involves the EC, member states and local authorities in new formal relationships and rescue the power of member states in influencing policy and delivery. Second, it has an important focus on changing policy making from sectors to geographic scales and increased the role of the place in informing policy development and delivery.

It is the FEA scale that is being privileged in this process and it is likely that as a consequence the local scale with be rescued in its influence (Cremer-Schulte, 2014).

Conclusions

FEAs and subregions are an important governance scale and one where the role of the territory is defined by its economic cohesion. This allows for more integrated approaches to infrastructure planning and can overcome traditional administrative boundaries and interests. As the pressure to act on climate change increases and more of the world's population is urbanised, democratic governance at this scale and the relationships between FEAs both within and between states may be critical to their longer-term success. The provision, quality and equitable access to integrated infrastructure will be critical to their role.

TEN

Local infrastructure delivery planning

Introduction

Infrastructure delivery planning at the local level is of significant importance to communities and their daily lives, including access to jobs health and facilities. It is a central responsibility of spatial planning to assess the quality, future adequacy and resilience of infrastructure in localities using plans, policies, regulation, development and direct delivery (Storbjörk, 2007; Bruton and Nicholson, 2013). This is also an important scale for climate change mitigation and adaption through the use of existing and new infrastructure (Measham et al, 2011).

In England, local plans are the only scale where infrastructure delivery planning is a statutory part of the plan's formulation and test of its deliverability (DCLG, 2012). Local plans are required in all English local authorities and since 1970, a series of methodologies and approaches have been applied (Bruton and Nicholson, 2013; Cullingworth et al, 2014). The 2004 Planning and Compensation Act introduced the deliverability test and this has subsequently been confirmed by the National Planning Policy Framework (NPPF) (DCLG, 2012). The local plan coincides with the administrative boundary of the local authority area and this means that urban and rural areas may be contained within it. The local plan has to be in conformity with any national planning policies and will be subordinate to any Nationally Significant Infrastructure Projects (NSIPs) in its area. Where there are neighbourhood plans made under the 2011 Localism Act, these will have to be in conformity with the local plan.

Local plans adopt a vision, identify deficits or gaps and then apply policies and programmes to meet them. The principle of access to the services embodied within local plans is a significant feature of social and economic justice and community welfare (Brown and Lloyd-Jones, 2002; Defra, 2003) although access may be difficult to measure (Howie et al, 2009). In the past, much local infrastructure delivery planning has been managed through the use of national access standards that have been used to assess the adequacy of infrastructure in any locality and followed by proposals to reduce any defined deficits. The use of national standards has now been dropped in some countries such as England (Morphet, 2011a). However, the need to assess localities against their access to services remains a priority within the EU Cohesion targets (CEC, 2013b). Local planning policy processes need to identify the evidence that may be used to define reasonable access strands and adopt policies to meet any deficits. There is also a need to consider additional development to support the maintenance of existing services as populations change.

While much of the infrastructure delivery planning debate is concerned with major investment in fixed links and built facilities, it is at the local level where smaller scale interventions and investment can have a major impact. These are particularly concerned with making localities more liveable (Urry et al, 2014) and sustainable. There can be major national advantages to implementing local SUDS (sustainable urban drainage systems) schemes to improve the resilience of any area against flooding and water shortage.

The quality and distribution of local infrastructure will be a major determinant of the popularity and success of any local administrative area. Local authorities are owners of land and buildings and use these infrastructure assets to provide services for their area. In some cases, local authorities have acquired land that is not directly used for service provision but for generating income to support service delivery. The ownership and distribution of property assets between local authorities is serendipitous and can be based on culture and practices over a long period. Some local authorities have also lost or gained land as a consequence of local government reviews as services have been transferred between tiers of local government (Morphet, 2008). Also, in the past, local authorities have provided more services than at present so although the police, justice, university and health services area now run independently of local government they still may share sites or be co-located for these historic reasons (Varney, 2006).

In addition to property assets local authorities may have financial reserves to use for infrastructure investment. These reserves may have been accumulated through the sale of the local authority's housing stock, income generation or low levels of expenditure on services. Local authorities also have traditionally invested part of their annual incomes in infrastructure through capital programmes comprising projects that may last over a three- to five-year period. Some local authority funding for infrastructure is provided by government. Schools have been provided through funding based on pupil numbers via capitation payments although this system is now fragmented between different national school types, some of which bypass local authorities. Other funding has been specifically provided for roads and transport. Local infrastructure expenditure from the government may be available through competitive or specific schemes or through annual funding equalisation mechanisms.

Role of infrastructure delivery planning at the local level

Economic role

Within local authority areas, the economic infrastructure has intra- and interspatial roles. Links with other local authority areas are important for access to social and community facilities, parks, schools and places of work. Linkages between the local authority areas will also be important for access to more specialist health or other services, events and strategic facilities, and for providing links into FEA (functional economic area) and state networks.

All types of physical infrastructure are important for the economy at the local level, including transport, waste, water, energy and telecommunications. The quality of this infrastructure may be a local concern and there may be competition for investment by infrastructure providers. Where areas have been developed over longer periods, then the infrastructure may need replacement or upgrading. This can be expensive and disruptive to communities. However, this is an important part of assessing sustainability, local resilience and potential for future expansion and growth. There may also be questions about retrofitting of older localities to meet with more modern standards, including broadband, energy management and recycling.

In newly developed areas, physical infrastructure may be provided by extending existing networks or by developing new ones. Some may be funded by new development, for others, costs are spread over all users, as for energy and water. Provision of new waste services and other physical infrastructure such as street lighting will be funded by local authorities but the extent to which this may be additional to current income will depend on net population and household changes year on year. If new development areas are increasing in population but other areas are losing population, or replacement development is reducing densities, then there will be an overall balance or loss in funding.

The provision of some physical infrastructure, including energy, water and telecommunications, will depend on suppliers that operate at state and FEA scales. Their programmes may not take a local focus and it can be particularly difficult for smaller local authorities to promote local infrastructure investment projects to organisations with a wide geographical remit. In all cases, working with organisations that are sectorally and nationally focused needs the building of long-terms relationships where this is possible. The networks between providers can be strong and it is possible that one contact can assist in attracting the attention of other infrastructure providers.

Similar concerns may occur in the provision of transport, which is critical to the local economy. Fixed links such as light and heavy rail will be supplied through strategic organisations that are concerned with specific routes and corridors as part of FEAs. However, the provision for bus, cycling, walking and car use modes will be local authority policy responsibilities. Also, each of these transport modes may be encouraged or discouraged through local policy interventions. Buses provide the most flexible public transport and with associated bus priority measures can be efficient and effective in road use and for passengers. Local transport hubs, with integrated timetables, can ensure that the links between different transport systems provide added value to each mode. This can also be supported through integrated ticketing systems which link across localities into FEAs and beyond.

One of the main challenges in physical infrastructure delivery planning in local authority areas is the extent of integration required between providers to create locally effective systems that support the economy. Many projects are developed by providers long before there are local plan discussions on them, and when these occur they may only be about detailed implementation rather than strategy. This may not provide the opportunity to discuss any alternatives in location, type of project and integration with other infrastructure. It may also be difficult to engage in earlier discussion on potential projects as providers may argue that their discussions are commercially sensitive and therefore confidential. Separation in service planning and infrastructure investment can also occur within local authorities where departments are using different demographic models and geographical areas. Where there is internal competition for capital funding within the local authority this may also encourage more opaque practices.

Therefore, one of the main challenges for infrastructure delivery planning in local authorities is maintaining contact with the provider institutions, discussing their plans for investment and bringing them together with other providers with similar responsibilities for physical infrastructure (Morphet, 2011b; Holt and Baker, 2014). Another challenge may the unwillingness of providers to share details of their policies, priorities and programmes with others and this may be difficult particularly where there is likely to be a need to service new development.

When working with major institutions with interests wider than the local area, it may also be difficult to attract their attention to the specific local situations that may need to be considered. Because these have not emerged through their own assessment processes they may not be willing to engage in local priority discussions. It may take some time to build trust and working relationships. It may also be possible to attempt to discuss them through strategic organisations at the FEA level so that major providers can discuss this within this wider context and the governance of the FEA may find it easier to bring these institutions to the table.

Without this kind of coordination between infrastructure providers the potential of any local authority area to fulfil its role in support of the economy and growth may be compromised. Even where no major change is planned, FEAs will depend on the relationship with their periphery for labour and access to jobs. Identifying the economic benefits of any infrastructure project at the local level may be critical in advocating its funding and delivery in ways that have local and wider benefit.

Environmental and green role

The role of environmental and green infrastructure at the local level is important for mental and physical health, waste water and habitats (Landscape Institute, 2011). The provision of parks and open spaces has a considerable contribution to local mental health and a sense of belonging. The quality of parks and play areas is important to residents and they provide places for community development. Parks and open spaces have links with the countryside and, with associated walking and cycling routes, can support physical recreation and biodiversity.

The management of local green spaces may be by public authorities and there have been anxieties about the quality and contribution of public parks as maintenance funding has fallen since 2007 (HLF, 2014). Visual green space is provided through landscaping around buildings, street trees and other meanwhile spaces (Nemeth, 2009; Carmona, 2010). Evidence for the provision of open space will be applied to the measurement of access by distance. Green space and play areas for younger children are provided nearer than those for older children and more formal sporting activity such as pitches. There is also a need for green spaces in town centres and locations where people work so that there are places to sit at lunchtime (Tzoulas et al, 2007).

The management of open and green spaces can be a major concern and the types of landscaping can have an effect on these costs. The least expensive planting such as grass may require most maintenance, unlike slower growing shrubs that if carefully chosen can provide green links and corridors but require less maintenance. Some areas, such as Milton Keynes, have put all their green spaces into a single trust and manage them as a whole in order to save costs.

In assessing the provision of green spaces within local areas there is a need to identify any shortfalls and consider how these can be met through development or other means. Given the interlinkages through corridors and habitats, then the preparation of open space strategies that identify how these components work together may be helpful. Although a strategy can be prepared at the local level, it will also need to link with wider scales and adjacent areas (Mayor of London and CABE, 2009). The maintenance and development of green corridors and river pathways may only be possible over long periods of time but the needs of consistently applied policies will support this provision and be completed over time.

In some localities communities have formed user and management groups for green spaces and these may be important in considering the role and management of parks within specific localities. They may also be important in encouraging volunteers in the park as part of the park's maintenance regime. In 2014, the London Borough of Hackney had 24 active park user groups that work together in the Hackney Parks Forum. Such groups can be central in the creation of open space strategies.

Local green spaces make an important contribution to carbon reduction as part of a wider climate change strategy at the local level. This may include a range of policies including conserving existing biodiversity and habitats, developing ecologically resilient landscape and managing coasts and rivers (Natural England, 2009).

Social and community role

Social and community facilities are important at the local level. While most will be within the local authority that is the focus of the local plan, communities may have easier access to services in neighbouring local plan areas including for schools, shops and libraries. In some cases, housing provision will have consequential effects on service use in adjacent areas.

Social and community infrastructure in local areas will have a focus on health and education facilities that are near to home. These will be accompanied by pharmacies, nurseries, police and fire services, retail and other services. One of the main considerations in the provision of local community and social infrastructure will be requirements that change over time. In areas with smaller catchment areas there may be pressures to close or combine facilities which may mean longer journeys to access them. In these cases, consideration of the size of the population and local growth in housing provision may help to support and maintain these facilities.

At the local level it will be important to plan in detail for social and community facilities, including assessments of their current condition and capacity. There is also a need to consider these facilities for new development where the existing facilities may only support some increases in populations levels (Taylor, 2011). One option for offering social and community facilities for transitional communities that are growing is to locate them within properties that may eventually become shops or use capacity within new or existing buildings such as schools. Smaller clinic and health facilities may be able to combine with pharmacies or leisure uses until the community population grows to the level that merits its own facilities.

Another aspect in the provision of social and community infrastructure at the local level is its role in promoting public health (Kidd, 2007). This may be through the design and layout of facilities and housing areas that encourage physical activity (NICE, 2008). There may also be a need to address public health issues such as obesity within existing areas where there is not much potential for physical change in the built environment. Changes can be associated with the management of local hot food takeaway shops through planning policies (HUDU, 2013). This can be extended to a consideration of access to fresh food through urban food planning (Morgan, 2009).

In England the relationship between spatial planning and health has always been strong but was separated through institutional frameworks. Since 2013, public health responsibilities have been returned to local authorities. This allows local health and local planning policies to be aligned (SPAHG, 2011). This may be through the physical environment, safety, and mental health aspects of the environment. However, it can also be through the control of specific types of retail facilities that are related to dependencies, such as betting shops, high street money lenders and shisha smoking bars (Ross with Chang, 2013).

Infrastructure provision also needs to acknowledge local culture and that can actively embody this through the retention of specific buildings as shadows of the past or specific pieces of machinery as urban sculpture. In some cases this might be through the use of the naming of new buildings and streets or cultural quarters that reflect the heritage of the locality. In some cases this cultural heritage may be used as a means of branding a place and to encourage new visitors. This may be through placemaking or the location of specific facilities such as national museums and galleries, for example Louvre-Lens Art Gallery in France, the Imperial War Museum North in Salford and the V&A Museum in Dundee.

The role of housing development

Planning has been concerned with the provision of adequate facilities for the current population and its future changes that may be in volume or specific age groups. However, since the early 1990s, local planning in England has been dominated by debates about the provision of adequate numbers of new homes. This has been generated by the then government's decision to stop public sector house building in the 1980s with the assumption that the private sector would increase their contribution to the former combined level. This has never happened and the private sector has continued to build at the same rate.

This failure to provide housing in population growth areas has generated a range of criticisms from the OECD (André, 2011), EU[1] (2014) and IMF (Inman, 2014) and also a range of policy reports and advice on how to improve house building (Griffith, 2011). Policies have included incentives and regulation to force local authorities to permit more housing development. The view of the Treasury and of its principal adviser (Barker, 2004, 2006) is that planning has been the source of restrictions on housing land supply. They argue that this has had consequential effects on the ability of developers to build housing, as land prices reflect this scarcity and that lack of housing supply has increased house prices and reduced mobility.

However, the removal of the public sector contribution to housing provision has allowed housing developers to benefit from shortages and they have used planning consents to improve their company's financial position. Despite many reviews and initiatives, this has not resulted in an increase in building rates, rather the shortage of supply has assisted in maintaining demand and price. This has had a major effect on skewing debate and the focus of local plan-making that has become dominated by housing supply.

Until 2004, housing provision was primarily related to demographic analysis undertaken at regional levels. The responsibility for the provision of evidence and supply for housing demand this was then transferred to local authorities. This has proved to be particularly difficult for local politicians as many communities do not want more housing development. When demographic projections were undertaken across a number of local authorities, it was possible to negotiate trade-offs between them. Once population numbers were agreed by the local authority, it could then blame the strategic process when challenged by local residents over housing growth. The local planning system has also been destabilised through successive government interventions. All these initiatives and changes to the planning system have not resulted in more new dwellings being built. Associated changes in the detailed use classes order has meant that more dwellings can be created from buildings formerly in other uses, such as offices.

A central concern in this debate is that public policy has been focused on new building as a means of increasing housing supply in England, although the introduction of the 'bedroom tax' in 2013 placed pressure on public sector tenants to move home if they were regarded as under-occupying stock. This has had some effect but has not released new homes to the market and has also been seen as a contributor to rises in homelessness. Further, local authorities are paying to rent accommodation for homeless families from landlords who have bought up housing stock previously in public sector ownership and now removed from the stock through Right to Buy initiatives.

One of the main approaches to providing more housing at the local level has been through the release of publicly owned land, including that of local authorities and the health service. In this approach public sector assets are released to housing developers and in some case it is proposed that this be for particular types in housing, including that for older people (Smith Institute, 2014b). This policy has resulted in an ecotown proposal for Bicester and some other smaller sites rereleases, but no major contribution to the housing stock.

The main shift in the consideration of housing at the local level has been to change its perceived role away from social to economic infrastructure to support growth and jobs in localities. The approaches that have been taken to localise housing provision through evidence-based assessments of local housing markets has not been accompanied by a willingness to accept the findings within local plan provision. Where higher numbers of houses are required then these plans have frequently been delayed. In 2011, the majority of local authorities delaying local plan preparation were Conservative administrations, the same party as the majority coalition partner in the government (Morphet, 2011b).

The provision of more housing to meet demand suggests a range of different approaches that include planning policies, among other measures, for their success. These include the development of housing in greater numbers by local authorities and housing associations. Greater focus on the reuse and densification of existing housing sites through redevelopment particularly near transport hubs would provide more transport oriented development. The use of higher densities in more suburban areas could contribute more dwellings. New ways of supporting older people to move into smaller accommodation, particularly using independent and local authority advisers that older people trust, are required. This needs to be accompanied by more suitable smaller housing developments for older people on the sites of former public sector services such as police and health locations that bring positive associations with them.

Governance and local planning

The development of local plans and programmes that result in infrastructure delivery plans are undertaken within local government frameworks that extend to the wider governance of the area, with the inclusion of community and civil society groups. The development of a local plan is a means of expressing a locality's objectives and response to managing change in a spatial, way. The plan that is prepared will be based both on evidence and on aspirations for the future. As such, it needs to be owned not only by the democratically elected politicians but also the communities that are served by it. Local plans may also be challenged to consider which areas of the local authority will receive priority for infrastructure investment projects while other locations may have to wait longer for any improvements. The allocations of projects and funding can also have a political element that may take higher precedence than evidence-based need.

Responsibility and decision making on the local plan will rest with the local authority and its elected councillors but institutions involved in the wider governance of the area will also be important in this process. These will include the public sector bodies that are operating within the area, even if they are located elsewhere. Similarly private sector organisations will have views on their requirements for expansion, the labour force and transport. Voluntary and community sector bodies may be part of the local service delivery system and have their own requirements for accommodation. Finally, the local authority will have many different requirements for the provision of its own services.

The governance of the local plan will include all these stakeholders and ways in which they can be involved in the vision, evidence, gap definition and proposals for the area. This will be in addition to formal consultation processes that exist as part of the statutory system. The role of the plan in identifying priorities including pressure on specific services or requirements for improved environmental resilience will also be important. The most crucial elements in plan-making are bringing these requirements together in a single plan and then developing an infrastructure delivery plan to meet these gaps.

Engaging organisations in these processes may be difficult and some may only join late in the day. In some local authorities, there are standing groups of infrastructure providers that consider how to coordinate individual investments and how to use any income generated through development and CIL (Community Infrastructure Levy) to support the infrastructure delivery programme (Peter Brett Associates, 2014). Even where it is not possible to bring together all the infrastructure providers, assessments will have to be made of their needs and how these might be met. These providers may also become engaged later in the process.

In some cases two or more local authorities may need to work together on some aspects of the plan and infrastructure provision. This may be for schools, transport or other services. There may be discussions between different local authorities for different infrastructure – so that one local authority may be in an estuarine or valley working partnership for environmental resilience and another for its housing market. In FEAs this cooperative working may be undertaken in a joint way and include some of the trans-boundary differences between local authorities. Local authorities have a duty to cooperate with each other on local plan-making and although this is a requirement it may be difficult to undertake in practice where there are different political administrations or dependencies such as between a city and its suburban periphery.

The governance of the local plan and the infrastructure delivery planning process is an important element in the trust and confidence that communities and investors have in the plan. If the plan has not engaged with providers and communities then questions may emerge late in process that can undermine the plan. Evidence of engagement with all parties is an important part of the process and repeat efforts at engagement may be required. Another element of a governance structure is that the local plan and its infrastructure delivery programme will be supported by those engaged who will also share and promote it with others. In this way more investment may be attracted to the area.

Local infrastructure delivery planning methods

In preparing infrastructure delivery plans as part of their local planning process, local authorities have adopted a range of methods that are discussed below. While these different methods have been applied in local plan-making, the sustainable steps method has been used by the majority of local authorities (Morphet, 2011a, 2011b, 2013b; UCL, 2014). The methods selected as the basis of infrastructure delivery planning are important as they will link to the methods of generating funding from development through the use of planning agreements or CIL payments. Further if infrastructure delivery planning is undertaken without discussions with service providers then development may be delayed or unable to proceed. Most importantly, infrastructure investment is across the whole of any local authority area and from a wide variety of bodies. The sum of this investment will be much greater than that provided in developer contributions and can have a greater role in implementing the local plan.

Predict and provide

The predict and provide method of infrastructure planning is based on the projected increase in population within an area, where there is an increase over current provision, making estimates of additional services required. This approach can take into account existing demography and capacity but has primarily been used by county councils to demonstrate need to district councils in their local plans and development negotiations. This method can generate multiple projects and infrastructure delivery plans that are high in cost and unlikely ever to be attained.

This approach has been difficult to sustain when challenged through the local plan or planning application appeal process. It is too general to relate to specific locations' infrastructure demand and does not take into account demographic changes, existing capacity and service reforms. Further, local authorities preparing local plans have been unwilling to collect and pass on the major proportion of infrastructure funds derived through the planning process without any guarantees about which projects they will be used for.

Linked with new housing

A more refined version of predict and provide has been that associated with new housing development. Here infrastructure estimates are based on the number of new dwellings and contributions from housing developers are calculated on this basis. Housing developers may contest the amounts of funding identified but may also offer to build the facilities within the development. This provides an added marketing feature for the new development and also guarantees that any funds generated by a development are spent within their area. This approach underpins the philosophy of CIL although in this case funds generated through development can be used anywhere within the local authority area.

This approach does not take into account existing capacity or the ways in which new development will interact with existing infrastructure provision. Where schools are provided they may not be in the most appropriate location and if there is an overall shortfall this funding will be provided by central government. In some cases provision for health facilities has been made but not used. This approach is also dependent on housing decisions once they have been made rather than basing the selection of housing sites on existing infrastructure capacity in a more sustainable approach. It also suggests that all housing provision is on greenfield land where there are no existing facilities. The method is less robust when housing is provided through a range of smaller urban or brownfield sites, implemented by a range of developers and with a cumulative impact on services. Lastly, tying infrastructure to new development might assist when capacity is required in locations where there has also been demographic change within existing stock. CIL can be applied although there will be pressure to align infrastructure contributions collected to the development where it has been generated.

Sustainable 'steps' method

The 'steps' method of infrastructure delivery planning was developed to assist local authorities to prepare infrastructure delivery plans to support their local planning functions (PAS, 2009; Morphet, 2011b) and by 2015, over 80% local authorities in England have adopted the method (Morphet, forthcoming). The approach is based on establishing a complete picture of their current infrastructure, its maintenance and capacity. It also includes agreed infrastructure projects by providers in their area. When new infrastructure is provided, local authorities have traditionally become involved at the latter stages in the process on a scheme-by-scheme basis. Most local authorities also assumed that there was little investment in their areas, particularly after the 2007 economic crisis. The 'steps' method is shown in Box 10.1.

Systematic gathering of capital programmes and information on committed projects revealed a different picture with committed schemes already in the pipeline. Until the local plan infrastructure delivery plan had been prepared, there had been no overall picture of this planned investment and individual investors had little or no knowledge of other schemes. Further, this had not been brought together with evidence of capacity and use. The loss of national standards also meant that there was little expectation of identifying under- or over-provision in specific areas.

The process of drawing together these schemes based on geography, themes or sectors has informed plan-making; it also provides a means by which different

Box 10.1: The 'steps' method for preparing Infrastructure Delivery Plans (IDPs)

Step 1: Vision:
- Set out a long-term vision and strategy for the area

Step 2: Governance:
- Establish a group comprising the local authority and those responsible for delivering infrastructure and asset management

Step 3: Evidence gathering:
- Identify the baseline for infrastructure in the area
- Undertake resource review
- Identify public and private capital programme commitments
- Identify public service outlets and potential for joint use
- Assess public sector assets for remodelling localities

Step 4: Standards and deficits:
- Identify service delivery standards
- Use infrastructure standards to identify existing local deficits
- Use infrastructure standards to identify future local deficits
- Use infrastructure standards to identify requirements for strategic sites

Step 5: Prepare the IDP:
- Identify infrastructure requirements in 5 year tranches
- Introduce any viability testing for capacity and process
- Undertake Sustainability Appraisal of infrastructure delivery plan schedule

Step 6: Validation:
- Consult on infrastructure delivery plan schedule
- Prepare an infrastructure delivery strategy
- Undertake risk assessment

Step 7: Delivery:
- Implement the Infrastructure delivery programme
- Undertake annual monitoring
- Review progress of delivery
- Update IDP regularly

providers have a better knowledge of other infrastructure investment and can create the potential for providers to work together. Further, it informed providers considering future programmes and could act as a means of attracting investment based on the certainty of committed projects.

The methods adopted suggest staged but iterative approaches to information collection, stakeholder engagement and identification of community priorities. Where schemes are agreed they are placed in the public domain preferably on a GIS (geographical information system) base. This approach then allows the application of standards to assess gaps and also can identify any problems with existing infrastructure by using a traffic light system. While most problems may be the condition of buildings, there can also be over-provision in specific locations. A map-based approach to create a baseline can also indicate the location of facilities within institutional settings such as universities, schools or hospitals that can make a contribution overall.

The establishment of the baseline, identification of gaps or over-provision can inform the plan-making process and provide the evidence to support investment in specific projects. It can be used to identify locations where there may be surplus capacity in the short term where demographic trends will change demand over time. This is particularly the case with school provision. This method may also identify where new development can support existing community facilities such as post offices, shops and schools. It can also take into account discussions about the reconfigurations of services, including health.

This method can provide an infrastructure delivery plan for three to ten years, depending on the project and the provider. It can also incorporate projects that are not yet fully funded but where there is commitment and project planning is underway. Inclusion in the infrastructure delivery plan may provide some benefits in business cases for funding by demonstrating commitment and interrelationships with other projects (HMT, 2014). This method has also being used to examine 'wish list' projects that are political objectives but for which there may be little demand or existing capacity.

The 'steps' approach is iterative and can be kept up to date. It can support infrastructure delivery groups and also inform strategic and neighbourhood plan-making. It can also be used by neighbouring authorities when considering their own infrastructure capacity and requirements, and help to prioritise specific projects when engaging developers in negotiation for new development. It can create a context for identifying gaps in infrastructure, particularly open space, walking and cycle routes that are linked across a wider area. Where future capacity for infrastructure such as schools is required, then land can be saved for future provision.

Local infrastructure delivery planning challenges

In undertaking local infrastructure delivery planning there are a number of challenges. Most of these relate to the way that the processes have to be undertaken through the use of soft power (Nye, 2004), that is through persuasion and advocacy rather than through direct control. Interpersonal relations, networking and negotiation skills are important, as are understanding the objectives of different organisations and finding common outcomes between them.

Agreeing a vision

Preparing a local plan includes agreeing a vision that will guide the formulation of the spatial policies for the area for the following 15–30 years. This vision is derived from a range of activities including stakeholder and community workshops as well as some contextual analysis of evidence and trends. The vision will be implemented in the local authority in different ways depending on the analysis that underpins it and the contribution that communities can make to achieve the overall objectives. This means that some areas may have considerable change while others have little.

Where the vision can only be achieved by working with neighbouring local authorities this has to be negotiated. Neighbouring local authorities may be preparing their local plan within a different time frame and have a vision that differs from and is not compatible with its neighbours. This may mean that the local authority has to modify its vision to take into account what can be achieved. Local authorities preparing local plans have a duty to cooperate but they do not have a duty to agree. Even when a local plan has been formulated and is being examined by an independent inspector, this inspector cannot make a neighbouring or co-terminus authority agree policies with the local authority whose plan is being examined.

Within many local plans in England, housing provision has been one of the most difficult to agree within local authorities and between them. Within local authorities, the debates will be around how new housing proposals can be allocated. There will be choices between densification, reuse of sites currently in other land uses or greenfield development. In the last case there will be choices about identifying land that adds to existing settlements, creates new urban or village extensions or freestanding communities. Many housing market areas stretch across local authority boundaries: this is where there can be most difficulty in agreeing a common approach (POS, 2014).

A variety of approaches can be taken to broker these differences between neighbouring local authority local plans. Preparation of a joint evidence base for the local authorities that are encompassed in the local plan vision can provide a starting point for vision and plan preparation. If common evidence can be agreed this will identify where there are differences and suggest the commissioning of new evidence or interpretation. This can be undertaken by a third-party broker agreed by all local authorities involved. Local authorities can agree to disagree but identify where they can work together nevertheless.

Another approach is to establish a local authority joint committee to make decisions for the local plans within the authorities in membership. Local authorities can go further than this and prepare a single local plan for more than one local authority. If local authorities do not wish to enter formal decision-making arrangement they can agree to align the timing of their plans so that the decisions on the vision, policies and proposals can be taken at the same time. This can be difficult to maintain if there is no formal agreement and can be broken by different electoral cycles in authorities – newly elected politicians can leave these agreements.

Local authorities can create voluntary joint working arrangements for strategic areas (DCN, 2014) or use the CA (combined authority) or LEP (Local Enterprise Partnership) organisations and strategy to provide a strategic framework for the local plans. Where there are FEA objectives it may make it easier for local authorities to agree the strategic plan or vision and then develop policies and projects to support delivery. This can remove local decision-making but incorporate democratic decision-making within the CA or joint committee at this wider scale. A CA may include strategic planning within its remit, creating joint decision-making for the local plans within its area. A CA or LEP may make infrastructure funding that it has available conditional on horizontal or vertically integrated or aligned plans for its area.

Different organisational objectives

A major challenge in preparing an infrastructure delivery plan that stretches across a range of organisations is that they may each have different objectives that result in different kinds of projects. In some cases these may not be shared with other organisations until they have been agreed and may be too late to amend. In some organisations such as charities, the potential to operate a more flexible approach to projects may be bounded by legislation, external funding sources or donors. In the private sector, the focus may be on achieving funding and return on investment. Working with other organisations in a more open way may be regarded as being risky as this may slow down decision making particularly where community groups do not support specific proposals.

The essence of local infrastructure delivery planning is to understand these differences in organisational objectives and to identify ways in which they can be enhanced through working together or at least in alignment with other organisations and projects. There may be financial appraisal benefits or positive public relations for the organisations involved in working together. For those bringing together the infrastructure delivery plan it may be helpful to know about other projects that organisations are involved in. This might provide some guidance on how the organisations' objectives are interpreted in practice, providing a means of assistance in delivery. Even where there are no synergies that can be achieved through the different objectives of organisations, it may be possible to demonstrate that multiple projects are being undertaken in the same locations through the use of GIS and other presentation methods. While individual projects may have different objectives, they can be grouped to identify a cumulative potential benefit.

Different planning cycles

When bringing together an infrastructure delivery planning process one of the central challenges will be the different planning cycles used by each organisation. These may vary from one to 30 years depending on the scale and type of investment and associated delivery requirements such as land purchase and funding. Given the processes that are used to identify each project, undertake an economic appraisal and secure funding, adding another stage that includes coordination with other projects creates difficulties. Those undertaking capital planning may already consider that their own tasks within the organisation are challenging enough and may not wish to engage in external discussions. Alternatively, some may use the external context and framing of the programme as a mechanism to reorder or prioritise specific projects within their own organisation. Where additional benefits can be achieved for a project through timing or joint working, this may change the business case assessment or viability of a project and change its priority order.

One way of approaching this may be through the use of shorter project cycles within a longer-term programme. By breaking down project delivery into small time frames within the whole it may be possible to identify potential decision points where synergies can be captured. There may also be some benefits in common appraisals for a range of projects that can assess their mutual influence on each other and the locality.

Even where there are no possibilities of changing institutional planning cycles for infrastructure delivery, knowledge of their processes and critical decision points can be logged into the operational infrastructure programme so that any benefits can be captured during these processes.

Conclusions

The role of spatial planning in infrastructure delivery is essential, particularly as many of the providers will have a wider remit and interests than local authority areas. Having a clear vision, process and methods of engaging in dialogue with and between infrastructure providers is important in understanding likely future investment and in influencing it. The role of communities in identifying infrastructure gaps and priorities is also an important part of this process. At this scale, provision may already be available and addressing infrastructure hoarding may be a central approach to sustainable infrastructure delivery.

Note
[1] See http://ec.europa.eu/europe2020/making-it-happen/country-specific-recommendations/index_en.htm

ELEVEN

Neighbourhood and community infrastructure planning

Introduction

Infrastructure planning at neighbourhood and community levels is concerned with local services and social infrastructure. Some communities are also the location of infrastructure that serves the needs of wider areas and sometimes of nations. This chapter discusses infrastructure planning and delivery at the community level and then considers associated processes and institutional arrangements. The methods of neighbourhood and community infrastructure planning are discussed, including similarities and differences with other spatial scales.

The approach to neighbourhood and community infrastructure delivery planning varies according the roles of each scale of governance in the state. In each of the UK nations these operate through different legal and institutional mechanisms, with different degrees of influence and delivery capability. The role of community-based planning in France has a longer legacy and has a different approach to relating to the wider institutional settings though on a 'contractual' basis (Le Galès, 2002). Further, the French system has adopted a different approach to working with communities where infrastructure which has regional or national significance is being delivered locally. This includes offering some financial compensation to communities and individual house owners. This approach was suggested in England but has not been adopted (DCLG, 2014a).

Neighbourhoods and communities are identified as being important in their contribution to local and national economic growth and the roles of community culture, work practices and entrepreneurship have all been identified as significant (HMT, 2003; Broughton et al, 2011). However, these contributions to national economic growth will also be dependent on the quality of the local infrastructure and the institutional processes available for its improvement and development. The relationship between infrastructure and the economy is set in a wider context but the same considerations apply at this micro scale. This is important in terms of transport access (Wilcox, 2014) broadband coverage, skills and training opportunities. It may also be a question of available accommodation, and access to research and to markets.

While neighbourhood and community contributions to the economy are important, communities that are relatively deprived require special measures to reduce unemployment and poverty and to help populations into economic activity. This focus of small-area urban and rural regeneration has been on infrastructure improvements, although it has rarely been cast within this language in policies and their evaluation. In the UK, neighbourhood regeneration has been a long-standing policy since 1945 when different policy waves have attempted to improve the life chances of deprived communities. In urban areas this also became a central policy consideration of the EU from 1972 onwards, followed by a focus on rural and coastal areas. Until the mid-2000s, local regeneration policies in the UK were based on compensating policies (Lawless, 1989; Imrie and Raco, 2003), generally through the provision of additional resources. Since this period, the focus has been on not rewarding failure and a different policy set is focused on reducing deprived areas from their peripheries rather than from their cores (HMT, 2003).

Infrastructure at the community level

Planning the type of infrastructure and when it is most likely to be required is a core competency of community-scale planning. There are also challenges in the local infrastructure process, including democratic accountability, potential fragmentation and power relations.

Neighbourhoods and communities – concepts and theories

What is a neighbourhood or community? As Jenks and Dempsey (2007) have stated, neighbourhood is a socio–spatial concept that has been growing in its use in public policy in the UK, although it remains slippery without an understood definition. While there has been much emphasis on neighbourhoods as social and community institutions, it is the relationship between these social constructs and the role of neighbourhoods as locations that can define infrastructure delivery. Talen (1998) has considered this from the perspective of access to services, including different modes, such as walking and cycling, and the way services provided are a good fit with the neighbourhood population. Some neighbourhoods are host to infrastructure serving wider communities and these are distinctive. However, neighbourhood areas are defined by the people who live or work in them, with an expectation that a range of services will be provided within easy walking or cycling access. These services will vary in their core components but may include shops, personal and health services, schools, and access to public transport to areas outside the neighbourhood. In some localities the neighbourhood may be defined by a place of worship.

The combination of services available may be distinctive and attract different groups of people. Those looking for a cafe culture if working from home may want something different from those with children or older people with more leisure. What also characterises a neighbourhood made up of a mixture of homes and businesses is that its life will extend over the whole of the day and into the evening. This may include breakfast clubs, daytime activities and evening events or cultural activities. There is also an expectation that meeting places such as restaurants and bars will be open in the evening. A neighbourhood may be distinguished from a suburb that is primarily defined as a dormitory and not have all the characteristics of a neighbourhood. Neighbourhood cultures are regarded as positive and something that people associate with through an expectation to contribute towards their community by volunteering and offering support to other neighbourhood members (Putnam, 2001). The quality and range of infrastructure are core elements in the desirability of any neighbourhood and action is generally focused towards improvement of this infrastructure through fundraising and advocacy.

Whereas most neighbourhoods are defined by their users (Jenks and Dempsey, 2007), they are also defined as units of development in new or expanded settlements including garden cities, suburbs and new towns. Neighbourhoods have also been used to define new housing development areas within urban redevelopment. More recently, neighbourhood definitions have been used as part of spatial differentiation and place marketing within urban revitalisation. Here specific characteristics or population groups are identified in locations where similar services or activities might cluster. Informal neighbourhoods may also develop as a consequence of migrations, where incoming migrants move to the same areas as people they know and then these areas can develop specialist services such as food stores to meet specific requirements of the incoming community.

The relationship between communities and neighbourhoods and the infrastructure that supports them can be significant. There may be expectations of services that are to be provided such as libraries, pubs or post offices and the UK government has requested high street banks to adopt a 'last man standing' policy for the closure of bank branches. Infrastructure needs and requirements can be assessed through a variety of means including community consultation and preference. Infrastructure providers rely on a range of criteria that may not provide much granularity in their application and determination. The difference in the application of infrastructure criteria may depend on the service provider but could also relate to population characteristics, the maturity of community development and general spatial characteristics, including its location in an urban, suburban or rural area (Barton et al, 2003; Bissonnette et al, 2012).

Institutional structures

In England, formal representation at the local level has been through a voluntary institutional process of creating parish councils. In urban areas these are termed town councils although there were no powers for parish councils to be formed in Inner London between 1935 and 2007 (Sandford, 2014). 'Parishes' are the smallest unit of government and originally intended as a form of specifically rural governance. Under the Local Government and Rating Act 1997 (Section 11), 'a community at the village, neighbourhood, town or similar level beneath a district or borough council in England can demand its own elected parish or town council'. In 2006, there were 9,500 parish councils in England, 730 community councils in Wales and 1,200 in Scotland (CRC, 2006).

Parish councils have always had a role in the delivery of services and Box 11.1 sets out the responsibilities that can be exercised. Through a series of legislative changes since 1999, parish councils now have the same powers as local authorities although, unlike local authorities, they do not have specific duties. In the 2011 Localism Act in England, parish councils were given a general power of competence that

Box 11.1: Parish councils: legal powers for services and infrastructure

Allotments

Burial grounds, cemeteries, churchyards and crematoria

Bus shelters

Bye-laws – the power to make bye-laws concerning: baths and washhouses (swimming pools), cycle parks, mortuaries and pleasure grounds

Clocks – public clocks can be provided and must be maintained

Community centres, conference centres, halls, public buildings

Drainage – of ditches and ponds

Entertainment and the arts

Footpaths

General spending – parish councils can spend a limited amount of money on anything they deem of benefit to the community that is not covered by the other specific responsibilities described in this list

Gifts – parish councils may accept gifts

Highways – lighting, parking places, right to enter into discussions about new roads and road widening, consent of parish council required for diversion or discontinuation of highway, traffic signs and other notices, tree planting and verge maintenance

Land – acquisition and sale of

Legal proceedings – power to prosecute and defend any legal proceedings in the interests of the community, power to take part in any public enquiry

Litter – provision of litter-bins and support for any anti-litter campaigns

Planning – parish councils must be notified of, and display for residents, any planning applications for the area. Any comments submitted to the planning authority by the parish council must be taken into account

Postal and telecommunication facilities – power to pay a public telecommunications operator any loss sustained in providing services in that area

Public conveniences – provision and maintenance of public toilets

Recreation – provision of recreation grounds, public walkways, pleasure grounds, open spaces, village greens, gymnasiums, playing fields, holiday camps and boating ponds

Rights of way – footpath and bridleway maintenance

Seats (public)

Signs – danger signs, place names and bus stops signs

Tourism – financial contributions to any local tourist organisations allowed

Traffic calming

War memorials

Water supply – power to utilise stream, well or spring water and to provide facilities for general use (www.localgov.co.uk/Parish-council-responsibilities/29135)

allows them to do anything not specifically prohibited by legislation. The use of these powers by any parish council is a matter of local choice.

In areas where there have been no formal parishes, other structures may be established that can be recognised and applied across local authority areas or exist in other informal ways. These alternative structures are shown in Box 11.2. These informal councils exist where communities have promoted specific projects for local infrastructure such as for leisure, children or older people. These activities have been ad hoc and based on individual groups generally constituted under charity legislation.

Box 11.2: Alternative groupings to parish councils

- Area committee
- Neighbourhood management arrangements
- Tenant management organizations
- Area/community forums
- Residents' and tenants' associations
- Community associations (DCLG/LGBCE, 2010, pp 29–41)

The opportunities that these frameworks create, for people to engage with the planning process, has been held up as evidence of a broader 'governance shift' (Jessop, 1997) towards a more 'participative' approach to strategising and decision-taking. In 2006, 30% of the English populations were included within a parish council (CRC, 2006). The Local Government White Paper 2006 (DCLG, 2006) called for the creation of more parish councils and an extension of responsibilities that occurred in the 2011 Localism Act.

> Parish councils are an established and valued form of neighbourhood democracy and management. They are not only important in rural areas but increasingly have a role to play in urban areas. We propose to build on the existing parish structure, so as to improve its capacity to deliver better services and represent the community's interests […] we will make it clear that there will be a presumption in favour of the setting up of parish councils so that local authorities will be expected to grant communities' requests to set up new parish councils, except where there are good reasons not to, and that existing parish councils are not to be abolished against the wishes of local people (DCLG, 2006: 42-3)

In Scotland, Wales and Northern Ireland there are community councils that undertake similar functions to parish councils. In Scotland and Wales, legislation has required that the whole territory has defined communities although not all have councils and they have fewer powers than parish councils in England. In 2011, the Scottish government set up a working group to review the ways in which community councils could be strengthened (Scottish Government, 2012). This group recommended that community councils should have more responsibilities although there was no unanimity as to whether this should include funding. In Northern Ireland, as part of the reform of local government that was implemented in 2015, there is a duty on local authorities to establish community planning.

Parish councils and planning

Where parish councils have been established in England, the local authority has a statutory obligation to consult them on all planning applications in their area and to include the views of the parish council in the determination of the application. Where there is no parish council there are no obligations for consultation although local authorities may consult local amenity societies or community groups for their views. This has created an unequal system where only some parts of the country can have their own form of community governance and a legal role in the planning applications system.

Until 2011, parish councils had no statutory planning powers for making plans. Before this, parish councils were encouraged by central government to 'connect' with statutory planning by becoming part of a wider process of local evidence-gathering and action–planning (Gallent et al, 2008). This informal role grew in importance as community-led plans and village design statements contributed to the formulation of strategy and policy at higher tiers (Bishop, 2007; Owen et al, 2007).

In the Localism Act 2011, provisions for neighbourhood planning fora and plans were included. The passage of the legislation generated a wave of discussion about the decisions that should be taken by parish councils. One of the objectives of central government was to encourage communities to take a more active engagement with the potential for new development. Local resistance to new housing has become a central political question in England and a main focus of the government–centred planning system. It was argued that if communities could plan their own approaches to new development together with the infrastructure that would accompany it, and receive a share of the development funds provided to mitigate the effects of any development, there would be greater interest and support from the community.

Inevitably, these messages were confused and many local communities assumed that undertaking a neighbourhood plan would be a means to prevent new development. However, the legislation and regulations provide for neighbourhood plans only where there is an acceptance of the planning policies of the local authority in which the forum area lies and a commitment to accepting new development. In return, neighbourhood plan areas were promised a proportion of CIL (Community Infrastructure Levy) to spend on infrastructure in their own areas. In 2013, this was set at 25% of the total levy. In order to consider the use of these funds, government suggests that neighbourhood fora will need their own version of an infrastructure delivery plan (DCLG, 2013), echoing that of the local authority, and they will need to manage some practical delivery mechanism for its implementation.

Local authorities are concerned that this approach will reduce the funds available to pursue the projects identified in the infrastructure delivery plan and lead to fragmentation in the delivery of facilities. Parish councils have the powers and some organisational experience in operating local infrastructure. Neighbourhood fora that have been established within the terms of the 2011 Localism Act will not have the same powers and experience in the management and maintenance of infrastructure. While CIL may provide the capital to build a facility, it will not fund its running and general maintenance costs. Further if the community decides that it wishes to have a new health facility, there may be no guarantee that any health provider will use it once built.

Neighbourhood and community demand for infrastructure

Within communities, there is an assumption that the main concerns will be for the provision of infrastructure to meet local needs. This will include social provision for education, health and leisure. Community infrastructure requirements may include sport and fitness, arts, and cultural activities such as libraries, cinema and spaces where arts events and local associations and societies can meet on a regular basis. However, communities also have wider concerns for provision of transport and access to larger centres and more services, and these can be redistributive in their location and provision. When more strategic public services are placed in town and city centres, they are supported by public transport networks. However, the removal of services to the periphery as part of asset capitalisation, such as hospitals, creates more access problems and can strongly disadvantage some communities.

Communities use infrastructure on a regular basis although some services, such as firefighting, may be for prevention or resilience. In Cornwall, a new service has a single person undertaking fire, ambulance and police roles in the community. Communities change primarily through growth in their population, but this is not always the case. In Eastern Germany, for example, many cities are reducing in size and housing is left empty. These may be shrinking cities but the impact on the loss of services – whether a shop or other social support services – will be a major consideration for the population. Those who can be economically mobile may decide to move elsewhere, leaving a greater proportion of dependent population even more reliant on dwindling services.

In other neighbourhoods there may not be any new building but the life cycle of the occupants of the existing building stock may be changing. In some areas, housing may have been purchased by young families in the 1950s or earlier but now these families have gone leaving only one or two people in a large dwelling. When these residents die or move to other accommodation, these family houses are occupied by families. This can create unexpected pressure on existing services, including schools and other social facilities.

Where social and cultural patterns change, with an increase in female activity rates, there is less time for other domestic activities. The rise in convenience stores near stations together with other services such as dry cleaning and health, parcel drop off and pick up after work has changed shopping habits and responsibilities within the household. Parcel collection is also available from stores through Click and Collect services, while in some cases, 50% of the parcels received by organisation post rooms are for the employees of the organisation rather than that organisation's own purposes.

New development

Infrastructure provision as part of new development may be an important consideration. While neighbourhoods may support new housing and other growth in their areas, there may concerns about the capacity of existing facilities such as schools and primary health services. Further, developers promoting new development to politicians and communities frequently include social infrastructure in order to make their development more attractive. In some parts of England there is evidence that this type of infrastructure is being offered as communities do not wish to have affordable housing located in their neighbourhoods.

The provision of other infrastructure to support new development may include physical infrastructure such as roads, sewerage, water, energy and flood prevention measures. The extent to which these are required will depend on existing capacity of this infrastructure and the scale of the new development. It will also depend on whether the infrastructure is on a brownfield site already serviced or a greenfield site that will require new infrastructure provision.

As indicated above, if there is a neighbourhood forum preparing a plan, then it will be eligible for a share of the CIL. However, even where formal arrangements do not exist, there will be some expenditure on the development in order to mitigate its impact. In addition, the local authority will receive its own CIL if it has a system set up, but there is no requirement for it to spend this funding in the immediate location of any new development or contribute to the neighbourhood.

National infrastructure provision

Some neighbourhoods and communities are the locations for major infrastructure. In some areas, existing infrastructure is well established, such as airports, railways or waste, water treatment, national parks or prisons. Communities grow up around these infrastructure locations with those employed in this particular infrastructure living locally and forming a major part of the community (Clifford and Tewdwr-Jones, 2013). In some cases these facilities are proposed for expansion and the response of the community may depend on the nature and scale of the expansion. In some locations, where more intrusive infrastructure is located such as break–bulk depots or energy locations, any negative response to these facilities may already be taken into account within the housing market in comparison with other areas. Additional facilities may increase pressure for demand on local facilities, including the housing market, although they may also incentivise people to relocate.

Some communities have to cope with infrastructure that changes its role. A local airport may commence more passenger services and generate more air and land travel movements. An airport may also change to ground-based development and the number of flight movements can be scaled back or stopped.

In some cases, major infrastructure can be introduced into new areas. This may be through the proposed development of a new town, high speed railway or energy provider. In these cases, the development of new infrastructure investment proposals will be undertaken within standard EU assessment processes (Therivel and Ross, 2007). This new infrastructure might be welcomed as it provides jobs or other social and cultural facilities, and improved transport. However, the extent of change and the time it takes to implement the development may be considerable and be preceded by a long period of uncertainty. In some cases the emergence of proposed infrastructure investment may appear suddenly such as proposals for fracking or in response to energy markets or subsidies provided to agriculture, for example energy farming.

Democratic accountability

One of the major concerns about planning for infrastructure in communities is democratic legitimacy. Where there are parish councils, these are directly elected although there may also be a lack of contestation between candidates at local elections. In Scotland, community planning has been included within local government legislation and community plans prepared by local partnerships of communities have a specific role although they may not draw up infrastructure plans.

In England, the 2011 Localism Act created neighbourhood planning powers. Here neighbourhood fora that are self-defining and composed of at least 21 stakeholders can be established, once they have the approval of the local authority. These neighbourhood fora can prepare plans for their areas within the context of the local plan for the area and on the basis that they accept growth. The proposed plan has to be examined by an independent person following it can only be accepted if a referendum on its content is positive. Parish councils have these powers and do not need to go through the local authority registration stage but have to use the rest of the stipulated institutional processes. As Davoudi and Cowie (2013) have suggested these new neighbourhood fora are not democratically accountable, as they are self-appointed. In some neighbourhoods, rival fora are vying to be recognised and the local authority has to choose between them.

Since the introduction of this legislation in England in 2011, over 1,000 communities have started to prepare neighbourhood plans (DCLG, 2014a). This plan-making is supported by the central government through grants to local authorities and specific grants to planning-aid organisations who have assisted over

700 of these (DCLG, 2014a), of which 34 have passed their referenda (DCLG, 2014a). Research commissioned by the government on the ways neighbourhood planning is working shows that in some areas the neighbourhood planning process has been stimulated by the local authority rather than the community (Parker and Mansfield, 2014, p 17) while the main reason for engaging in neighbourhood planning was given as participants wanting a greater say in the planning of their area (DCLG, 2014a, p 18), although it does not investigate the relative representation of the neighbourhood forum instigators and how representatives were selected for each forum.

In England, each neighbourhood forum plan is required to engage in community consultation and demonstrate to the independent examiner how this has been undertaken. Requirements for a referendum before adoption of the plan is another safeguard to wider community interests but the relationship between the forum and wider democratic institutions, outside parish council-led plan areas, is nebulous and might be conflictual (Parker and Mansfield, 2014, p 51). This may bring difficulties in the implementation of the neighbourhood plans, an area where there is little experience as yet.

While the neighbourhood plan might be in compliance with local plans, its proposals may not be a priority. Similarly, the neighbourhood plan might identify infrastructure requirements but there may not be funds to provide the buildings or works or to run or maintain the resulting facilities. Neighbourhood plans might be prepared in order to gain attention in a local authority area where priorities are directed elsewhere. While this might be recognised it may not have any effect in changing priorities. It may also cause resentment or political contestation, particularly where the elected representative is from a different political party from that of the overall majority of the local authority area.

If the local authority has a CIL scheme, fora will be provided with a share of the funding for any development in their area. Other projects, including those of the local authority and other tiers of government, for example central and the emerging subregional arrangements, also have to be managed and implemented in ways that bring community benefit.

Fragmentation

One major consideration when planning infrastructure at the community scale is that of fragmentation. If all small communities and neighbourhoods are seeking their own swimming pools or leisure centres, will there be a loss in the economies of scale? Also, there may be concerns where some communities progress neighbourhood plans and others do not. Will those with neighbourhood plans be privileged in comparison with others? Are communities with existing social and economic advantages more likely to progress neighbourhood plans, leaving behind those with less income?

A major consideration is the way that concerns are defined within smaller areas. This may lead to a lack of a strategic approach (Holman and Rydin, 2013), and more fragmentation and competition between areas for resources or the location of strategic infrastructure. While all neighbourhood plans have to be prepared within the framework of local plans, this may be regarded as bidding or advocacy for resources in a specific neighbourhood area. The effort and resources taken to support neighbourhood plans within a local authority area may also undermine and reduce the resources available to undertake local authority-wide plans or contribute to more strategic planning discussions at the subregional scale. They may use resources in disproportion to their total value.

Creating social capital – bonding, bounding, binding or bridging?

Neighbourhood planning is identified as means to devolve decision making to the local level by government. It is also a means of creating social capital (Putnam, 2001) where the development of a forum and plan provides a means to bind people together in ways that reduce conflict. This is particularly an objective of neighbourhood planning in England where there has been opposition to new development. Can incorporating the whole community together start to overcome these conflicting voices?

Some neighbourhood fora have been set up in response to perceived external development threats where the coming together of disparate interests in an area can be bridged by a common response to this external threat (Holman and Rydin, 2013). Where there is a neighbourhood plan that is agreed through referenda, then those dissident voices will find that they are less able to continue their opposition. The plan will serve to bind the whole community into the agreed proposals together with priorities for infrastructure investment.

Neighbourhood planning may also be used develop coalescence through exclusion. In setting up a neighbourhood forum it is possible to define boundaries that enclose socially homogenous areas and exclude those that may be regarded as socially less desirable. It may also be drawn to exclude specific tenure groups if social housing is located in specific areas. Where this bounding is exclusionary then this could be evidence of the 'dark side' of social capital emerging (Holman and Rydin, 2013) where existing social values can become entrenched and a bunker mentality may emerge.

Capturing social value

The use of neighbourhood planning is now being harnessed with traditional community regeneration methods to capture their social value. Pietrzyk-Kaszyńska and Grodzińska-Jurczak (2015) argue that neighbourhood planning should be extended and incorporated within partnership agreements as part of multilevel governance. The Neighbourhood Partnership approach could have the benefit that it creates an institutional structure for delivery of the proposals in the plan and a vehicle that could be used more widely. In the EU's Cohesion policy (CEC, 2013b) these institutional structures are named as Community Led

Local Development (CLLD) and can be for communities of over 10,000 people. This might be larger than neighbourhood planning areas in most cases but they include a common methodology and approach that can be applied (Miller, 2014). Neighbourhood planning areas could join together to make a larger area if that is useful. The methodology set out by the European Commission for CLLD is set out in Box 11.3.

Box 11.3: Community Led Local Development

What is meant by Community Led Local Development (CLLD)?
A single methodology regarding CLLD for the ESIF Funds that:

- focuses on specific sub-regional areas;
- is community-led, by local action groups composed of representatives of local public and private socio-economic interests;
- is carried out through integrated and multi-sectoral area-based local development strategies, designed taking into consideration local needs and potential; and
- takes into consideration local needs and potential, includes innovative features in the local context, networking and, where appropriate, co-operation.

This single methodology will allow for connected and integrated use of the Funds to deliver local development strategies (CEC, 2014g).

Neighbourhood infrastructure planning processes

Neighbourhood plans identify local infrastructure requirements including new and improved facilities, and include social and community facilities, flood presentation and transport improvements. Neighbourhood plans can also be a means for organisations focused on neighbourhood regeneration to progress their priorities. This demands greater coordination and integration between neighbourhood plan proposals, programmes and projects (Broughton et al, 2011) and results are enhanced where the partners operate at the same neighbourhood scale (Cole et al, 2011).

Neighbourhood planning practices

Defining the area

Identifying the area for a neighbourhood plan will be defined by a parish boundary where this exists. Otherwise it will need to be defined in ways shown in Box 11.4.

Scoping the issues and priorities

The issues and priorities within the neighbourhood area need to be identified through scoping methods and consultation with the community in the area. This

Box 11.4: Issues to consider when setting a boundary for a neighbourhood plan area

Where to begin Perceived boundaries might depend on the logic of the character of the area, street patterns, landscape, catchment areas of services, natural features (rivers, canals, and/or green areas) and prevalent social networks.

Negotiation and agreement Negotiating and agreeing the perceived boundaries with the local authority and local interests, is required to build consensus early on. If conducted openly, it has the potential to strengthen relationships between all those involved.

Justification The group will need to justify and explain clearly how and why the boundaries have been defined. This might be supported by a local neighbourhood identity survey or a web-based questionnaire.

Data/evidence base Perceived boundaries rarely match ward boundaries. Finding appropriate statistics will require desk research, local surveys and statistical techniques to extrapolate data. The practicality of data collection should be considered.

Engagement and consultation Finding out how different people understand, identify with and use their neighbourhood can not only promote the initiative, but avoid charges that the neighbourhood has been carved up wrongly by failing to take account of the views of social groups who may not be represented on the forum (LGA, 2013).

is particularly important throughout the process not least as any proposals can only be adopted following a local referendum. Failing to identify these priorities and address them may lead to failure.

Identifying infrastructure needs

Central government guidance on preparing neighbourhood plans in England includes the provision of infrastructure, as shown in Box 11.5. However, like the government's guidance on infrastructure delivery planning at the subnational level this focuses solely on infrastructure to support new development. There is no assessment of the capacity of existing infrastructure in considering sites for development, shortfalls or reconfigurations of infrastructure in areas where no development is proposed. This focus on new development is unsustainable and may make residents resent it. Development that can support the maintenance of local shops, schools and services through focusing on their spare capacity and ensuring their future for the community might be better received.

Box 11.5: Government guidance on preparing a neighbourhood plan

Should a neighbourhood plan consider infrastructure?

A qualifying body may wish to consider what infrastructure needs to be provided in their neighbourhood area alongside development such as homes, shops or offices. Infrastructure is needed to support development and ensure that a neighbourhood can grow in a sustainable way.

The following may be important considerations for a qualifying body to consider when addressing infrastructure in a neighbourhood plan:

- what additional infrastructure may be needed to enable development proposed in a neighbourhood plan to be delivered in a sustainable way
- how any additional infrastructure requirements might be delivered
- what impact the infrastructure requirements may have on the viability of a proposal in a draft neighbourhood plan and therefore its delivery
- what are the likely impacts of proposed site allocation options or policies on physical infrastructure and on the capacity of existing services, could help shape decisions on the best site choices

Qualifying bodies should engage infrastructure providers (e.g. utility companies, transport infrastructure providers and local health commissioners) in this process, advised by the local planning authority.

Paragraph: 046 Reference ID: 41-046-20140306
What should a qualifying body do if it identifies a need for new or enhanced infrastructure?

A qualifying body should set out in their draft neighbourhood plan the prioritised infrastructure required to address the demands of the development identified in the plan.

Source: DCLG, 2014b

Infrastructure delivery

While neighbourhoods may be good at developing projects: 'communities can play an especially strong role in defining needs and validating the "additionality" of new proposals emerging from mainstream delivery agencies; they tend to be less interested in, and may lack the skills for, delivering projects' (Batty et al, 2010, p 9).

The delivery of the plan is a core component of its work. Some neighbourhood plans have addressed this through the preparation of a delivery plan. One example of this is Thame (2012) in South Oxfordshire, shown in Box 11.6. A similar approach has been taken in the Winsford Neighbourhood Plan delivery strategy

(April, 2013), although it focuses on the use of funds generated by the local authority through CIL rather than taking a wider approach. Some neighbourhood plan delivery groups are protectionist in their style and are more focused on commenting on planning applications and new development than identifying how the plan and its associated infrastructure is to be delivered (for example, the Ascot, Sunninghill and Sunningdale Neighbourhood Plan Delivery Group).

Box 11.6: Thame Neighbourhood Plan Delivery Strategy

Key components:

1. Objective: that infrastructure requirements are clearly identified
2. Types of infrastructure: physical, social and green
3. Projects identified and linked to specific policies
4. Identified projects linked to specific institutions holding responsibility for delivery
5. Delivery mechanisms:
6. Specific policy requirements set out
   - e.g. dwelling tenure mix
   - Process of design briefs
   - Reference to overriding documents on green living and sport
7. Flexibility about role:
   - In negotiation with land owners
   - On other site requirements
   - Acting as arbiter between interests
   - Supporting partner bids for funding
   - Consider revising all or part of plan
8. Risk assessment criteria: crucial necessary, preferred
9. Monitoring framework

Source: Adapted from Thame Neighbourhood Plan Delivery Strategy: www.southoxon.gov. uk/sites/default/files/Delivery%20Strategy_0.pdf

---

The ownership, management and maintenance of community buildings has been a long-term community and neighbourhood role in many places although the experience of undertaking this may vary. In some places this will be community or social centres whereas in others it may through sports clubs and youth organisations. Community groups set up to run these services have different levels of expertise and experience and the way that this interrelates within neighbourhood planning and delivery may be significant. These groups may be fully engaged in neighbourhood fora where they exist and may also be major project promoters or beneficiaries through neighbourhood planning processes or through CIL contributions associated with development in their area, whether there is a neighbourhood plan or not. Many retail developments, for example, have included the provision of community facilities as part of their planning consent and frequently house builders will contribute a school or other community facilities particularly where these can be provided as the housing development is built out.

In England, the government has also developed a strong policy line on the passing over of assets to the community following the Quirk Review (Quirk, 2007) that focused on the transfer of assets from the public sector into the control or joint control (with public sector agencies) of community organisations. '[N] ew, neighbourhood-level, physical developments can provide guaranteed rental income after regeneration funding ceases; but the management costs of such projects can be underestimated, it may be difficult to maintain full occupancy rates and rental income will not be sufficient to maintain the same scale of activity' (Batty et al, 2010, p 9).

Some of this experience may be useful where a neighbourhood plan has been developed and delivered but there is no other experience of developing community facilities. Holman and Rydin (2013) argue that although delivery is central at neighbourhood plan-making level, the system introduced in 2011 did not bring any additional delivery features with it. This particularly relates to the survival and development of neighbourhood fora after a plan has been agreed through a referendum. Skills and commitment in the community are required to deliver the plan. These might exist through voluntary associations or groups or may be transferable between them through knowledge and skills pooling. However, some neighbourhood fora may have less experience or an unwillingness to take responsibility for delivery.

The ability to pursue the delivery of the plan proposals or projects may depend on networking with those who have these skills. Where projects are proposed but there is no commitment by the local authority or infrastructure provider then the ability to advocate and network may be central to success (Holman and Rydin, 2013). Once plans have been adopted, local communities may think that their work is done and lose confidence or interest in the process if further work is required to promote the plan's delivery. This may particularly be the case where a plan has been prepared without any significant new development proposals in a small number of locations and growth is more distributed.

Where neighbourhood fora take an active role in infrastructure delivery, then skills are required in the client role, specifying what is required and how it is managed. There may also be opportunities to develop infrastructure projects in partnership with others, where the contribution of the neighbourhood's funding could be delivered by others. Eventually neighbourhood fora may need to manage and maintain facilities and in these cases, transition to a parish council may be a more effective route.

Conclusions

Increased focus on devolution and subsidiarity will encourage more focus on spatial planning at the neighbourhood scale. While neighbourhood and community plans have important roles in identifying priorities and in some local expenditure within a democratically accountable framework, as organisations many are not sufficiently robust to engage in implementation of their projects. This may change in the future and groups of neighbourhood plans may emerge with a critical mass to be determinants of spatial planning over larger areas.

TWELVE

Effective infrastructure delivery planning

Introduction

Infrastructure is an essential element of making places. It is delivered through spatial, territorial and strategic planning. It supports all aspects of life through existing and new infrastructure. Infrastructure delivery planning is concerned ensuring that this investment is focused on achieving sustainability, equity and economic objectives. As shown in Box 12.1, spatial planning is about place–shaping and placemaking. The use of infrastructure is central to achieving these ends.

> ### Box 12.1: Defining spatial planning
>
> **Spatial planning is the practice of place-shaping... that aims to:**
>
> - enable a vision for the future of places that is based on evidence, local distinctiveness and community derived objectives;
> - translate this vision into a set of policies, priorities, programmes and land allocations together with the public sector resources to deliver them;
> - create a framework for private sector investment and regeneration that promotes economic, environmental and social wellbeing for the area; and
> - coordinate the delivery of the vision with other agencies and processes.
>
> Source: adapted from Morphet, 2007

In this book, infrastructure delivery planning has been considered by types of infrastructure – physical, environmental/green and social/community and by scale of governance. There has also been a consideration of the methods used in these process of accessing existing infrastructure needs and those of the future. It has also been concerned with the funding that can be applied to infrastructure delivery. In this last chapter, the key principles of effective infrastructure delivery planning are discussed.

Introduction to the principles of effective infrastructure delivery planning

When engaging in infrastructure delivery planning, specific negotiations of development applications or pressures from providers can narrow the consideration of infrastructure requirements. Developers may offer infrastructure that appears attractive, creating new facilities, whereas providers will argue the case for investment based on their own criteria and priorities. These factors are important in spatial planning but they also need to be set into a wider context to ensure that infrastructure decision–making is not within silos or taken in isolation from the rest of the infrastructure investment for the scale of territory under consideration. Modes of transport, for example, may be delivered separately but unless they work together their investment will be underutilised.

Overcoming these pressures can be difficult, particularly when having to make a wider case against specific providers and strong arguments for specific investment. The principles set out here are about widening the context for these specific infrastructure investment discussions as well considerations in their longer–term planning. These principles provide a means of examining the proposals for investment and are not meant to be rigid or fixed but rather to assist in locating any investment within a wider context.

Principles of effective infrastructure delivery planning

Cumulative

The provision of infrastructure is not in isolation. It is always located within an existing development and investment context. The provision of any infrastructure will contribute to or replace existing provision whether this is for specific facilities, networks or services. Planning for infrastructure delivery in isolation, for example as in predict and provide methods for new development will always be unsustainable. Even where these schemes may be large or free–standing they will operate within energy and telecommunications systems, access to strategic centres and transport systems and framed within standards of delivery that are recognisable and applied to the contextual location. Sites for new development need to be assessed against the provision of existing infrastructure, the costs of connecting to the networks and any capacity concerns that this might create.

In areas of urban redevelopment or renewal, new infrastructure may be required to upgrade or replace what exists. If this is provided for specific developments, it will also be important for the wider area. Also, the cumulative benefits of infrastructure investment need to be considered in its design. This will also be important for open space corridors and the siting of larger than local facilities that will be used by a wider population. When infrastructure is historic or has a cultural role, access and promotion of cultural tourism may be a major factor in its preservation and presentation within its locality. No infrastructure investment is isolated, individual or free–standing. All infrastructure connects or contributes to spaces and to other infrastructure that exists now or will exist in the future. Effective infrastructure delivery planning is based on the cumulative principle.

Pipeline and flow

The process of effective infrastructure delivery planning includes a continuing assessment of the pipeline and flow of infrastructure projects for the area. While spatial planning commences with a baseline that will include an assessment of the current provision of infrastructure to support the area, this baseline may be changed when projects that are in development come into the public domain.

It is important to recognise that projects exist even if they are not yet announced. In examining the published capital programmes of infrastructure providers, it will be possible to make an assessment of the likely value of their annual investment programme and the kinds of projects that the organisation will be prioritising. In engaging in discussion with the organisation on the published projects, informal briefings on future projects, not yet approved, may be available that can be fed into some of the pipeline and revised baseline considerations.

The combined influence of a range of infrastructure projects from different providers may also offer synergies for localities and organisations. Holding regular briefing discussions about the plan area or those parts undergoing most change will be a good mechanism to verify knowledge of infrastructure projects. Project and programme managers are frequently aware of other projects going on in the same area and although not all infrastructure providers may attend these sessions, the information shared will be passed around through informal networks.

Effective spatial planning includes these dynamic investment practices and without this part of the process there may be mistaken assumptions about development capacity or investment focus. Similarly where new projects are anticipated by the spatial plan, discussion with infrastructure providers will enable these considerations to be included within the plan assessment and for infrastructure providers to include projects within their own pipelines.

Plan-led

Effective infrastructure delivery planning will always be plan-led although these plans may be sectoral or organisational rather than spatial and integrated. Understanding the planning process of organisations will be an important part of the spatial plan-making process.

When developing a new spatial plan, effective infrastructure delivery will depend on the baseline and principles applied to existing infrastructure use. Infrastructure delivery may be influenced by policies as well as through specific projects. Where there is an oversupply of specific types of infrastructure policy changes may allow more flexibility to widen its role. Where there is an oversupply of specific infrastructure then this may need specific discussions on management that are reinforced by plan policies to overcome infrastructure hoarding.

In areas where planning proposals for new development are submitted there will be pressures for infrastructure to be provided that accompanies the development but may not fit the wider plan priorities. These may be pressure to accept additional built facilities but not guarantees that that they will be used by service providers such as health. These facilities can be used to enhance the apparent value of the development to the community but in the longer term not provide any real value and may be a drain on resources. With a plan-led approach, then negotiations with developers can be focused on specific requirements for infrastructure already identified. If there is uncertainty about new requirements, then developers can gift the land to the public authority to be used in the future if required. Within a Community Infrastructure Levy regime, funding raised as part of the development's contributions can be used on other infrastructure priorities elsewhere.

One of the greatest impediments to effective infrastructure delivery planning is the gap between the spatial plan and those negotiating specific development applications in development management. For those responsible for infrastructure delivery planning, this has to be a close working relationship so that there is a good knowledge of what is required in any particular area, the standards that are being applied for access and any specific management conditions that might be placed on facilities that are provided. Effective practice makes this a continuing dialogue and benefit to those negotiating on specific developments.

Evidence based

Effective infrastructure delivery planning is evidence based. This evidence will be derived from different sources and needs to be considered together. It will include demographic analysis of the population, its current and its expected future needs. It will also include other population evidence of work locations, models of travel and household formation rates. This evidence will provide analysis of the likely requirements for housing, transport and jobs.

Evidence is also needed on environmental conditions including propensity to flood and mechanisms for developing resilience to sudden changes. These questions will need to be considered within a system–wide approach and include not only weather events but the potential influence of changing management and maintenance regimes that could have an effect on the way that infrastructure will perform in changing conditions.

Some of this evidence will be used to model changing conditions and examine alternative scenarios so that ranges of resilience and supply of infrastructure can be considered. Models will need to be carefully calibrated and considered within contemporaneous reality as far as possible rather than on past trends. There may be other evidence that will be included in this analysis including the monitoring of development trends in any area. There may also be effects of changes within the planning regulation regime that cannot be controlled by planning policy but that will have some influence on decisions for other land uses.

Contextual evidence for neighbouring areas of the FEA (functional economic area) may need to be considered, or connections within and between nations and states. These decisions may place pressure on existing infrastructure in the future where networks cannot connect with equivalent capacity such as grids or broadband networks. The effect of EU and government regulation may also influence infrastructure and this may need to be modelled using the evidence that is available.

Finally it is important to include qualitative as well quantitative evidence. There may be community or user perceptions about the quality of infrastructure interoperability, capacity and suitability for needs. This may include sports and leisure provision, community facilities such as parks, and experience of broadband speeds and 'not spots'. Qualitative evidence can be useful if collected over a period of time and using consistent methodologies. It may be most useful at the local and neighbourhood levels, but views about the quality of infrastructure in FEAs may also influence investment in specific locations if transport services exist but are not reliable in the experience of users. This may also apply to congestion and quality of other services.

Evidence has to be collected, collated, analysed and interpreted to provide some potential tests and options to be considered in infrastructure delivery planning. This evidence may assist in making the case for more investment and initiating discussions about improvements in access, equity and resilience.

Standards of provision

While infrastructure providers may have their own standards against which they measure the quality, capacity and condition of their facilities, these standards may differ from those that will be applied in spatial plans and strategies. Providers from the public sector and regulators of utilities will have a public interest in infrastructure provision although this may need to be moderated through evidence from communities in the adoption and application of any standards used.

Infrastructure provided by the charity and third sectors may have a specific and specialist focus based on the terms under which their organisations are established. They may have a primary interest in a type of sport, a particular age group or those with specific needs. In these cases there may be a need to integrate these specific interests within the spatial plan or to introduce the charity into an area when there are specific gaps in provision that it may be able to assist in providing or advising on.

The private sector will be concerned with providing infrastructure when it can maximise its profit for shareholders. In these cases they may be reliant on business models that have worked in other locations. If there is an assumption that different conditions apply then there will be a requirement to demonstrate these potential differences through the submission and examination of evidence. Another approach to encouraging private sector infrastructure investment may be through attempting to encourage a number of providers to invest at the same time or in the same location so that risks are mitigated through agglomerations and other supporting policies.

Community led

As infrastructure is provided for the community it is important that it has a role in identifying the quality, provision and location of infrastructure that it provided.

In the private sector, if infrastructure is provided in locations that do not meet with community requirements then it will not be used and the facilities, including retail, sport, leisure and other services may fail commercially.

Public sector services may be provided using decisions made on behalf of communities by democratically elected politicians or professionals working for them. In these cases the standards may not have been subjected to community validation. It may also be that some communities are more effective at voicing their needs and preferences than others.

All public providers will have limited budgets and it may be necessary to engage communities in determining priorities in the use of funding that is available. This may be through community-based budgeting systems or other forms of participative decision-making.

The communities' views on infrastructure provision can be obtained through evidence gathering via surveys focus groups and meetings. However, these approaches will need to ensure that they reflect the population as a whole and not only those that might be more interested in attending. Here telephone and school gate surveys can add to those views supplied through meetings and other events. Community preferences may vary and those democratically elected may have to decide between them. In these cases, explanation of the options chosen and the reasons for them need to be communicated clearly and widely.

Resilient

One of the principles that all infrastructure delivery planning has to consider is resilience. What resilience does the current provision of infrastructure provide and how will any new infrastructure contribute to strengthening it or meeting gaps? Assessments of resilience at all scales need to be undertaken in real time and on a continuous basis. Specific stimulus to examine new aspects of resilience may come from experiences of disasters, failures or events elsewhere. While most resilience assessment of infrastructure will be based on the past, it will also be necessary to consider scenarios of what might happen in the future.

The way in which resilience is included within infrastructure delivery planning may be through the application of standards. There may be other types of cumulative impacts and stress that may need to be applied within any system. This may occur when new facilities are added into these systems or different services are provided. There also needs to be test of what will occur when things go wrong, including diversion of people, water and transport and access for disaster management. Operation of phone services and hospital equipment is important at times of power failures or surges.

In some cases there will be political choices about the levels of resilience to apply for different types of infrastructure. Where there is coastal erosion, decisions may be taken not to continue to reinforce existing coastal defences but to move people away and abandon the coast to the sea. This will be problematic and will lead to loss of property and a reduction in property values. However, if the forces creating the erosion are sufficiently powerful this may be the only course of action. Other situations where there are conflicts between resilience and other forms of action may be in historic environments or buildings where improving resilience may damage what is being preserved.

The application of resilience principles will offer a new set of standards to apply as part of the examination of infrastructure by emergency services and others concerned with emergency planning but it is also a central feature of infrastructure planning. It may form part of an environmental impact assessment or sustainability appraisal as well as tests for specific types of building.

Flexible

One of the major principles of infrastructure delivery planning is a measure of flexibility. If there are specific gaps in provision then there may be numerous ways in which they can be met. Additional facilities can be provided through repurposing existing buildings or land, by sharing facilities or through joint commissioning with others.

There may also be possibilities to meet gaps when new development is proposed. Although gaps in infrastructure may have been identified and included in the spatial plan, those submitting proposals for development may not have reinforced any synergies between their proposals and other requirements and early discussion may be useful. Those engaged in infrastructure delivery planning may be able to introduce different providers to discuss the potential for joint facilities or commission when neither has considered it.

Proactive

One of the central principles of infrastructure delivery planning is proactivity on the part of those responsible for developing and delivering the plan. Creating a plan and then expecting others to implement it will not result in infrastructure delivery. Instead, development will be uncoordinated and there may be few opportunities for added value to be achieved in providing the infrastructure.

The proactive approach needs to be adopted at all scales – in the identification of the infrastructure baseline, of the gaps and the potential, and for providing infrastructure to meet them. This will include attempting to engage providers, meeting them, remaining in contact with them as their programmes develop and finding opportunities to bring them together so that the issues of providing infrastructure for the specific location can be more clearly understood by those whose primary focus is in their own service or sectoral provision.

This approach also needs to be promoted with public bodies where planning for infrastructure may also have been within specific service silos, and there is competition for budgets. Where possible incentivising the allocation of budgets through the multiservice use of infrastructure may assist in encouraging a more joined-up approach to infrastructure delivery. As well as being proactive with the infrastructure providers, it is also important to be proactive with communities about their needs and communicating the ways in which decisions about infrastructure will be taken.

The proactive approach also has to be taken by the planning department with those who are responsible for negotiating development permissions and master plans. Continuing engagement with progress in assessing gaps and any success in provision can encourage a more joined-up approach for delivery and the adopted and implementation of common objectives.

Integrated

An infrastructure delivery plan is both an integrator and integrated within the place. The identification of the roles of all infrastructure within a place and how it is used together is a significant feature of placemaking and quality of life. Also, places link to others and infrastructure has an important role in delivering this in a seamless way. People cross administrative boundaries and choose to access services in locations that are easiest for them.

There are other important considerations in the application of integration within infrastructure delivery. They include the need to recognise the range of providers and their differential objectives. In encouraging providers to work together on these organisational objectives, those engaged in infrastructure delivery planning may be able to demonstrate how their interests can be enhanced through joint working.

Another challenge of integration is where infrastructure delivery planning and providers range across different scales of government. Providers may not be concerned about specific borders and administrative areas and focus only on their own delivery objectives. Engaging with infrastructure providers at different scales can be challenging and may need collaborative working or may need intermediaries to make introductions or to point out these concerns at different delivery planning scales.

Funded

While many infrastructure projects may be needed to improve existing infrastructure or provide new, the only projects that will be implemented are those that are funded. The principles of infrastructure delivery planning include an understanding of the funding models that support infrastructure investment, the models that are used for facilities and maintenance, and the ways in which organisations and institutions that formulate their investment programmes. Without this, together with some knowledge of the criteria used to prioritise specific projects, infrastructure delivery planning may be more theoretical than practical. Institutional funding programmes will comprise both existing and potential projects and those engaged in delivery will always attempt to have a range of projects 'oven' or 'shovel' ready in case there is some underspend towards the end of the year or a project is prevented from being implemented within its programme slot.

Many infrastructure projects also comprise a number of elements and stages. These may be broken up into different projects for the purposes of funding and while there may be commitment to fund some stages, others may have to be engaged in competitive bidding for delivery. Where no funding is likely in the immediate future but the infrastructure project is supported then some funding may be available to undertake a feasibility assessment, develop a project plan and obtain any necessary planning consents. These preparatory projects may then be permitted to enter the capital programme for preliminary work or for detailed designs to be prepared.

The development of projects can be funded from the capital programme and once funding has been agreed the costs of scheme development will be attributed to the project. If the schemes fails and does not go ahead then these costs will be attributed to an abortive fees entry in the capital programme.

Once a scheme has been developed, funding may have to be collected to support it and this may need to be undertaken in a proactive way. This may be from a development tariff, such as that for Crossrail across all London developments, or loans based on land value capture through tax increment financing. Schemes may also be funded through loans and bonds raised on the markets or through contributions or donations from charitable bodies or individuals. Some larger infrastructure may be part-funded by the European Investment Bank and smaller schemes funded through Cohesion fund loans.

Functional

Finally all infrastructure provided has to be functional and fit for purpose. If this is not the case it cannot fulfil its primary purpose nor contribute to the added value provided through an integrated approach to infrastructure provision. Functional infrastructure can be well designed, fit in to the site or location and contribute positively to it. It should be easy to access and to understand by its users. If infrastructure is provided that is overdesigned or not fit for purpose then it may never fulfil its intended role and justify its initial investment. Well-designed and functional infrastructure is a component of well-being and placemaking.

Conclusions

Effective infrastructure delivery planning is a perpetual process although its constituent projects have discrete deliverables and end points. It requires technical, financial, networking and negotiation skills and will benefit from experience of similar projects or processes. It is an essential service for all communities and without it they will not function efficiently nor receive value for money for the investment made. Without effective infrastructure delivery planning, the quality of life will be reduced and places may require more support in the longer run. Effective infrastructure planning can ensure that the experience of places is positive, that people feel safe and that the places are designed for their needs.

References

6, P, 2010, When forethought and outturn part, in H. Margetts, P. 6 and C. Hood (eds) *Paradoxes of modernization: unintended consequences of public policy reform*, Oxford: Oxford University Press, 44-62

Aberdeen City Council, 2015, *Sustainable urban mobility plan*, www.aberdeencity. gov.uk/SUMP/

Abraham, A, Sommerhalder, K and Abel, T, 2010, Landscape and well-being: a scoping study on the health-promoting impact of outdoor environments, *International Journal of Public Health*, 55, 1, 59-69

Abrate, G, Piacenza, M and Vannoni, D, 2009, The impact of integrated tariff systems on public transport demand: Evidence from Italy, *Regional Science and Urban Economics*, 39, 2, 120-7

Adams, D and Watkins, C, 2014, *The value of planning*, London: RTPI

Adams, D, Hardman, M and Larkham, P, 2014, Exploring guerrilla gardening: Gauging public views on the grassroots activity, *Local Environment* (ahead-of-print), 1-16

Adlung, R, 2009, Services liberalization from a WTO/GATS perspective: in search of volunteers, *WTO Staff working paper*, No. ERSD-2009-05, Leibniz: ZBW, www.econstor.eu/bitstream/10419/26732/1/592490718.PDF

Adshead, M, 2014, EU cohesion policy and multi-level governance outcomes in Ireland: How sustainable is Europeanization? *European Urban and Regional Studies*, 21, 4, 416-31

Agénor, PR and Moreno-Dodson, B, 2006, Public infrastructure and growth: New channels and policy implications, *World Bank Policy Research Working Paper 4064*, Washington, DC: World Bank

Agnello, L and Schuknecht, L, 2011, Booms and busts in housing markets: Determinants and implications, *Journal of Housing Economics*, 20, 3, 171-90

Ahrend, R and Schumann, A, 2014, Approaches to metropolitan area governance: A country overview, *OECD Regional Development Working Papers*, 2014/03, Paris: OECD Publishing

Ahrend, R, Farchy, E, Kaplanis, J and Lembcke, AC, 2014, What makes cities more productive? Evidence on the role of urban governance from five OECD countries, *OECD Regional Development Working Papers*, 2014/05, Paris: OECD Publishing

Akerman, J, Banister, D, Dreborg, K, Nijkamp, P, Schleicher-Tappeser, R, Stead, D and Steen, P, 2000, *European transport policy and sustainable mobility*, Abingdon: Routledge

Albalate, D, Bel, G, Bel-Pinana, P and Geddes, RR, 2015, Risk mitigation in Motorway PPPs: A comparative analysis of alternative approaches, *Journal of Comparative Policy Analysis: Research and Practice*, DOI: 10.1080/138769988.2015.1010788

Alber, G and Kern, K, 2008, Governing climate change in cities: Modes of urban climate governance in multi-level systems, in *Competitive cities and climate change OECD Conference Proceedings* Milan, Italy, 9–10 October 2008, 171–96

Albrechts, L, Healey, P and Kunzmann, KR, 2003, Strategic spatial planning and regional governance in Europe, *Journal of the American Planning Association*, 69, 2, 113–29

Alesina, A, Angeloni, I and Schuknecht, L, 2005, What does the European Union DO? *Public Choice*, 123, 3/4, 275–319

Almunia, J, 2011, Reforming EU state aid rules on public services: The way forward, speech to EC Policy Dialogue, Brussels, 2 May

Alpkokin, P, 2012, Historical and critical review of spatial and transport planning in the Netherlands, *Land Use Policy*, 29, 3, 536–47

Álvarez, IC, Prieto, ÁM and Zofío, JL, 2014, Cost efficiency, urban patterns and population density when providing public infrastructure: A stochastic frontier approach', *European Planning Studies*, 22, 6, 1235–58

Anable, J, 2005, 'Complacent car addicts' or 'aspiring environmentalists'? Identifying travel behaviour segments using attitude theory, *Transport Policy*, 12, 1, 65–78

Andersson, M, 2007, Region branding: The case of the Baltic Sea region, *Place Branding and Public Diplomacy*, 3, 2, 120–30

André, C, 2011, Improving the functioning of the housing market in the United Kingdom, *OECD Economics Department Working Papers*, N° 867, Paris: OECD

Ang, G and Marchal, V, 2013, Mobilising private investment in sustainable transport: The case of land-based passenger transport infrastructure, OECD Environment Working Papers, No 56, Paris: OECD

Antikainen, J, 2005, The concept of functional urban areas, *Informationen zur Raumentwicklung*, 4, 447–52

Armstrong, A, 2015, Tesco abandons three times as many supermarkets as its rivals, *Daily Telegraph*, 25 July 2015, available at www.telegraph.co.uk/finance/newsbysector/retailandconsumer/11762283/Tesco-abandons-three-times-as-many-supermarkets-as-its-rivals.html

Arts, J, Hanekamp, T and Dijkstra, A, 2014, Integrating land-use and transport infrastructure planning: Towards adaptive and sustainable transport infrastructure, *Transport research arena 2014*, Paris: OECD

Athreye, S, 2000, *Agglomeration and growth: A study of the Cambridge hi-tech cluster*, Milton Keynes: Open University

Audit Commission, 2009, *Room for improvement: Strategic asset management in local government*, London: Audit Commission

Audit Commission, 2010, *Countdown to IFRS implementation in local government*, London: Audit Commission

Baker, M and Wong, C, 2013, The delusion of strategic spatial planning: what's left after the Labour government's English regional experiment? *Planning Practice & Research*, 28, 1, 83–103

Banister, D, 2008, The sustainable mobility paradigm, *Transport Policy*, 5, 2, 73–80

Barber, BR, 2014, *If mayors ruled the world: Dysfunctional nations, rising cities*, London: Yale University Press

Barbosa, O, Tratalos, JA, Armsworth, PR, Davies, RG, Fuller, RA, Johnson, P and Gaston, KJ, 2007, Who benefits from access to green space? A case study from Sheffield, UK, *Landscape and Urban Planning*, 83, 2, 187-95

Barca, F. (2009) *An Agenda for a reformed cohesion policy A place-based approach to meeting European Union challenges and expectations* , Brussels: CEC.

Bardens, J and Rhodes, C, 2013, *Infrastructure policy*, SN/EP/6594 London: House of Commons Library

Barker, K, 2004, *Review of housing supply*, London: HMT

Barker, K, 2006, *Review of land-use planning*, London: HMT

Barker, K, 2014, *Housing where's the plan?* London: London Publishing Partnership

Barlow Report, 1940, *Report of the Royal Commission on the Distribution of the Industrial Population*, London: HMSO

Barton, H, Grant, M and Guise, R, 2003, *Shaping neighbourhoods: a guide for health, sustainability and vitality*. Abingdon: Taylor & Francis

Bateman, IJ, Harwood, AR, Mace, GM, Watson, RT, Abson, DJ, Andrews, Binner, A, Crowe, A, Day, BH, Dugdale, S, Fezzi, C, Foden, J, Hadley, D, Haines-Young, R, Hulme, M, Kontoleon, A, Lovett, AA, Munday, P, Pascual, U, Paterson, J, Perino, G, Sen, A, Siriwardena, G, van Soest, D and Termansen, M, 2013, Bringing ecosystem services into economic decision-making: land use in the United Kingdom, *Science*, 341, 6141, 45-50

Batty, E, Beatty, C, Foden, M, Lawless, P, Pearson, S and Wilson, I, 2010, *The New Deal for Communities Experience: A Final assessment* (The New Deal for Communities Evaluation: Final report–Volume 7). London: DCLG

Benedict, MA and McMahon, ET, 2012, *Green infrastructure: linking landscapes and communities*, London: Island Press

Berkes, F and Folke, C, 2000, Linking social and ecological systems for resilience and sustainability, in F Berkes, C Folke and J Colding (eds) *Linking social and ecological systems: Management practices and social mechanisms for building resilience*, Cambridge: Cambridge University Press, 1-25

Berkes, F, Folke, C and Colding, J, 2000, *Linking social and ecological systems: Management practices and social mechanisms for building resilience.*, Cambridge: Cambridge University Press.

Biermann, F and Pattberg, P, 2008, Global Environmental Governance: Taking stock, moving forward, *Annual Review of Environment and Resources*, 33, 277-94

Bigotte, JF and Antunes, AP, 2007, Social infrastructure planning: A location model and solution methods, *Computer-Aided Civil and Infrastructure Engineering*, 22, 8, 570-83

Bishop, J, 2007, Plans without planners?, *Town and Country Planning*, 76, 340-44

Bishop, M, 2014, New state spaces and contested territories: A critical analysis of joint regional planning panels, *Urban Policy and Research*, 32, 2, 185-201

Bissonnette, L, Wilson, K, Bell, S and Shah, TI, 2012, Neighbourhoods and potential access to health care: The role of spatial and aspatial factors, *Health and Place*, 18, 4, 841–53

Blackden, R, 2014, The Canadian pensioners who own Britain, *The Telegraph*, 11 August, www.telegraph.co.uk/finance/globalbusiness/9469070/The-Canadian-pensioners-who-own-Britain.html

Blythe, PT, 2004, Improving public transport ticketing through smart cards, *Proceedings of the ICE-Municipal Engineer*, 157, 1, 47–54

Boateng, N, Castaing Gachassin, M, Gay, E and Recuero-Virto, L, 2014, Public financial management in infrastructure in Africa, *OECD Development Centre Working Papers*, No 323, Paris: OECD

Boin, A and McConnell, A, 2007, Preparing for critical infrastructure breakdowns: the limits of crisis management and the need for resilience, *Journal of Contingencies and Crisis Management*, 15, 1, 50–59

Börjesson, M, Jonsson, D and Lundberg, M, 2012, The long term social benefits of transit, in Transportation Research Board (ed.) *Transportation Research Board 91st Annual Meeting* (No 12-2286), Washington, DC: Transportation Research Board

Boterman, WR and Karsten, L, 2014, On the spatial dimension of the gender division of paid work in two-parent families: The case of Amsterdam, the Netherlands, *Tijdschrift voor economische en sociale geografie*, 105, 1, 107–16

Boussabaine, A and Kirkham, R, 2008, *Whole life-cycle costing: Risk and risk responses*, Oxford: John Wiley and Sons

Boyd, J and Banzhaf, S, 2007, What are ecosystem services? The need for standardized environmental accounting units, *Ecological Economics*, 63, 2, 616–26

Boyes, SJ and Elliott, M, 2015, The excessive complexity of national marine governance systems: Has this decreased in England since the introduction of the Marine and Coastal Access Act 2009? *Marine Policy*, 51, 1, 57–65

Braconier, H, Nicoletti, G and Westmore, B, 2014, Policy challenges for the next 50 years, *OECD Economic Policy Papers*, 9, Paris: OECD

Breheny, MJ, 1978, The measurement of spatial opportunity in strategic planning, *Regional Studies*, 12, 4, 463–79

Brenner, N, 2004, Urban governance and the production of new state spaces in Western Europe, 1960–2000. *Review of international political economy*, *11*(3), pp.447–488

Brezzi, M and Veneri, P, 2014, Assessing polycentric urban systems in the OECD: Country, regional and metropolitan perspectives, *OECD Regional Development Working Papers*, 2014/01, Paris: OECD Publishing

Brezzi, M, Dijkstra, L and Ruiz, V, 2011, *OECD extended regional typology*, Paris: OECD

Broughton, K, Berkeley, N and Jarvis, D, 2011, Where next for neighbourhood regeneration in England? *Local Economy*, 26, 2, 82–94

Brown, A and Lloyd-Jones, T, 2002, Spatial planning, access and infrastructure, in C Rakodi with T Lloyd-Jones (eds) *Urban livelihoods: A people-centred approach to reducing poverty*, Abingdon: Earthscan, 188–204

Brown, J and Barber, A, 2012, Social infrastructure and sustainable urban communities, *Proceedings of the ICE-Engineering Sustainability*, 165, 1, 99–110

Brueckner, JK, 2000, Urban sprawl: diagnosis and remedies, *International Regional Science Review*, 23, 2, 160–71

Bruton, MJ and Nicholson, DJ, 2013, *Local planning in practice*, Abingdon: Routledge

Buchan, D, 2010, Energy policy; sharp challenges and rising ambitions, in H Wallace, MA Pollack and AR Young (eds) *Policy making in the European Union* (6th edn), Oxford: Oxford University Press, 357–79

Bunker, R, 2014, How is the compact city fairing in Australia? *Planning Practice and Research*, 29, 5, 449–60

Burns, P, Hope, D and Roorda, J, 1999, Managing infrastructure for the next generation, *Automation in Construction*, 8, 6, 689–703

Burstow, P, 2014, *Key to care*, London: LGIU

Butcher, L, 2013, Railways: EU policy, *Standard Note*, House of Commons Library SN 184 published 14 February

Cabinet Office, 2013, *What works network*, London: Cabinet Office

Cairney, P, 2015, Debate: What is complex government and what can we do about it? *Public Money and Management*, 35, 1, 3–6

Callois, JM and Aubert, F, 2007, Towards indicators of social capital for regional development issues: The case of French rural areas, *Regional Studies*, 41, 6, 809–21

Cameron, RW, Blanuša, T, Taylor, JE, Salisbury, A, Halstead, AJ, Henricot, B and Thompson, K, 2012, The domestic garden: Its contribution to urban green infrastructure, *Urban Forestry & Urban Greening*, 11, 2, 129–37

Canadell, JG and Raupach, MR, 2008, Managing forests for climate change mitigation, *Science*, 320, 5882, 1456–7

Caragliu, A, Del Bo, C and Nijkamp, P, 2011, Smart cities in Europe, *Journal of Urban Technology*, 18, 2, 65–82

Carbonell, A and Yaro, RD, 2005, American spatial development and the new megalopolis, *Land Lines*, 17, 2, 1–4

Carina, E and Keskitalo, ECH, 2010, Adapting to climate change in Sweden: National policy development and adaptation measures in Västra Götaland, in ECH Keskitalo (ed.) *Developing adaptation policy and practice in Europe: Multi-level governance of climate change*, Berlin: Springer, 189–232

Carmona, M, 2010, Contemporary public space: Critique and classification, part one – critique, *Journal of Urban Design*, 15, 1, 123–48

Carsjens, GJ and Ligtenberg, A, 2007, A GIS-based support tool for sustainable spatial planning in metropolitan areas, *Landscape and Urban Planning*, 80, 1, 72–83

Carter, JG, 2011, Climate change adaptation in European cities, *Current Opinion in Environmental Sustainability*, 3, 3, 193–8

CBI-URS, 2014, *Taking the long view: a new approach to infrastructure: CBI-URS infrastructure Survey 2014*, www.cbi.org.uk/media/3590298/cbi_urs_infrastructure_survey.pdf

CEC (Commission of the European Communities), 1957, *Treaty of Rome, Treaty establishing the European Economic Community*, Brussels: CEC

CEC, 1991a, Directive 91.440/EC 29 July Railways, Brussels: CEC

CEC, 1991b, *Europe 2000*, Brussels: CEC

CEC, 1994, *Europe 2000+*, Brussels: CEC

CEC, 1996a, *Directive of landfill tax*, Brussels: CEC

CEC, 1996b, *Revitalizing the Community's railways*, COM 96(41) final 30 July, Brussels: CEC

CEC, 1996c, *Council Directive 96/48/EC of 23 July 1996 on the interoperability of the trans-European high-speed rail system*, Brussels: CEC

CEC, 1999, *ESDP*, Brussels: CEC

CEC, 2000, *E-commerce Directive 2000/31/EC*, Brussels: CEC

CEC, 2001a, *Large combustion plant directive*, 2001/80/EC, Brussels: CEC

CEC, 2001b, *European governance a white paper*, Brussels: CEC

CEC, 2003, *Directive 2003/41/EC of the European Parliament and of the Council of 3 June 2003 on the activities and supervision of institutions for occupational retirement provision*, Brussels: CEC

CEC, 2004, *Directive 2004/35/CE of the European Parliament and of the Council of 21 April 2004 on environmental liability with regard to the prevention and remedying of environmental damage*, Brussels: CEC

CEC, 2006, *Decision No 1364/2006/laying down guidelines for trans-European energy networks*, Brussels: CEC

CEC, 2007a, *European Agenda for Culture*, Brussels: CEC

CEC, 2007b, *Green paper: Towards a new culture for urban mobility*, COM 2007 551 final 25 September, Brussels: CEC

CEC, 2007c, *Lisbon treaty*, Brussels: CEC

CEC, 2008, *Directive 2008/98/EC on waste (Waste Framework Directive)*, Brussels: CEC

CEC, 2009, *Action plan on urban mobility*, COM (2009) 490 final 30 September, Brussels: CEC

CEC, 2010, *White Paper: European transport policy for 2010: Time to decide*, COM(2001) 370 Brussels: CEC

CEC, 2011a, *White Paper: Roadmap to a Single Transport Area: Towards a competitive and resource efficient transport system*, COM 2011 144 final, Brussels: CEC

CEC, 2011b, *Energy roadmap 2050*, COM/2011/0885 final, Brussels: CEC

CEC, 2011c, *Our life insurance, our natural capital: An EU biodiversity strategy to 2020*, COM/2011/0244 final, Brussels: CEC

CEC, 2011d, *Connecting Europe: The new EU core transport network*, MEMO/11/706, Brussels: CEC

CEC, 2011e, *The EU biodiversity strategy to 2020*, Brussels: CEC

CEC, 2012a, *Commission Regulation (EU) No 360/2012 of 25 April 2012 on the application of Articles 107 and 108 of the Treaty on the Functioning of the European Union to de minimis aid granted to undertakings providing services of general economic interest*, CEC: Brussels

CEC, 2012b, *Road transport: A change of gear*, Brussels: CEC

CEC, 2012c, *Growth and stability pact*, Brussels: CEC

CEC, 2013a, *TEN-T Regulation*, Brussels: CEC

CEC, 2013b, *Cohesion Regulation*, Brussels: CEC

CEC, 2013c, *Fourth railway package*, Brussels: CEC

CEC, 2013d, *Ports: An engine for growth – where we're headed one year on*, Brussels: CEC

CEC, 2013e, *List of sea ports in the core and comprehensive networks*, http://ec.europa.eu/transport/modes/maritime/ports/doc/2014_list_of_329_ports_june.pdf

CEC, 2013f, Maps of ports and inland ports designated as art of the TEN-T core networks http://ec.europa.eu/transport/themes/infrastructure/doc/com%282011%29_650_final_2_annex_i_part02.pdf, Brussels: CEC

CEC, 2013g, *Annex a concept for sustainable urban mobility: Together towards competitive and resource-efficient urban mobility*, Brussels, 17 December COM(2013) 913 final, Brussels: CEC

CEC, 2013h, *Together towards competitive and resource-efficient urban mobility*, Brussels, 17 December COM(2013) 913 final, http://ec.europa.eu/transport/themes/urban/doc/ump/com(2013)913_en.pdf

CEC, 2013i, *Green Infrastructure (GI): Enhancing Europe's natural capital*, SWD (2013) 155 final 6 May, Brussels: CEC

CEC, 2013j, *Commission Staff Working Document Technical information on Green Infrastructure (GI)*, Brussels: CEC

CEC, 2013k, *Interpretation Manual of European Union Habitats*, Brussels: CEC

CEC, 2014a, *A policy framework for climate and energy in the period from 2020 to 2030*, COM/2014/015 final, Brussels: CEC

CEC, 2014b, *European energy security strategy*, COM/2014/0330 final, Brussels: CEC

CEC, 2014c, *Directive 2014/89/: Establishing a framework for maritime spatial planning*, Brussels: CEC

CEC, 2014d, *An investment plan for Europe*, Brussels, 26.11.2014 COM(2014) 903 final, Brussels: CEC

CEC, 2014e, *Communication on the exploration and production of hydrocarbons (such as shale gas) using high volume hydraulic fracturing in the EU* COM/2014/023 final/2, Brussels: CEC

CEC, 2014f, *Europe mid term review public consultation on the Europe 2020 strategy*, Brussels: CEC

CEC, 2014g, *Guidance on community-led local development for local actors*, Brussels: CEC

CEC, 2015a, *A framework strategy for a resilient energy union with a forward-looking climate change policy*, COM/2015/080 final, Brussels: CEC

CEC, 2015b, Commission launches work on Energy Union European Commission Press Release Brussels, 4 February, Brussels: CEC, http://europa.eu/rapid/press-release_IP-15-4103_en.htm

CEC, 2015c, *An aviation strategy for Europe*, Brussels: CEC

Centre for Cities, 2014, *Industrial revolutions: Unlocking potential in the UK's thriving cluster sectors*, London: Centre for Cities

CEC, 2015d, *REFIT – making EU law lighter, simpler and less costly*, http://ec.europa.eu/smart-regulation/refit/index_en.htm

CEC, 2015e, *COM(2015) 595 final Directive amending Directive 2008/98/EC on waste*, London: Centre for Cities

Centre for Cities, 2015, *Cities Outlook 2015*, London: Centre for Cities

Charbit, C, 2011, Governance of public policies in decentralised contexts, *Regional development Working Papers,* Paris: OECD

Choo, K, 2011, Plowing over: Can urban farming save Detroit and other declining cities-will the law allow it? *American Bar Association Journal*, www.abajournal.com/magazine/article/plowing_over_can_urban_farming_save_detroit_and_other_declining_cities_will

Clarke, E, Nohrová, N and Thomas, E, 2014, *Delivering change: Building homes where we need them*, London: Centre for Cities

Clarke, T and Beaney, P, 1993, Between autonomy and dependence: Corporate strategy, plant status, and local agglomeration in the Scottish electronics industry, *Environment and Planning A*, 25, 2, 213-32

Clayton, N, 2011, *Access all areas*, London: Centre for Cities

Clifford, B and Morphet, J, 2015, A policy on the move? Spatial planning and state actors in the post-devolutionary UK and Ireland, *The Geographical Journal*, 181, 1, 16–25

Clifford, B and Tewdwr-Jones, M, 2013, *The collaborating planner?* Bristol: Policy Press

Cockfield, A, 1994, *The European Union*, London: John Wiley

Coelho, M and Ratnoo, V with Dellepiane, S, 2014, *The political economy infrastructure in the UK*, London: Institute for Government

Colasanti, KJ, Hamm, MW and Litjens, CM, 2012, The city as an 'agricultural powerhouse'? Perspectives on expanding urban agriculture from Detroit, Michigan, *Urban Geography*, 33, 3, 348-69

Cole, I, Batty, E and Green, S, 2011, *Low-income neighbourhoods in Britain: the gap between policy ideas and residents' realities*, York: Joseph Rowntree Foundation

Collinge, C and Gibney, J, 2010, Connecting place, policy and leadership, *Policy studies, 31*(4), 379-391

Colomb, C and Santinha, G, 2012, European competition policy and the European Territorial Cohesion Agenda: An impossible reconciliation? State aid rules and public service liberalization through the European spatial lens, *European Planning Studies*, 22, 3, 459-80

Conteh, C, 2013, *Policy governance in multi-level systems: Economic development and policy implementation in Canada*, Montreal: McGill-Queen's University Press

Cooke, P and De Propris, L, 2011, A policy agenda for EU smart growth: The role of creative and cultural industries, *Policy Studies*, 32, 4, 365-75

Cooke, PN and Lazzeretti, L (eds) 2008, *Creative cities, cultural clusters and local economic development*, Cheltenham: Edward Elgar Publishing

Cooper, CB, Dickinson, J, Phillips, T and Bonney, R, 2007, Citizen science as a tool for conservation in residential ecosystems, *Ecology and Society*, 12, 2, 11

Cooper, Z, Gibbons, S, Jones, S and McGuire, A, 2011, Does hospital competition save lives? Evidence from the English NHS patient choice reforms, *The Economic Journal*, 121, 554, F228-F260

CoR (Committee of the Regions) 2014, *On the mid-term review of Europe 2020: A territorial vision for growth and jobs*, Brussels: CoR

Corfee-Morlot, J, Marchal, V, Kauffmann, C, Kennedy, C, Stewart, F, Kaminker, C and Ang, G, 2012, Towards a green investment policy framework: The case of low-carbon, climate-resilient infrastructure, *OECD Environment Working Papers*, No 48, Paris: OECD

Costa, JD, 2012, *Factors of air-rail passenger intermodality*, Lisbon: Technical University

Coventry City Council, 1971, *Coventry-Solihull-Warwickshire – a strategy for the sub-region: The report on the sub-regional planning study*, Coventry: Coventry City Council

Cox, E, 2014, *Home economics the role of housing in rebalancing the economy*, Newcastle-upon-Tyne: IPPR North

Cox, E and Raikes, L, 2014, *The state of the North: Setting a baseline for the devolution decade*, Newcastle-upon-Tyne: IPPR North

Crampton, G, 2002, International comparison of urban light rail systems: The role of integrated ticketing, pedestrianisation and population density, *European Regional Science Association (ERSA) Conference 2000*, paper 167 Dortmund: ERSA, www-sre.wu.ac.at/ersa/ersaconfs/ersa02/cd-rom/papers/167.pdf

Crane, A, Viswanathan, L and Whitelaw, G, 2013, Sustainability through intervention: A case study of guerrilla gardening in Kingston, Ontario, *Local Environment*, 18, 1, 71-90

CRC (Commission of Rural Communities) 2006, *Community empowerment awards*, London: Commission of Rural Communities/DEFRA

Cremer-Schulte, D, 2014, With or without you? Strategic spatial planning and territorial re-scaling in Grenoble urban region, *Planning Practice and Research*, 29, 3, 287-301

Cruz, AM and Okada, N, 2008, Consideration of natural hazards in the design and risk management of industrial facilities, *Natural Hazards*, 44, 2, 213-27

Cullingworth, B, Nadin, V, Hart, T, Davoudi, S, Pendlebury, J, Vigar, G, Webb, D and Townsend, T, 2014, *Town and country planning in the UK*, Abingdon: Routledge

Currie, G, Ahern, A and Delbosc, A, 2011, Exploring the drivers of light rail ridership: An empirical route level analysis of selected Australian, North American and European systems, *Transportation*, 38, 3, 545-60

Dabrowski, M, 2014, EU cohesion policy, horizontal partnership and the patterns of sub-national governance: Insights from Central and Eastern Europe, *European Urban and Regional Studies*, 21, 4, 355-363

Davies, S, 2012, Powering the games [energy efficiency], *Engineering and Technology*, 7, 7, 40–3

Davies, H, 2015, *Airports Commission: Final Report*, London: Airports Commission

Davoudi, S, 2000, Planning for waste management: Changing discourses and institutional relationships, *Progress in Planning*, 53, 165–216

Davoudi, S and Strange, I, eds, 2008, *Conceptions of space and place in strategic spatial planning*, London: Routledge

Davoudi, S and Cowie, P, 2013, Are English neighbourhood forums democratically legitimate? *Planning Theory and Practice*, 14, 4, 562–66

Davoudi, S, Brooks, E and Mehmood, A, 2013, Evolutionary resilience and strategies for climate adaptation, *Planning Practice and Research*, 28, 3, 307–22

Dayson, C, Lawless, P and Wilson, I, 2013, *The Economic Impact of Housing Organisations on the North*, Sheffield: CRESR Sheffield Hallam University

DCLG (Department of Communities and Local Government), 2006, *Strong and prosperous communities The Local government White Paper*, London: DCLG

DCLG, 2008, *Planning and optimal geographical levels for economic decision making – the sub-regional role*, London: DCLG

DCLG, 2010, *Functional economic market areas: An economic note*, London: DCLG

DCLG, 2011a, *Accelerating the release of public sector land update, overview and next steps*, London: DCLG

DCLG, 2011b, *Community infrastructure: Levy, an overview*, London: DCLG

DCLG, 2012, *National planning policy framework*, London: DCLG

DCLG, 2013, *Notes on neighbourhood planning* (3rd edn), London: DCLG

DCLG, 2014a, Flood risk and coastal change, site specific flood risk assessment, *Planning Practice Guidance*, http://planningguidance.planningportal.gov.uk/blog/guidance/flood-risk-and-coastal-change/site-specific-flood-risk-assessment/

DCLG, 2014b, Community infrastructure levy, *Planning Practice Guidance*, http://planningguidance.communities.gov.uk/blog/guidance/community-infrastructure-levy/spending-the-levy/

DCLG/LGBCE (Department of Communities and Local Government/Local Government Boundary Commission for England) 2010, *Guidance on community governance reviews*, London: DCLG

DCMS (Department of Culture, Media and Sport) 2014, *Gambling protections and controls*, London: DCMS

DCN (District Councils' Network) 2012, *Local enterprise partnerships: The role and contribution of district councils in unlocking growth*, London: DCN

DCN, 2014, *Streamlining and supporting the local plan process: A discussion paper*, London: DCN

De Groot, RS, Alkemade, R, Braat, L, Hein, L and Willemen, L, 2010, Challenges in integrating the concept of ecosystem services and values in landscape planning, management and decision making, *Ecological Complexity*, 3, 260–72

De Roo, G and Porter, G (eds) 2009, *Fuzzy planning the role of actors in a fuzzy governance environment*, Farnham: Ashgate

Deas, IA, 2013, Towards post–political consensus in urban policy? Localism and the emerging agenda for regeneration under the Cameron Government, *Planning Practice & Research*, 28, 1, 65–82

Defra (Department for Environment, Food and Rural Affairs) 2003, *Rural services standard*, London: Defra

Defra, 2011a, *Evidence requests on reducing the impact of heavy goods vehicles and buses on air quality: summary of responses*, London: Defra

Defra, 2011b, *Biodiversity 2020: A strategy for England's wildlife and ecosystem services*, London: Defra

Defra/DCLG (2014) *Delivering sustainable drainage systems*, London: Defra

Della Croce, R and Yermo, J, 2013, *Institutional investors and infrastructure financing*, Paris: OECD

Dennis, C, Marsland, D and Cockett, T, 2002, Central place practice: Shopping centre attractiveness measures, hinterland boundaries and the UK retail hierarchy, *Journal of Retailing and Consumer Services*, 9, 4, 185–99

Dewe, MM, 2012, *Planning public library buildings: Concepts and issues for the librarian*, Farnham: Ashgate

DfT (Department for Transport), 2014, *National policy statement for national networks*, London: HMSO

DHS (Department of Homeland Security), 2010, *National infrastructure protection plan*, Washington, DC: Department of Homeland Security

Dijkstra, L and Poelman, H, 2012, *Cities in Europe: The new OECD definition*, RF 01/2012, Brussels: CEC

DIUS (Department for Innovation, Universities and Skills) 2008, *A new 'university challenge': Unlocking Britain's talent*, London: DIUS

Dixon, T, Otsuka, N and Abe, H, 2011, Critical success factors in urban brownfield regeneration: An analysis of hardcore sites in Manchester and Osaka during the economic recession, *Environment and Planning A*, 43, 961–80

Dobbin, F, 2001, Why the economy reflects the polity: Early rail policy in Britain, France, and the United States, *The Sociology of Economic Life* (2nd edn), Boulder, CO: Westview, 401–24

Dobbs, R, Smit, S, Remes, J, Manyika, J, Roxburgh, C and Restrepo, A, 2011, *Urban world: Mapping the economic power of cities*, np: McKinsey Global Institute

Dolowitz, D and Marsh, D, 1996, Who learns what from whom: A review of the policy transfer literature, *Political Studies*, 44, 2, 343–57

Dolowitz, DP and Marsh, D, 2000, Learning from abroad: The role of policy transfer in contemporary policy-making, *Governance*, 13, 1, 5–23

Dolphin, T and Griffith, M, 2011, *Forever blowing bubbles: Housing's role in the UK economy*, London: IPPR

DRD (Department for Regional Development), 2001, *Shaping our Future, Regional Development Strategy for Northern Ireland*, Belfast: DRD

Du, H and Mulley, C, 2007, The short-term land value impacts of urban rail transit: Quantitative evidence from Sunderland, UK, *Land Use Policy*, 24, 1, 223–33

Duffy, JE, Cardinale, BJ, France, KE, McIntyre, PB, Thébault, E and Loreau, M, 2007, The functional role of biodiversity in ecosystems: Incorporating trophic complexity, *Ecology Letters*, 10, 6, 522–38

Dühr, S, Colomb, C and Nadin, V, 2010, *European spatial planning and territorial cooperation*, Abingdon: Routledge

Dwyer, C, 2013, Religion and place: Landscape, politics and piety, *AREA*, 45, 3, 386–87

Dwyer, C, 2014, On the edge: The contested cultures of English suburbia, *Urban Geography*, 35, 4, 631–2

Eddington, R, 2006, *The Eddington transport study*, London: HMT

EEDA (East of England Development Agency) 2011, *Lessons learnt in promoting economic development in the East of England: A toolkit for economic development practitioners*, Bury St Edmunds: EEDA

Ellis, JB, 2013, Sustainable surface water management and green infrastructure in UK urban catchment planning, *Journal of Environmental Planning and Management*, 56, 1, 24–41

Elson, MJ, 1986, *Green belts: Conflict mediation in the urban fringe*, Oxford: Butterworth–Heinemann

Engel, E, Fischer, R and Galetovic, A, 2013, The basic public finance of public–private partnerships, *Journal of the European Economic Association*, 11, 1, 83–111

Environment Agency, 2008, *Guidance on the permeable surfacing of front gardens*, London: DCLG

Erkip, F, Kızılgün, Ö and Mugan, G, 2013, The role of retailing in urban sustainability: The Turkish case, *European Urban and Regional Studies*, 20, 3, 329–42

ESPON (European Observation Network for Territorial Development and Cohesion) 2012, *EDORA – European Development Opportunities for Rural Areas: Final report*, Luxembourg: ESPON

ESPON, 2013, *ESPON ATLAS – Territorial Dimensions of the Europe 2020 Strategy*, Luxembourg: ESPON, www.espon.eu/main/Menu_Publications/Menu_ATLAS2020/

European Environment Agency, 2012, *Streamlining European biodiversity indicators 2020: Building a future on lessons learnt from the SEBI 2010 process*, Luxembourg: European Environment Agency

Evans, G, 2015, Rethinking place branding and place making through creative and cultural quarters, in M Kavaritzis, G Warnaby and GJ Ashworth (eds) *Rethinking Place Branding*, Cham: Springer International Publishing, 135–58

Evans, G and Foord, J, 2008, Cultural mapping and sustainable communities: Planning for the arts revisited, *Cultural Trends*, 17, 2, 65–96

Fabbro, S and Dean, M, 2014, Regional planning on the European corridors: the Italian case of Friuli Venezia Giulia region, in I Vinci (ed) *In spatial strategies of Italian regions*, Milan: Franco Angeli, 89–107

Falk, N and Hall, P, 2009, Why not here? Nicholas Falk and Peter Hall sift through the lessons from two recent TCPA study tour trips to Germany and the Netherlands and consider how European experience can best be applied in British towns and cities, *Town and Country Planning*, 78, 1, 27

Faludi, A, 2004, The European spatial development perspective and North-West Europe: Application and the future, *European Planning Studies*, 12, 3, 391–408

Faludi, A, 2010, *Cohesion, coherence, cooperation: European spatial planning coming of age?*, Abingdon: Routledge

Farthing, S and Carrière, JP, 2007, Reflections on policy-oriented learning in transnational visioning processes: The case of the Atlantic Spatial Development Perspective (ASDP), *Planning, Practice & Research*, 22, 3, 329–45

Feinstein, L, Lupton, R, Hammond, C, Mujtaba, T, Salter, E and Sorhaindo, A, 2008, *The public value of social housing: A longitudinal analysis of the relationship between housing and life chances*, London: The Smith Institute

Feinstein, SS, 2008, Mega-projects in New York, London and Amsterdam, *International Journal of Urban and Regional Research*, 32, 4, 768–85

Fisher, B, Turner, RK and Morling, P, 2009, Defining and classifying ecosystem services for decision making, *Ecological Economics*, 68, 3, 643–53

FIT (Fields in Trust) 2012, *Planning and design for outdoor sport and play*, London: FIT

Florida, R, 2003, *Cities and the creative class*, New York: Routledge

Flyvbjerg, B, 2014, What you should know about megaprojects and why: an overview, *Project Management Journal*, 45, 2, 6–19

Flyvbjerg, B, Bruzelius, N and Van Wee, B, 2008, Comparison of capital costs per route-kilometre in urban rail, *European Journal of Transport and Infrastructure Research*, 8, 1, 17–30

Fobker, S and Grotz, R, 2006, Everyday mobility of elderly people in different urban settings: The example of the city of Bonn, Germany, *Urban Studies*, 43, 1, 99–118

Foray, D, 2013, The economic fundamentals of smart specialisation, *Ekonomiaz*, 83, 2, 55–82

Forrest, R and Kearns, A, 2001, Social cohesion, social capital and the neighbourhood, *Urban Studies*, 38, 12, 2125–43

Foster, J, Lowe, A and Winkelman, S, 2011, *The value of green infrastructure for urban climate adaptation*, Washington, DC: Center for Clean Air Policy

Franchino, F and Mainenti, M, 2013, Electoral institutions and distributive policies in parliamentary systems: An application to state aid measures in EU countries, *Western European Politics*, 36, 3, 498–520

Fryd, O, Jensen, MB, Ingvertsen, ST, Jeppesen, J and Magid, J, 2010, Doing the first loop of planning for sustainable urban drainage system retrofits: A case study from Odense, Denmark, *Urban Water Journal*, 7, 6, 367–78

Gale, R, 2008, Locating religion in urban planning: Beyond 'race' and ethnicity? *Planning, Practice and Research*, 23, 1, 19–39

Gale, R and Naylor, S, 2002, Religion, planning and the city: The spatial politics of ethnic minority expression in British cities and towns, *Ethnicities*, 2, 3, 387–409

Gallent, N, Morphet, J and Tewdwr-Jones, M, 2008, Parish plans and the spatial planning approach in England, *Town Planning Review*, 79, 1, pp.1–29

Ganser, A, 2009, *Roads of her own: Gendered space and mobility in American women's road narratives, 1970-2000*, New York, NY: Rodopi

Garcia, M and McDowell, T, 2010, Mapping social capital: A critical contextual approach for working with low–status families, *Journal of Marital and Family Therapy*, 36, 1, 96–107

Gardiner, B, Martin, R, Pike, A and Tyler, P, 2014, *The case for a more balanced approach to spatial economic growth and development policy within the UK*, Seaford: Regional Studies Association

Garreau, J, 2011, *Edge city: Life on the new frontier*, New York: Random House

Germain, A and Gagnon, JE, 2003, Minority places of worship and zoning dilemmas in Montréal, *Planning Theory and Practice*, 4, 3, 295–318

Getis, A and Getis, J, 2008, Christaller's central place theory, in RG Putnam, FJ Taylor and PK Kettle (eds) *A Geography of Urban Places*, Abingdon: Routledge, 68–72

Gill, SE, Handley, JF, Ennos, AR and Pauleit, S, 2007, Adapting cities for climate change: The role of the green infrastructure, *Built Environment*, 33, 1, 115–33

Gill, SE, Handley, JF, Ennos, R and Nolan, P, 2009, Planning for green infrastructure: Adapting to climate change, in S Davoudi, J Crawford and A Mehmood (eds) *Planning for climate change: Strategies for mitigation and adaptation for spatial planners*, Abingdon: Routledge, 252-60

Givoni, M, 2006, Development and impact of the modern high–speed train: A review, *Transport Reviews*, 26, 5, 593–611

GLA (Greater London Authority) 2012, *Takeaways toolkit tools: Interventions and case studies to help local authorities develop a response to the health impacts of fast food takeaways*, London: GLA

Glasson, J and Marshall, T, 2007, *Regional planning*, Abingdon: Routledge

Glasson, J, Therivel, R and Chadwick, A, 2013, *Introduction to environmental impact assessment*, Abingdon: Routledge

Goetz, KH and Meyer-Sayling, JH, 2009, Political time in the EU: Dimensions, perspectives, theories, *Journal of European Public Policy*, 16, 2, 180-201

Goh, G, 2004, The World Trade Organization, Kyoto and energy tax adjustments at the border, *Journal of World Trade*, 38, 3, 395-423

Golden, JS and Kaloush, KE, 2006, Mesoscale and microscale evaluation of surface pavement impacts on the urban heat island effects, *The International Journal of Pavement Engineering*, 7, 1, 37-52

Goldthau, A and Sitter, N, 2014, A liberal actor in a realist world? The Commission and the external dimension of the single market for energy, *Journal of European Public Policy*, 21, 10, 1452-72

Goodsell, TL, 2013, Familification: Family, neighbourhood change, and housing policy, *Housing Studies*, 28, 6, 845-68

Goodwin, P, 2012, Peak travel, peak car and the future of mobility: Evidence, unresolved issues, and policy implications, and a research agenda, *International Transport Forum Discussion Papers*, No 2012/13, Paris: OECD

Gordon, K and Dion, M, 2008, *Protection of 'critical infrastructure' and the role if investment policies relating to national security*, Paris: OECD

Graham, S, 2000, Constructing premium network spaces: Reflections on infrastructure networks and contemporary urban development, *International Journal of Urban and Regional Research*, 24, 1, 183–200

Graham, S and Marvin, S, 2001, *Splintering urbanism: Networked infrastructures, technological mobilities and the urban condition*, London: Routledge

Gray, R, 2002, The social accounting project and *Accounting Organizations and Society*: Privileging engagement, imaginings, new accountings and pragmatism over critique? *Accounting, Organizations and Society*, 27, 7, 687–708

Greater Manchester, 2015, Police and crime: Making Greater Manchester a safer place, www.agma.gov.uk/greater-manchester-prepared

Greater Manchester LEP, 2010, *Single Assessment Framework*, Manchester: AGMA

Greenhalgh, P, Furness, H and Hall, A, 2012, Time for TIF? The prospects for the introduction of Tax Increment Financing in the UK from a local authority perspective, *Journal of Urban Regeneration and Renewal*, 5, 4, 367–80

Greenwood, J and Aspinwall, M (eds) 2013, *Collective action in the European Union: Interests and the new politics of associability*, Abingdon: Routledge

Griffith, M, 2011, *We must fix it*, London: IPPR

Griffith, M and Jeffreys, P, 2013, *Solutions for the housing shortage: How to build the 250,000 homes a year that we need*, London: Shelter

Grimsey, D and Lewis, M, 2007, *Public private partnerships: The worldwide revolution in infrastructure provision and project finance*, Cheltenham: Edward Elgar Publishing

Grodach, C and Loukaitou-Sideris, A, 2007, Cultural development strategies and urban revitalization: A survey of US cities, *International Journal of Cultural Policy*, 13, 4, 349–70

Groth, NB, Smidt-Jensen, S and Nielsen, T, 2011, Polycentricity: an issue in local development strategies? Findings from the Baltic Sea region, *European Planning Studies*, 19, 5, 727–51

Groves, C, Munday, M and Yakovleva, N, 2013, Fighting the pipe: Neoliberal governance and barriers to effective community participation in energy infrastructure planning, *Environment and Planning C: Government and Policy*, 31, 2, 340–56

Gunderson, LH, 2001, *Panarchy: understanding transformations in human and natural systems*, Washington: Island press

Gurria, A, 2014, Smart Investment in Regions and Cities, Remarks by Angel Gurría, OECD Secretary-General, delivered at the Opening Session of the OPEN DAYS 2014 European Week of Regions and Cities, 6 October 2014, Brussels, Belgium, www.oecd.org/about/secretary-general/smartinvestmentinregionsandcities.htm

Guy, C, 2006, Retail productivity and land-use planning: Negotiating joined-up retail planning policy, *Environment and Planning C: Government and Policy*, 24, 5, 755-70

Hagler, Y, 2009, *Defining U.S. megaregions*, New York: RPA, www.america2050.org/upload/2010/09/2050_Defining_US_Megaregions.pdf

Haigh, N, 1987, *EEC environmental policy and Britain*, Harlow: Longman

Haigh, N, 1996, *Climate change policies and politics in the European Community*, in T O'Riordan and J Jager (eds) *Politics of climate change: A European perspective*, London: Routledge, 155-87

Hall, P, 1977, *The containment of urban England*, London: Allen and Unwin

Hall, P, 1980, *Great planning disasters*, London: Weidenfeld

Hall, RE and Jones, CI, 1998, Why do some countries produce so much more output per worker than others? *NBER paper w6564*, Cambridge, MA: National Bureau of Economic Research

Halliday, S, 2013a *Underground to everywhere: London's underground railway in the life of the capital*, Stroud: The History Press

Halliday, S, 2013b, *The great stink of London: Sir Joseph Bazalgette and the cleansing of the Victorian metropolis*, Stroud: The History Press

Hammami, M, Ruhashyankiko, J-F and Yehoue, EB, 2006, Determinants of public–private partnerships in infrastructure, *Working Paper No 06/99*, Washington: IMF

Hansman, RJ, Magee, C, De Neufville, R and Robins, R, 2006, Research agenda for an integrated approach to infrastructure planning, design and management, *International Journal of Critical Infrastructures*, 2, 2, 146-59

Hare, P, 2013, PPP and PFI: The political economy of building public infrastructure and delivering services, *Oxford Review of Economic Policy*, 29, 1, 95-112

Harguindéguy, JB and Bray, Z, 2009, Does cross-border cooperation empower European regions? The case of INTERREG III-A France-Spain, *Environment and Planning C: Government and Policy*, 27, 4, 747-60

Harker, L, 2007, *Chance of a lifetime: The impact of bad housing on children's lives*, London: Shelter

Harrison, P, Todes, A and Watson, V, 2008, *Planning and transformation*, Abingdon: Routledge

Haughton, G, Allmendinger, P, Counsell, D and Vigar, G, 2010, *The New Spatial Planning Territorial management with soft spaces and fuzzy boundaries,* Abingdon: Routledge

Haughton, G, Bankoff, G and Coulthard, TJ, 2015, In search of 'lost' knowledge and outsourced expertise in flood risk management, *Transactions of the British Institute of Geographers*, 40, 3, 375-86

HCA (Homes and Communities Agency) 2009, *Investment and planning obligations responding to the downturn*, London: HCA

Headicar, P, 2013, The changing spatial distribution of the population in England: Its nature and significance for 'Peak Car', *Transport Reviews*, 33, 3, 310-24

Healey, P, 2004, The treatment of space and place in the new strategic spatial planning in Europe, *International Journal of Urban and Regional Research*, 28, 1, 45–67

Healey, P, 2009, In search of the 'strategic' in spatial strategy making, *Planning Theory and Practice*, 10, 4, 439–57

Helm, D, 2013, British infrastructure policy and the gradual return of the state, *Oxford Review of Economic Policy*, 29, 2, 287–306

Helm, D, 2015, The road to re-regulation, *Energy Futures Network Paper, No. 7*, www.dieterhelm.co.uk/sites/default/files/The%20road%20to%20re-regulation.pdf

Herbert, D and Thomas, C, 2013, *Cities in space: City as place*, Abingdon: Routledge

Hess, DB and Almeida, TM, 2007, Impact of proximity to light rail rapid transit on station-area property values in Buffalo, New York, *Urban Studies*, 44, 5/6, 1041–68

Hjorthol, R and Vågane, L, 2014, Allocation of tasks, arrangement of working hours and commuting in different Norwegian households, *Journal of Transport Geography*, 35, 75–83

HLF (Heritage Lottery Fund) 2014, *State of UK public parks: Renaissance or risk?* London: Heritage Lottery Fund

HMG (Her Majesty's Government) 2014a, *Better connected: A practical guide to utilities for home builders*, London: HMG

HMG, 2014b, *United Kingdom Partnership Agreement Official Proposal April*, London: HMG

HMG, 2014c, *United Kingdom Partnership Agreement Official Proposal October*, London: HMG

HMG, 2015, *Plymouth and South West Peninsula city deal*, London: HMG

HMT (Her Majesty's Treasury), 2003, *Productivity in the UK 4 - The local dimension*, London: HMT

HMT, 2007, *Sub-national economic development and regeneration review*, London: HMT

HMT, 2011, *Valuing infrastructure spend: Supplementary guidance to the Green Book*, London: HMT

HMT, 2014, *National infrastructure plan*, London: HMT

HMT and DCLG, 2010, *Total place: A whole area approach to public services*, London: HMT

HoC (House of Commons) 2015, *Strategic flood risk management*, London: House of Commons Environmental Audit Select Committee, www.publications.parliament.uk/pa/cm201415/cmselect/cmpubacc/737/73702.htm

Hodge, GA and Greve, C, 2007, Public–private partnerships: an international performance review, *Public Administration Review*, 67, 3, 545–58

Hodson, M and Marvin, S, 2010, Can cities shape socio-technical transitions and how would we know if they were? *Research Policy*, 39, 4, 477–85

Hogland, W, Hogland, M, and Marques, M, 2010, Enhanced Landfill Mining: Material recovery, energy utilisation and economics in the EU (Directive) perspective, in *International Academic Symposium on Enhanced Landfill Mining. Houthalen-Helchteren, Belgium, October 2010*, 233–47

Holman, N and Rydin, Y, 2013, What can social capital tell us about planning under localism? *Local Government Studies*, 39, 1, 71–88

Holt, V and Baker, M, 2014, All hands to the pump? Collaborative capability in local infrastructure planning in the north west of England, *Town Planning Review*, 85, 6, 757–76

Hood, C, 2012, *The blame game*, London: Princeton Press

Hoppe, T, Graf, A, Warbroek, B, Lammers, I and Lepping, I, 2015, Local governments supporting local energy initiatives: Lessons from the best practices of Saerbeck (Germany) and Lochem (the Netherlands), *Sustainability*, 7, 2, 1900–31

Hostetler, M, Allen, W and Meurk, C, 2011, Conserving urban biodiversity? Creating green infrastructure is only the first step, *Landscape and Urban Planning*, 100, 4, 369–71

Hovden, E, 2004, Norway: Top down Europeanization by fax, in A Jordan and D Liefferink (eds) *Environmental policy in Europe: The Europeanization of national environmental policy*, London: Routledge, 154–71

Howie, P, Murphy, SM and Wicks, J, 2009, An application of the stated preference methods to value urban amenities, *Urban Studies*, 47, 2, 235–56

HUDU (Healthy Urban Development Unit) 2013, Using the planning system to control hot food takeaways: A good practice guide, London: National Health Service London Healthy Urban Development Unit

Hughes, B, 2014, Demographic growth in Ireland since 2011: Some geographic implications for future spatial planning, housing and infrastructure provision, Dublin Institute of Technology School of Surveying and Construction Management, *Other Resources, Paper 35*, http://arrow.dit.ie/beschreoth/35

IGU (International Gas Union) 2014, Unconventional gas: From perplexity to confidence, *Concerns versus Facts International Energy Forum Ministerial Meeting in Moscow, 15-16 May 2014*, IGU Background Paper, Fornebu: IGU

IMF (International Monetary Fund) United Kingdom: Staff Report for the 2012 Article IV Consultation, Country Report No. 12/190, Washington, DC: IMF, www.imf.org/external/pubs/cat/longres.aspx?sk=26083.0

Imrie, R and Raco, M, 2003, *Urban renaissance? New Labour, community and urban policy*, Bristol: Policy Press

Inderst, G and Della Croce, R, 2013, Pension fund investment in infrastructure: A comparison between Australia and Canada, *OECD Working Papers on Finance, Insurance and Private Pensions*, No 32, Paris: OECD Publishing

Inman, P, 2014, IMF sounds alarm on UK house prices but changes its tune on austerity, *The Guardian*, 6th June, www.theguardian.com/politics/2014/jun/06/george-osborne-concedes-threat-rising-house-prices-uk-economy

IPPR North, 2014, *Great north plan*, Newcastle-upon-Tyne: IPPR North

Irwin, A, 1995, *Citizen science: A study of people, expertise, and sustainable development*, London: Psychology Press

Jaffe, M, 2011, Environmental reviews and case studies: Reflections on green infrastructure economics, *Environmental Practice*, 12, 4, 357–65

Jay, S, Jones, C, Slinn, P and Wood, C, 2007, Environmental impact assessment: Retrospect and prospect, *Environmental Impact Assessment Review*, 27, 4, 287–300

Jeffery, C, 2000, Sub-national mobilization and European integration: Does it make any difference? *JCMS: Journal of Common Market* Studies, 38, 1, 1–23

Jenkins, P and Pickard, J, 2015, Cash-strapped local councils to raise millions with new municipal bonds, *Financial Times*, 2 February, 1

Jenks, M and Dempsey, N, 2007, Defining the neighbourhood: challenges for empirical research, *Town Planning Review*, 78, 2, 153–77

Jensen, S, Corkery, A and Donald, K, 2015, *Realizing rights through the sustainable development goals: The role of national human rights institutions*, Copenhagen: Danish Institute of Human Rights, www.humanrights.dk/publications/realizing-rights-through-sustainable-development-goals-role-national-human-right

Jensen, OB and Richardson, T, 2004, *Making European space: Mobility, power and territorial identity*, Abingdon: Routledge

Jessop, B, 1997, The entrepreneurial city: re-imaging localities, redesigning economic governance, or restructuring capital, in J Newsom and S MacGregor (eds) *Transforming cities: Contested governance and new spatial divisions*, London: Routledge, 28–41

Jim, CY, 2004, Green-space preservation and allocation for sustainable greening of compact cities, *Cities*, 21, 4, 311–20

Jones, P, Hillier, D and Comfort, D, 2009, Primary health care centres in the UK: Putting policy into practice, *Property Management*, 27, 2, 109–18

Jordan, A, 2008, The governance of sustainable development: Taking stock and looking forwards, *Environment and Planning C: Government & Policy*, 26, 1, 17–33

Jordan, A and Lenschow, A, 2010, Environmental policy integration: A state of the art review, *Environmental Policy and Governance*, 20, 3, 147–58

Jordan, A and Schout, A, 2006, *The coordination of the European Union: Exploring the capacities of networked governance*, Oxford: Oxford University Press

Jordan, A, van Asselt, H, Berkhout, F, Huitema, D and Rayner, T, 2012, Understanding the paradoxes of multilevel governing: climate change policy in the European Union, *Global Environmental Politics*, 12, 2, 43–66

Kaiser, C, 2014, Functioning and impact of incentives for amalgamations in a federal state: The Swiss case, *International Journal of Public Administration*, 37, 10, 625–37

Kallis, G and Butler, D, 2001, The EU water framework directive: measures and implications, *Water Policy*, 3, 2, 125–42

Kambites, C and Owen, S, 2006, Renewed prospects for green infrastructure planning in the UK, *Planning, Practice & Research*, 21, 4, 483–96

Karsten, L, 2003, Family gentrifiers: Challenging the city as a place simultaneously to build a career and to raise children, *Urban Studies*, 40, 12, 2573–84

Katz, B and Bradley, J, 2013, *The metropolitan revolution*, Washington, DC: Brookings Institute

Kavanagh, D and Richards, D, 2001, Departmentalism and joined-up government, *Parliamentary Affairs*, 54, 1, 1–18

Kawachi, I and Berkman, L, 2000, Social cohesion, social capital, and health, in L Berkman and I Kawachi (eds) *Social epidemiology*, Oxford: Oxford University Press

Kazmierczak, A and Carter, J, 2010, Adaptation to climate change using green and blue infrastructure: A database of case studies, University of Manchester, GRaBS project, www.grabs-eu.org/membersArea/files/Database_Final_no_hyperlinks.pdf

Keeling, R, 2013, Transforming the community budget pilots, *Local Government Chronicle*, 24 October, 10–11

Kibert, CJ, 2012, *Sustainable Construction: Green Building Design and Delivery: Green Building Design and Delivery*, London: John Wiley & Sons

Kidd, S, 2007, Towards a framework of integration in spatial planning: an exploration from a health perspective, *Planning Theory & Practice*, 8, 2, 161–81

Kingdon, JW, 2003, *Agendas, alternatives and public policies* (2nd edn), New York: Longman

Knill, C and Lenschow, A, 2005, Compliance, communication and competition: Patterns of EU environmental policy making and their impact on policy convergence, *European Environment*, 15, 2, 114–28

Knill, C and Liefferink, D, 2007, *Environmental politics in the European Union*, Manchester: Manchester University Press

Kohijoki, AM, 2011, The effect of aging on consumer disadvantage in grocery retail services among the Finnish elderly, *Journal of Retailing and Consumer Services*, 18, 4, 370–7

Koźluk, T, 2011, Greener growth in the Belgian Federation, *OECD Economics Department Working Papers*, No 894, Paris: OECD Publishing

Krawczyk, E and Ratcliffe, J, 2005, Predict and provide vs explore, envision and plan: Transforming the urban planning approach towards the future, *Futures Academy*, Dublin: Dublin Institute of Technology

Krugman, P, 1991, *Geography and trade*, Cambridge, MA: MIT Press

Krugman, P, 2004, The 'new' economic geography: Where are we?, Unpublished manuscript. Department of Economics, Princeton University, pp.1–14

Krugman, P, 2011, The new economic geography, now middle-aged, *Regional Studies*, 45, 1, 1–8

Kunzmann, KR, 2004, Culture, creativity and spatial planning, *Town Planning Review*, 75, 4, 383–404

Kuo, FE, 2001, Coping with poverty: Impacts of environment and attention in the inner city, *Environment and Behavior*, 33, 1, 5–34

Kuo, FE and Sullivan, WC, 2001, Aggression and violence in the inner city: Effects of environment via mental fatigue, *Environment and Behavior*, 33, 4, 543–71

Kuppinger, P, 2011, Vibrant mosques: Space, planning and informality in Germany, *Built Environment*, 37, 1, 78-91

Kushner, JA, 2010, Affordable housing as infrastructure in the time of global warming, *The Urban Lawyer*, 42/43, 179-221

Kux, S and Sverdrup, U, 2000, Fuzzy borders and adaptive outsiders: Norway, Switzerland and the EU, *Journal of European Integration*, 22, 3, 237-70

Lal, D, 2001, The development and spread of economic norms and incentives, in R Rosecrance and AA Stein (eds) *The new great power coalition: Toward a world concert of nations*, Lanham, MD: Rowman and Littlefield Publishers

Lam, JSL and Notteboom, T, 2014, The greening of ports: A comparison of port management tools used by leading ports in Asia and Europe, *Transport Reviews*, 34, 2, 169-89

Lamie, J and Ball, R, 2010, Evaluation of partnership working within a community planning context, *Local Government Studies*, 36, 1, 109-27

Landscape Institute, 2011, *Local green infrastructure*, London: Landscape Institute

Lang, RE and LeFurgy, J, 2003, Edgeless cities: Examining the noncentered metropolis, *Housing Policy Debate*, 14, 3, 427-60

Lawless, P, 1989, *Britain's inner cities*, London: Paul Chapman Publishing

Layard, R, 2011, *Happiness: Lessons from a new science* (2nd edn), London: Penguin

Le Galès, P, 2002, *European cities: Social conflicts and governance*, Oxford: Oxford University Press

Lee, ACK and Maheswaran, R, 2011, The health benefits of urban green spaces: A review of the evidence, *Journal of Public Health*, 33, 2, 212-22

Leichenko, R, 2011, Climate change and urban resilience, *Current Opinion in Environmental Sustainability*, 3, 3, 164-8

Lennon, M, Scott, M and O'Neill, E, 2014, Urban design and adapting to flood risk: the role of green infrastructure. *Journal of Urban Design*, 19,5, 745-58

Letki, N, 2008, Does diversity erode social cohesion? Social capital and race in British neighbourhoods, *Political Studies*, 56, 1, 99-126

Levi, M, 1996, Social and unsocial capital: A review essay of Robert Putnam's Making Democracy Work, *Politics and Society*, 24, 1, 45-55

Levy, DT, Chaloupka, F and Gitchell, J, 2004, The effects of tobacco control policies on smoking rates: A tobacco control scorecard, *Journal of Public Health Management and Practice*, 10, 4, 338-53

Lewis, M, 2014, Flash Boys: A Wall Street Revolt W. W. Norton & Company

LGA (Local Government Association), 2013, *Neighbourhood planning: a simple guide for councillors*, London: LGA

Liberatore, A, 1997, The integration of sustainable development objectives into EU policy-making, in S Baker, M Kousis, D Richardson and S Young (eds) *The Politics of Sustainable Development: Theory, Policy and Practice in the European Union*, London/New York: Routledge, 107-27

Ligtvoet, W, Knoop, J, Strengers, B and Bouwman, A, 2009, *Flood protection in the Netherlands: Framing long-term challenges and options for a climate-resilient delta*, The Hague: The Netherlands Environmental Assessment Agency (PBL)

Limao, N and Venables, AJ, 2001, Infrastructure, geographical disadvantage, transport costs, and trade, *The World Bank Economic Review*, 15, 3, 451–79

Lindner, M, Garcia-Gonzalo, J, Kolström, M, Green, T, Reguera, R, Maroschek, M and Corona, P, 2008, Impacts of climate change on European forests and options for adaptation, *Report to the European Commission Directorate-General for Agriculture and Rural Development* www.metla.eu/tapahtumat/2009/JFNW2009/Lindner.pdf

Lipton, S, 2011, *Setting cities free: Releasing the potential of cities to drive growth*, London: City Finance Commission

Lodge, M, 2003, Institutional choice and policy transfer: Reforming British and German railway regulation, *Governance*, 16, 2, 159–78

London Borough of Croydon, 2014, *Infrastructure delivery plan*, London: London Borough of Croydon www.croydon.gov.uk/sites/default/files/articles/downloads/Infrastructure%20delivery%20plan%202014.pdf

Lund, H and Mathiesen, BV, 2009, Energy system analysis of 100% renewable energy systems: The case of Denmark in years 2030 and 2050, *Energy*, 34, 5, 524–53

Lundquist, KJ and Trippl, M, 2009, Towards cross-border innovation spaces: A theoretical analysis and empirical comparison of the Öresund region and the Centrope area, *SRE Discussion Papers, 2009/05*, Vienna: Institut für Regional- und Umweltwirtschaft, WU Vienna University of Economics and Business

Lyons, M, 2007, Place-shaping: a shared ambition for the future of local government Lyons Inquiry final report and recommendations, www.lyonsinquiry.org.uk/

Lyons, M, 2011, The Lyons Housing review, www.yourbritain.org.uk/uploads/editor/files/The_Lyons_Housing_Review_2.pdf

Maes, J, Paracchini, ML, Zulian, G, Dunbar, MB and Alkemade, R, 2012, Synergies and trade-offs between ecosystem service supply, biodiversity, and habitat conservation status in Europe, *Biological Conservation*, 155, 1–12

Magnani, N and Struffi, L, 2009, Translation sociology and social capital in rural development initiatives: A case study from the Italian Alps, *Journal of Rural Studies*, 25, 2, 231–8

Mahon, R and McBride, S, 2009, Standardizing and disseminating knowledge: The role of the OECD in global governance, *European Political Science Review*, 1, 1, 83–101

Mäntysalo, R, Kangasoja, JK and Kanninen, V, 2015, The paradox of strategic spatial planning: A theoretical outline with a view on Finland, *Planning Theory & Practice*, 6, 2, 169–83

Margetts, H and Hood, C (eds) 2012, *Paradoxes of modernization: Unintended consequences of public policy reform*, Oxford: Oxford University Press

Markusen, A, 2007, A consumption base theory of development: An application to the rural cultural economy, *Agricultural and Resource Economics Review*, 36, 1, 9–23

Markusen, A and Gadwa, A, 2010, Arts and culture in urban or regional planning: A review and research agenda, *Journal of Planning Education and Research*, 29, 3, 379–91

Marsan, GA and Maguire, K, 2011, Categorisation of OECD regions using innovation–related variables, *OECD Regional Development Working Paper 2011/03*, Paris: OECD Publishing

Marsh, D and Sharman, JC, 2009, Policy diffusion and policy transfer, *Policy Studies*, 30, 3, 269–88

Marshall, S and Banister, D, 2007, *Land use and transport: European research towards integrated policies*, Oxford: Elsevier

Marshall, T, 2009a, Infrastructure and spatial planning, Netherlands Working Paper, Oxford: Oxford Brookes University http://planning.brookes.ac.uk/research/spg/projects/infrastructure/resources/NLWPmay182009final.pdf

Marshall, T, 2009b, Infrastructure planning in the Netherlands the benefit of long-term thinking, *Town and Country Planning*, 78, 10, 429–32

Marshall, T, 2009c, Infrastructure planning in Spain: A complex dynamic, *Town and Country Planning*, December, 78, 12, 536–40

Marshall, T, 2009d, Planning and New Labour in the UK, *Planning, Practice & Research*, 24, 1, 1–9

Marshall, T, 2009e, Infrastructure planning in France – context is critical, *Town and Country Planning*, 78, 11, 487

Marshall, T, 2011, Reforming the process for infrastructure planning in the UK/England 1990–2010, *Town Planning Review*, 82, 4, 441–67

Martens, K and Jakobi, AP, 2010, *Mechanisms of OECD governance: International incentives for national policy-making?* Oxford: Oxford University Press

Martí-Henneberg, J, 2013, European integration and national models for railway networks (1840–2010), *Journal of Transport Geography*, 26, 126–38

Martinez-Fernandez, C, Audirac, I, Fol, S and Cunningham-Sabot, E, 2012, Shrinking cities: Urban challenges of globalization, *International Journal of Urban and Regional Research*, 36, 2, 213–25

Marvin, S and Guy, S, 1997, Infrastructure provision, development processes and the co-production of environmental value, *Urban Studies*, 34, 12, 2023–36

Mashayekh, Y, Hendrickson, C and Matthews, HS, 2012, Role of brownfield developments in reducing household vehicle travel, *Journal of Urban Planning and Development*, 138, 3, 206–14

Masiol, M, Agostinelli, C, Formenton, G, Tarabotti, E and Pavoni, B, 2014, Thirteen years of air pollution hourly monitoring in a large city: Potential sources, trends, cycles and effects of car-free days, *Science of the Total Environment*, 494, 84–96

Matas, A, 2004, Demand and revenue implications of an integrated public transport policy: The case of Madrid, *Transport Reviews*, 24, 2, 195–217

Maussen, M, 2004, Policy discourses on mosques in the Netherlands 1980–2002: Contested constructions, *Ethical Theory and Moral Practice*, 7, 2, 147–62

Mayor of London, 2011, *Delivering London's energy future: The mayor's climate change mitigation and energy strategy*, London: GLA

Mayor of London, 2015, *London infrastructure plan 2050*, London: Mayor of London, www.london.gov.uk/file/19038/download?token=1Zj5uQZf

Mayor of London and CABE (Chartered Association of Building Engineers) 2009, *Open space strategies: Best practice guidance*, London: CABE

McCall, MK and Dunn, CE, 2012, Geo-information tools for participatory spatial planning: Fulfilling the criteria for 'good' governance? *Geoforum*, 43, 1, 81–94

McCormick, J, 2001, *Environmental policy in the European Union*, Basingstoke: Palgrave

McDaniels, T, Chang, S, Cole, D, Mikawoz, J and Longstaff, H, 2008, Fostering resilience to extreme events within infrastructure systems: Characterizing decision contexts for mitigation and adaptation, *Global Environmental Change*, 18, 2, 310–18

McLoughlin, S, 2005, Mosques and the public space: Conflict and cooperation in Bradford, *Journal of Ethnic and Migration Studies*, 31, 6, 1045–66

Mcrit, 2014, *Territorial scenarios and vision for Europe*, Luxembourg: ESPON

Measham, TG, Preston, BL, Smith, TF, Brooke, C, Gorddard, R, Withycombe, G and Morrison, C, 2011, Adapting to climate change through local municipal planning: Barriers and challenges, *Mitigation and Adaptation Strategies for Global Change*, 16, 8, 889–909

Mehiriz, K and Marceau, R, 2013, The politics of intergovernmental grants in Canada: The case of the Canada–Quebec infrastructure works 2000 program, *State and Local Government Review*, 45, 2, 73–85

Meiner, A, 2010, Integrated maritime policy for the European Union: Consolidating coastal and marine information to support maritime spatial planning, *Journal of Coastal Conservation*, 14, 1, 1–11

Mejia-Dorantes, L and Lucas, K, 2014, Public transport investment and local regeneration: A comparison of London's Jubilee Line extension and the Madrid Metrosur, *Transport Policy*, 35, 241–52

Melhuish, E, Sammons, P, Siraj-Blatchford, I and Taggart, B, 2004, *The effective provision of pre-school education (EPPE) project: Findings from pre-school to end of key stage 1*, London: Department for Education and Skills–SureStart

Mendez, C, 2012, The post-2013 reform of EU cohesion policy and place-based narrative, *Journal of European Public Policy*, 20, 5, 639–59

Merk, O, 2014, Metropolitan governance of transport and land use in Chicago, *OECD Regional Development Working Papers, 2014/08*, Paris: OECD

Merk, O and Dang, T, 2012, Efficiency of world ports in container and bulk cargo (oil, coal, ores and grain), OECD Regional Development Working Papers, No. 2012/09, Paris: OECD Publishing

Metz, D, 2013, Peak car and beyond: The fourth era of travel, *Transport Reviews*, 3, 3, 255–70

Meunier, S, 2005, *Trading voices: The European Union in international commercial negotiations*, Woodstock: Princeton University Press

Milio, S, 2014, The conflicting effects of multi-level governance and the partnership principle: Evidence from the Italian experience, *European Urban and Regional Studies*, 21, 4, 384–97

Miller, S, 2014, Emerging trends and challenges in community-led local development (CLLD), *European Structural and Investment Funds Journal*, 2, 4, 302–7

Miller, V, 2010, *Implementing the Lisbon Treaty*, SN/IA/5331 8 February, London: House of Commons Library

Millie, A, 2012, Police stations, architecture and public reassurance, *British Journal of Criminology*, 52, 6, 1092–112

Mills, DE and Keast, RL, 2009, Achieving better stewardship of major infrastructure assets through configuration of governance arrangements utilising Stewardship Theory, *13th International Research Society for Public Management Conference (IRSPM XIII)*, Fredericksberg, Denmark, 6–8 April, IRSPM

Milner, C, 2009, Constraining and enhancing policy space: The WTO and adjusting to globalisation, *The Journal of International Trade and Diplomacy*, 3, 1, 127–54

Mishan, EJ and Quah, E, 2007, *Cost–benefit analysis*, Abingdon: Routledge

Mongon, D, Allen, T, Farmer, L and Atherton, C, 2010, *Emerging patterns of leadership: Co-location, continuity and community*, Nottingham: National College for Leadership of Schools and Children's Services

Montgomery, J, 2003, Cultural quarters as mechanisms for urban regeneration, Part 1: Conceptualising cultural quarters, *Planning, Practice & Research*, 18, 4, 293–306

Monti, M, 2010, *A new strategy for the single market at the service of Europe's economy and society*, Brussels: CEC

Morgan, K, 2009, Feeding the city: The challenge of urban food planning, *International Planning Studies*, 14, 4, 341–8

Morgan, K, 2013, The regional state in the era of Smart Specialisation, *Ekonomiaz*, 83, 2, 103–26

Morphet, J, 1994, *Parks, open space and the future of urban planning*, Stroud: Demos Comedia

Morphet, J, 2007, *Delivering inspiring places: The role and status of planning*, IDOX report, London: National Planning Forum

Morphet, J, 2008, *Modern local government*, London: Sage

Morphet, J, 2011a, *Effective practice in spatial planning*, Abingdon: Routledge

Morphet, J, 2011b, Infrastructure investment in local enterprise partnerships: The contribution of local infrastructure delivery plans – an updated view including London, *Working Paper 2*, London: Bartlett School of Planning London

Morphet, J, 2011c, Reflections on alterity in Irish and Scottish spatial planning: fragmentation or fugue?, *Journal of Irish and Scottish Studies*, 4, 2, 173–94

Morphet, J, 2013a, *How Europe shapes British public policy*, Bristol: Policy Press

Morphet, J, 2013b, *Infrastructure delivery planning in England: Local infrastructure delivery planning results of a survey of local authorities responsible for local plans and local enterprise partnerships*, www.bartlett.ucl.ac.uk/planning/FilesForNewsItems/ LEP_IDP_REVIEW_v8_June_2013.pdf

Morphet, J, 2015, *Applying leadership and management in planning*, Bristol: Policy Press

Morphet, J, forthcoming, *Updated review of the role and use of infrastructure delivery plans in England*

Morphet, J, and Pemberton, S, 2013, 'Regions out—sub-regions In'—can sub-regional planning break the mould? The view from England, *Planning Practice & Research*, 28, 4, 384–99

Morphet, J, Burton, T and Hughes, L, 2007, *Delivering inspiring places: The role and status of planning*, IDOX report, London: National Planning Forum

Moseley, MJ, Parker, G and Wragg, A, 2004, Multi-service outlets in rural England: The co-location of disparate services, *Planning Practice and Research*, 19, 4, 375–91

Mulligan, GF, Partridge, MD and Carruthers, JI, 2012, Central place theory and its re-emergence in regional science, *The Annals of Regional Science*, 48, 2, 405–31

NAO (National Audit Office) 2010, *Ministry of Defence The Major Projects Report 2010*, London: NAO

NAO, 2013, *Planning for economic infrastructure*, London: NAO

Natural England, 2009, *European landscape convention*, York: Natural England, http://publications.naturalengland.org.uk/publication/6361194094919680?c ategory=31019

Nauwelaers, C, Maguire, K and Ajmone Marsan, G, 2013a, The case of Oresund (Denmark-Sweden) – regions and innovation: collaborating across borders, *OECD Regional Development Working Papers*, 2013/21, Paris: OECD Publishing

Nauwelaers, C, Maguire, K and Ajmone Marsan, G, 2013b, The case of Ireland-Northern Ireland (United Kingdom) – regions and innovation: collaborating across borders, OECD Regional Development Working Papers, No. 2013/20, Paris: OECD Publishing

Nauwelaers, C, Maguire, K and Ajmone Marsan, G, 2013c, The case of the Bothnian Arc (Finland-Sweden) – regions and innovation: collaborating across borders, *OECD Regional Development Working Papers*, 2013/17, Paris: OECD

Nauwelaers, C, Maguire, K and Ajmone Marsan, G, 2013d, The case of Hedmark-Dalarna (Norway-Sweden) – regions and innovation: collaborating across borders, *OECD Regional Development Working Papers*, 2013/18, Paris: OECD Publishing.

Neill, WJV, 2011, The debasing of the myth: The privatization of the Titanic memory in designing the post-conflict city, *Urban Design*, 16, 1, 67–86

Nemeth, J, 2009, Defining a public: The management of privately owned public space, *Urban Studies*, 46, 11, 2463–90

NHS England, 2013, *Improving health and patient care through community pharmacy: A call to action*, London: NHS England

NICE (National Institute for Health and Care Excellence) 2008, Promoting and creating built or natural environments that encourage and support physical activity, *NICE Public Health Guidance 8*, London: NICE

Nielsen, TS and Hansen, KB, 2007, Do green areas affect health? Results from a Danish survey on the use of green areas and health indicators, *Health and Place*, 13, 4, 839-50

Niemelä, J, Saarela, SR, Söderman, T, Kopperoinen, L, Yli-Pelkonen, V, Väre, S and Kotze, DJ, 2010, Using the ecosystem services approach for better planning and conservation of urban green spaces: A Finland case study, *Biodiversity and Conservation*, 19, 11, 3225-43

Nordås, HK and Piermartini, R, 2004, Infrastructure and trade, *WTO Staff Working Paper*, No ERSD-2004-04, Geneva: World Trade Organization

Nowak, DJ, 2006, Institutionalizing urban forestry as a 'biotechnology' to improve environmental quality, *Urban Forestry and Urban Greening*, 5, 2, 93-100

Nye, JS, 1990, Soft power, *Foreign policy*, 80, 153-171

Nye, JS, 2004, *Soft power: The means to success in world politics*, New York: Public Affairs

Oates, WE, 2008, On the evolution of fiscal federalism: theory and institutions, *National Tax Journal*, 61, 2, 313-34

Oc, T and Tiesdell, S, 1991, The London Docklands Development Corporation (LDDC), 1981-1991: A perspective on the management of urban regeneration, *Town Planning Review*, 62, 3, 311-30

Odeck, J, 1996, Ranking of regional road investment in Norway, *Transportation*, 23, 2, 123-40

OECD (Organisation for Economic Co-operation and Development) 2002, *Improving policy coherence and integration for sustainable development: A checklist*, Paris: OECD

OECD, 2006, *Territorial Reviews: Newcastle in the North East, the United Kingdom*, Paris: OECD

OECD, 2007a, *Territorial Reviews: Madrid, Spain*, Paris: OECD

OECD, 2007b, *Territorial Reviews: Randstad Holland, Netherlands*, Paris: OECD

OECD, 2008, *Climate change mitigation: What do we do?* Paris: OECD

OECD, 2009, *The impact of culture on tourism*, Paris: OECD

OECD, 2011a, *Strategic transport infrastructure needs to 2030*, Paris: OECD

OECD, 2011b, *Pension funds investment in infrastructure: A survey*, Paris: OECD

OECD, 2011c, *Economic policy reforms going for growth*, Paris: OECD

OECD, 2012, *Energy and climate policy: Bending the technological trajectory*, OECD Studies on Environmental Innovation, OECD Publishing

OECD, 2013, *How's life? 2013 Measuring well-being*, Paris: OECD

OECD, 2014a, *Tourism and the creative economy*, Paris: OECD

OECD, 2014b, *Recommendation of the Council on effective public investment across levels of government*, Paris: OECD

OECD, 2015, *Governing the city*, Paris: OECD

Omega Centre, 2012, *MEGA PROJECTS Centre for Mega Projects in Transport and Development. A global Centre of Excellence in Future Urban Transport sponsored by Volvo Research and Educational Foundations (VREF) OMEGA Centre Lessons for Decision-makers: An Analysis of Selected International Large-scale Transport Infrastructure Projects*, London: UCL, www.omegacentre.bartlett.ucl.ac.uk/wp-content/uploads/2014/11/Mega-Projects-Executive-Summary.pdf

Owen, S, Moseley, M and Courtney, P, 2007, Bridging the gap: an attempt to reconcile strategic planning and very local community-based planning in rural England, *Local Government Studies*, 33, 49-76

Owen, R and Walker, A, 2012, *The new planning process for national infrastructure*, London: Bircham Dyson Bell

Pagano, MA and Perry, D, 2008, Financing infrastructure in the 21st century city, *Public Works Management & Policy*, 13, 1, 22-38

Pagliara, F and Papa, E, 2011, Urban rail systems investments: An analysis of the impacts on property values and residents' location, *Journal of Transport Geography*, 19, 2, 200-11

Palomo, I, Martín-López, B, López-Santiago, C and Montes, C, 2011, Participatory scenario planning for protected areas management under the ecosystem services framework: The Doñana social–ecological system in southwestern Spain, *Ecology and Society*, 16, 1, art 23

Parker, S and Mansfield, C, 2014, *As tiers go by: A collaborative future for counties and districts*, London: NLGN

Parsons, W, 2002, From muddling through to muddling up–evidence based policy making and the modernisation of British Government, *Public Policy and Administration*, 17, 3, 43-60

PAS (Planning Advisory Service) 2009, *A steps approach to infrastructure planning and delivery*, London: PAS

PAS, 2014, *Doing your duty: Practice update*, London: LGA

Pemberton, S and Morphet, J, 2014, The rescaling of economic governance: Insights into the transitional territories of England. *Urban Studies*, *51*(11), pp.2354-2370

Peter Brett Associates (2014) *This paper is about your responses to building infrastructure: Achieving growth,* Reading: PBA, www.peterbrett.com/media/1341/biag-book.pdf

Pettersson, P, 2013, From words to action: Concepts, framings of problems and knowledge production practices in regional transport infrastructure planning, *Transport Policy*, 29, C, 13-22

Phan, PH, Siegel, DS and Wright, M, 2005, Science parks and incubators: Observations, synthesis and future research, *Journal of Business Venturing*, 20, 2, 165-82

PHE (Public Health England) 2013, *Obesity and the environment: Increasing physical activity and active travel*, London: Public Health England

PHE, 2014, *Obesity and the environment: Regulating the growth of fast food outlets*, London: Public Health England

Phelps, NA and Fuller, C, 2000, Multinationals, intracorporate competition, and regional development, *Economic Geography*, 76, 3, 224-43

Pickard, J, Wigglesworth, R and Goff, S, 2012, Housing groups tap markets for capital, *Financial Times*, May 29, 3

Pickup, L, 1978, Women's gender-role and its influence on travel behaviour, *Built Environment*, 10, 1, 61-8

Pielke, RA, Marland, G, Betts, RA, Chase, TN, Eastman, JL, Niles, JO and Running, SW, 2002, The influence of land-use change and landscape dynamics on the climate system: Relevance to climate-change policy beyond the radiative effect of greenhouse gases, *Philosophical Transactions of the Royal Society of London A: Mathematical, Physical and Engineering Sciences*, 360, 1797, 1705-19

Pietrzyk-Kaszyńska, A and Grodzińska-Jurczak, M, 2015, Bottom-up perspectives on nature conservation systems: The differences between regional and local administrations, *Environmental Science & Policy*, 48, 20-31

Piris, J-C, 2010, *The Lisbon Treaty: A legal and political analysis*, Cambridge: Cambridge University Press

Pitt, M, 2007, *The Pitt Review: Learning lessons from the 2007 floods*, London: Cabinet Office

Pollitt, C and Bouckaert, G, 2000, *Public management reform: A comparative analysis*, Oxford: Oxford University Press

Porta, DD and Andretta, M, 2002, Changing forms of environmentalism in Italy: The protest campaign on the high speed railway system, *Mobilization: An International Quarterly*, 7, 1, 59-77

POS (Planning Officers Society) 2014, *Implementing our manifesto: An evolutionary approach to improving local plans*, London: POS

Preston, J and Almutairi, T, 2013, Evaluating the long term impacts of transport policy: An initial assessment of bus deregulation, *Research in Transportation Economics*, 39, 1, 208-14

Preston, P, Cawley, A and Metykova, M, 2007, Broadband and rural areas in the EU: From technology to applications and use, *Telecommunications Policy*, 31, 6, 389-400

Priemus, H and Zonneveld, W, 2003, What are corridors and what are the issues? Introduction to special issue: the governance of corridors, *Journal of Transport Geography*, 11, 3, 167-77

Pucher, J, Buehler, R, Bassett, DR and Dannenberg, AL, 2010, Walking and cycling to health: A comparative analysis of city, state, and international data, *American Journal of Public Health*, 100, 10, 1986-92

Pugh, TA, MacKenzie, AR, Whyatt, JD and Hewitt, CN, 2012, Effectiveness of green infrastructure for improvement of air quality in urban street canyons. *Environmental science & technology*, 46(14), pp.7692-7699

Putnam, R, 2001, *Bowling alone: The collapse and revival of American community*, New York: Simon and Schuster

Putnam, R and Bayne, N, 1987, *Hanging together: Cooperation and conflict in the seven-power summits*, Cambridge, MA: Harvard University Press

Qualtrough, J, 2011, *Planning Act 2008 Community Infrastructure Levy*, London: Bircham Dyson Bell

Quirk, B. (2007) *Making assets work: The Quirk Review*, London: DCLG

Rae, A, 2013, English urban policy and the return to the city: A decade of growth, 2001-2011, *Cities*, 32, 94-101

Reckien, D, Flacke, J, Dawson, RJ, Heidrich, O, Olazabal, M, Foley, A, Hamann, JJ-P, Orru, H, Salvia, M, De Gregorio Hurtado, S, Geneletti, D and Pietrapertosa, F, 2014, Climate change response in Europe: What's the reality? Analysis of adaptation and mitigation plans from 200 urban areas in 11 countries, *Climatic Change*, 122, 1/2, 331-40

Redman, L, Friman, M, Gärling, T and Hartig, T, 2013, Quality attributes of public transport that attract car users: A research review, *Transport Policy*, 25, C, 119-27

Regeneris Consulting and Oxford Economics, 2010, *The role of housing in the economy: A final report*, London: HCA

Reh, C, Héritier, A, Bressanelli, E and Koop, C, 2013, The informal politics of legislation explaining secluded decision making in the European Union, *Comparative Political Studies*, 46, 9, 1112-42

Rérat, P, 2012, Gentrifiers and their choice of housing: Characteristics of the households living in new developments in Swiss cities, *Environment and Planning-Part A*, 44, 1, 221-36

Rérat, P and Lees, L, 2011, Spatial capital, gentrification and mobility: Evidence from Swiss core cities, *Transactions of the Institute of British Geographers*, 36, 1, 126-42

Rhodes, C, 2014, Infrastructure policy, *Library Standard Note*, 9 December SN06594, London: House of Commons Library

RIBA (Royal Institute of British Architects) nd, Designing for flood risk, *Climate Change Toolkit 07*, London: RIBA

Rigg, C and O'Mahoney, N, 2013, Frustrations in collaborative working, *Public Management Review*, 15, 1, 83-108

Rodrigue, JP, Comtois, C and Slack, B, 2013, *The geography of transport systems* (3rd edn), Abingdon: Routledge

Rodrigue, JP, Debrie, J, Fremont, A and Gouvernal, E, 2010, Functions and actors of inland ports: European and North American dynamics, *Journal of Transport Geography*, 18, 4, 519-29

Roe, M and Mell, I, 2013, Negotiating value and priorities: Evaluating the demands of green infrastructure development, *Journal of Environmental Planning and Management*, 56, 5, 650-73

Rose, R, 1993, What is lesson drawing? *Journal of Public Policy*, 11, 3, 3-30

Rosenbaum, MS, 2006, Exploring the social supportive role of third places in consumers' lives, *Journal of Service Research*, 9, 1, 59-72

Rosenberg, G and Carhart, N, 2013, A systems-based approach to creating value from infrastructure interdependencies, *International Symposium for Next Generation Infrastructure*, 1-4 October 2013, Wollongong, Australia, http://ro.uow.edu.au/cgi/viewcontent.cgi?article=1040&context=isngi2013&sei-redir=1&referer=https%3A%2F%2Fscholar.google.co.uk%2Fscholar%3Fas_ylo%3D2011%26q%3Dvalue%2Bof%2Binfrastructure%26hl%3Den%26as_sdt%3D0%2C5#search=%22value%20infrastructure%22

Roskill, 1971, *Roskill Commission report on the London Airport expansion*, London: HMSO

Roskruge, M, Grimes, A, McCann, P and Poot, J, 2011, Social capital and regional social infrastructure investment: Evidence from New Zealand, *International Regional Science Review*, 35, 1, 3-25

Ross, A with Chang, M, 2013, *Planning healthier places: Report from the reuniting health with planning project*, London: TCPA

Rothaermel, FT, Agung, SD and Jiang, L, 2007, University entrepreneurship: A taxonomy of the literature, *Industrial and Corporate Change*, 16, 4, 691-791

Roumboutsos, A and Pantelias, A, 2014, Allocating revenue risk in transport infrastructure public private partnership projects: How it matters, *Transport Reviews*, 35, 2, 183-203

RPA (Regional Plan Association) 2014, *Megaregions 2050*, New York: RPA

RSA (Royal Society for the Encouragement of Arts, Manufactures and Commerce) 2014a, *Connected cities: The link to growth*, Report of the City Growth Commission, London: RSA

RSA, 2014b, *Unleashing metro growth: Final recommendations of the City Growth Commission*, London: RSA

RTPI (Royal Town Planning Institute) 2014, Creating economically successful places, *Planning Horizons no 4*, London: RTPI

Sala-i-Martín, X, Bilbao-Osorio, B, Di Battista, A, Drzeniek Hanouz, M, Geiger, T and Galvan, C, 2014, The global competitiveness index 3 2014-2015: Accelerating a robust recovery to create productive jobs and support inclusive growth, in K Schwab (ed.) *The global competitiveness report 2014-15*, Geneva: World Economic Forum, 3-52

Salet, WG, Thornley, A and Kreukels, A (eds) 2003, *Metropolitan governance and spatial planning: Comparative case studies of European city-regions*, Abingdon: Taylor and Francis

Salvati, L, 2013, Urban containment in action? Long-term dynamics of self-contained urban growth in compact and dispersed regions of southern Europe, *Land Use Policy*, 35, 213-25

Sandford, M, 2014, *Parish and town councils: Recent issues*, SN/PC/04827, 4 November, London: House of Commons Library

Sandstrom, UG, 2002, Green infrastructure planning in urban Sweden, *Planning Practice and Research*, 17, 4, 373-86

Santamouris, M, 2007, Heat island research in Europe: The state of the art, *Advances in Building Energy Research*, 1, 1, 123-50

Sarmiento-Mirwaldt, K, 2015, Can multiple streams predict the territorial cohesion debate in the EU? *European Urban and Regional Studies*, 22, 4, 431–45

Sassatelli, M, 2002, Imagined Europe: The shaping of a European cultural identity through EU cultural policy, *European Journal of Social Theory*, 5, 4, 435–51

Saxena, S, Thornicroft, G, Knapp, M and Whiteford, H, 2007, Resources for mental health: Scarcity, inequity, and inefficiency, *The Lancet*, 370, 9590, 878–89

Schilling, J and Logan, J, 2008, Greening the rust belt: A green infrastructure model for right sizing America's shrinking cities, *Journal of the American Planning Association*, 74, 4, 451–66

Schmitt, P, Harbo, LG, Diş, AT and Henriksson, A, 2013, Urban resilience and polycentricity: The case of the Stockholm urban agglomeration, in A Eraydin and Tuna Taşan-Kok (eds) *Resilience thinking in urban planning*, Dordrecht: Springer, 197–209

Schmuecker, K, 2011, *The good, the bad and the ugly: Housing demand 2025*, London: IPPR

Schumann, JW, 1997, Rail in multimodal transit systems: Concept for improving urban mobility by increasing choices for travel and lifestyle, *Transportation Research Record: Journal of the Transportation Research Board*, 157, 1, 208–17

Schwab, K (ed) 2014, *The global competitiveness report 2014-2015*, Geneva: World Economic Forum

Scottish Government, 2012, *Community councils short-life working group report and recommendations*, Edinburgh: Scottish Government

Scottish Government, 2014, *National planning framework 3*, Edinburgh: Scottish Government, www.gov.scot/Publications/2014/06/3539

Sellberg, MM, Wilkinson, C and Peterson, GD, 2015, Resilience assessment: A useful approach to navigate urban sustainability challenges, *Ecology and Society*, 20, 1, art 43, http://dx.doi.org/10.5751/ES-07258-200143

Shaffer, G, 2001, The World Trade Organization under challenge: Democracy and the law and politics of the WTO's treatment of trade and environment matters, *Harvard Environmental Law Review*, 25, 1–93

Shaw, J, 2000, *Competition, regulation and the privatisation of British Rail*, Aldershot: Ashgate

Sheppard, SRJ, Shaw, A, Flanders, D, Burch, S, Wiek, A, Carmichael, J, Robinson, J and Cohen, S, 2011, Future visioning of local climate change: A framework for community engagement and planning with scenarios and visualisation, *Futures*, 43, 4, 400–12

Short, J and Kopp, A, 2005a, Summary of discussions, in ECMT (ed.) National systems of transport infrastructure planning, ECMT Round Tables, No 128, Paris: OECD Publishing

Short, J and Kopp, A, 2005b, Transport infrastructure: Investment and planning – policy and research aspects, *Transport Policy*, 12, 4, 360–7

Shortall, S, 2008, Are rural development programmes socially inclusive? Social inclusion, civic engagement, participation, and social capital: Exploring the differences, *Journal of Rural Studies*, 24, 4, 450–7

Siemens, PWC and Berwin Leighton Paisner, 2014, *Investor ready cities*, London: Siemens

Simpson, LE, 2005, Community informatics and sustainability: Why social capital matters, *The Journal of Community Informatics*, 1, 2, www.ci-journal.net/index.php/ciej/article/view/210/169

Skaburskis, A, 2012, Gentrification and Toronto's changing household characteristics and income distribution, *Journal of Planning Education and Research*, 32, 2, 191-203

Smeets, S and Vennix, J, 2014, How to make the most of your time in the Chair: EU presidencies and the management of Council debates, *Journal of European Public Policy*, 21, 10, 1435-51

Smith Institute, 2014a, *All change: Delivering future city transport*, London: PWC

Smith Institute, 2014b, *NHS surplus land for supported housing*, London: Smith Institute

Smith, L, 2014, *Planning for nationally significant infrastructure projects*, SN/SC/6881, London: House of Commons Library

SPAHG (Spatial Planning and Health Group) 2011, *Steps to healthy planning: Proposals for action*, June, London: SPAHG

Squires, G and Lord, AD, 2012, The transfer of tax increment financing (TIF) as an urban policy for spatially targeted economic development, *Land Use Policy*, 29, 4, 817-26

Stabiner, K, 2011, New Lives for 'dead' suburban malls, *New York Times*, January 21 http://newoldage.blogs.nytimes.com/2011/01/21/new-lives-for-dead-suburban-malls/?_r=0

Starfield, B, Shi, L and Macinko, J, 2005, Contribution of primary care to health systems and health, *The Milbank Quarterly*, 83, 3, 457-502

Stead, D, 2014, European integration and spatial rescaling in the Baltic region: Soft spaces, soft planning and soft security. *European Planning Studies*, 22(4), pp.680-693

Stead, D and Meijers, E, 2009, Spatial planning and policy integration: Concepts, facilitators and inhibitors, *Planning Theory and Practice*, 10, 3, 317-32

Steeneveld, GJ, Koopmans, S, Heusinkveld, BG, Van Hove, LWA and Holtslag, AAM, 2011, Quantifying urban heat island effects and human comfort for cities of variable size and urban morphology in the Netherlands, *Journal of Geophysical Research: Atmospheres (1984-2012)*, 116, D20, 2156-202

Steiner, A, 2014, *Policy statement on UNEP*, June 27, Nairobi, www.unep.org/newscentre/Default.aspx?DocumentID=2791&ArticleID=10930&l=en

Stern, N, 2007, *The economics of climate change: The Stern Review*, Cambridge: Cambridge University Press

Stevens, B, Schieb, PA and Gibson, A (2011) *Strategic transport infrastructure needs to 2030*, Paris: OECD

Stevens, P, 2012, The 'shale gas revolution': Developments and changes, *Chatham House Briefing Paper*, 4, London: Chatham House

Stewart, F, Kaminker, C and Ang, G, 2012, Towards a green investment policy framework: The case of low-carbon, climate-resilient infrastructure, *OECD Environment Working Papers*, No. 48, Paris: OECD

Stiglitz, J, 2015, *The great divide*, London: Allen Lane

Stiglitz, J, Sen, A and Fitoussi, JP, 2009, The measurement of economic performance and social progress revisited: Reflections and overview, Commission on the Measurement of Economic Performance and Social Progress 2009-33, Paris: OFCE – Centre de recherche en économie de Sciences Po

Stigsdotter, UK, Ekholm, O, Schipperijn, J, Toftager, M, Kamper-Jørgensen, F and Randrup, TB, 2010, Health promoting outdoor environments: Associations between green space, and health, health-related quality of life and stress based on a Danish national representative survey, *Scandinavian Journal of Public Health*, 38, 4, 411-17

Stockholm Resilience Centre, 2015, Ecosystem resilience, *Resilience Dictionary*, www.stockholmresilience.org/21/research/resilience-dictionary.html

Stoelinga, A and Luikens, H, 2005, National systems of transport infrastructure planning: the case of the Netherlands, in ECMT (ed.) *National systems of transport infrastructure planning*, ECMT Round Tables, No 128, Paris: OECD Publishing

Stone, D, 2004, Transfer agents and global networks in the 'transnationalization' of policy, *Journal of European Public Policy*, 11, 3, 545-66

Storbjörk, S, 2007, Governing climate adaptation in the local arena: Challenges of risk management and planning in Sweden, *Local Environment*, 12, 5, 457-69

Stott, M, Stott, N and Wiles, C, 2009, *Learning from the past: Building community in new towns, growth areas and new communities*, Thetford: Keystone Development Trust

Sugiyama, T, Leslie, E, Giles-Corti, B and Owen, N, 2008, Associations of neighbourhood greenness with physical and mental health: Do walking, social coherence and local social interaction explain the relationships? *Journal of Epidemiology and Community Health*, 62, 5, e9-e9

Sugrue, TJ, 2014, *The origins of the urban crisis: Race and inequality in postwar Detroit*, Princeton, NJ: Princeton University Press

Susca, T, Gaffin, SR and Dell'Osso, GR, 2011, Positive effects of vegetation: Urban heat island and green roofs, *Environmental Pollution*, 159, 8, 2119-26

Symons, T, 2011, *Capital futures*, London: NLGN

Talen, E, 1998, Visualizing fairness: equity maps for planners, *Journal of the American Planning Association*, 64, 1, 22-38

Tanguay, GA, Rajaonson, J, Lefebvre, JF and Lanoie, P, 2010, Measuring the sustainability of cities: An analysis of the use of local indicators, *Ecological Indicators*, 10, 2, 407-18

Taylor, BD, Kim, EJ and Gahbauer, JE, 2009, The thin red line: A case study of political influence on transportation planning practice, *Journal of Planning Education and Research*, 29, 2, 173-93

Taylor, M, 2011, Community infrastructure in new residential developments, briefing paper, York: Joseph Rowntree Foundation

Tett, G, 2015, *The Silo Effect* , London: Simon and Schuster

Thaler, R and Sunstein, C, 2009, *Nudge*, London: Penguin

Therivel, R and Ross, B, 2007, Cumulative effects assessment: Does scale matter? *Environmental Impact Assessment Review*, 27, 5, 365–85

Thomson, A and Wilkes, P, 2014, *Public land, public good*, London: Localis

Thornley, A, 1991, *Urban planning under Thatcherism: The challenge of the market*, Abingdon: Taylor and Francis

Tochtermann, L and Clayton, N, 2011, *Moving on up, moving on out? Overcoming the jobs-skills mismatch,* London: Centre for Cities

Todes, A, 2004, Regional planning and sustainability: Limits and potentials of South Africa's integrated development plans, *Journal of Environmental Planning and Management*, 47, 6, 843–61

Turok, I, 2004, Cities, regions and competitiveness, *Regional Studies*, 38, 9, 1069–83

Turok, I, Bailey, N, Atkinson, R, Bramley, G, Docherty, I, Gibb, K, Goodlad, R, Hastings, A, Kintrea, K, Kirk, K and Leibovitz, J, 2004, Sources of city prosperity and cohesion: the case of Glasgow and Edinburgh, in M Boddy and M Parkinson (eds) *City matters: Competitiveness, cohesion and urban governance*, Bristol: Policy Press, 13–31

Tyler, S and Moench, M, 2012, A framework for urban climate resilience, *Climate and Development*, 4, 4, 311–26

Tzoulas, K, Korpela, K, Venn, S, Yli-Pelkonen, V, Kaźmierczak, A, Niemela, J and James, P, 2007, Promoting ecosystem and human health in urban areas using green infrastructure: A literature review, *Landscape and Urban Planning*, 81, 3, 167–78

UCL (University College London) 2014, Infrastructure investment to promote sustainable growth, REF Case Study, www.ucl.ac.uk/impact/case-study-repository/infrastructure-investment-to-promote-sustainable-growth

Ulrich, RS, 1979, Visual landscapes and psychological well-being, *Landscape Research*, 4, 1, 17–23

UNEP (United Nations Environment Programme) nd, *Ecosystem management*, Nairobi: UNEP

Urbed, 2010, *Growth cities: Local investment for national prosperity*, Norwich: Regional Cities East

Urry, J, Birtchnell, T, Caletrio, J and Pollastri, S, 2014, Living in the city, *Future of Cities Working Paper* Foresight, London: Government Office for Science

USDOT (United States Department of Transportation), 2009, *Vision for high speed rail in America*, Washington DC: DOT

Van den Brande, L, 2014, *Multilevel governance and partnership: The Van den Brande Report*, Brussels: CEC

Van den Hurk, M, Brogaard, L, Lember, V, Peterson, OH and Witz, P, 2015, National varieties of public –private partnerships (PPP): A comparative analysis of PPP supporting units in 19 European countries, *Journal of Comparative Policy Analysis: Research and Practice*, DOI: 10.1080/13876988.2015.1006814

Van der Heijden, H, Dol, K and Oxley, M, 2011, Western European housing systems and the impact of the international financial crisis, *Journal of Housing and the Built Environment*, 26, 3, 295–313

Van der Krabben, E and Jacobs, HM, 2013, Public land development as a strategic tool for redevelopment: Reflections on the Dutch experience, *Land Use Policy*, 30, 1, 774–83

Van Exel, J and Rietveld, P, 2010, Perceptions of public transport travel time and their effect on choice-sets among car drivers, *Journal of Transport and Land Use*, 2, 3/4, 75–86

Van Herzele, A and Wiedemann, T, 2003, A monitoring tool for the provision of accessible and attractive urban green spaces, *Landscape and Urban Planning*, 63, 2, 109–26

Varney, D, 2006, *Service transformation: A better service for citizens and businesses, a better deal for the taxpayer*, London: HMT

Veenstra, G, 2005, Location, location, location: Contextual and compositional health effects of social capital in British Columbia, Canada, *Social Science & Medicine*, 60, 9, 2059–71

Verhoeven, P, 2010, *European port governance: Report of an enquiry into the current governance of European seaports*, Brussels: European Sea Ports Organisation

Walker, BH, Anderies, JM, Kinzig, AP and Ryan, P, 2006, Exploring resilience in social-ecological systems through comparative studies and theory development: introduction to the special issue, *Ecology and Society*, 11, 1, www.researchgate.net/profile/Brian_Walker6/publication/26987477_ Exploring_Resilience_in_Social-Ecological_Systems_Through_Comparative_ Studies_and_Theory_Development_Introduction_to_the_Special_Issue/ links/54b47dbd0cf26833efd02636.pdf

Wallis, I, Wignall, D and Parker, C, 2012, *The implications of road investment* (No 507), Wellington: New Zealand Transport Agency

Wannop, U, 2013, *The regional imperative: Regional planning and governance in Britain, Europe and the United States*, Abingdon: Routledge

Wärnbäck, A and Hilding-Rydevik, T, 2009, Cumulative effects in Swedish EIA practice: Difficulties and obstacles, *Environmental Impact Assessment Review*, 29, 2, 107–15

Warner, AM, 2014, Public Investment as an engine of growth, *IMF working paper 14/148*, Washington: International Monetary Fund

Waterhout, B, 2008, *The institutionalisation of European spatial planning*, vol 18, Delft: IOS Press

Wates, N, 2014, *The community planning handbook: How people can shape their cities, towns and villages in any part of the world* (2nd edn), Abingdon: Routledge

WEF (World Economic Forum) 2012, *Strategic infrastructure: Steps to prioritize and deliver infrastructure effectively and efficiently*, Geneva: WEF

WEF, 2013, *The green investment report: The ways and means to unlock private finance for green growth*, Geneva: WEF

WEF, 2014, *Infrastructure investment policy blueprint*, Geneva: WEF

Welsh Government, 2013, *Wales infrastructure investment plan for growth and jobs 2012*, Cardiff: Welsh Government

Welsh Government, 2015, *The Wales infrastructure investment plan annual report 2015 and project pipeline*, Cardiff: Welsh Government

Westerink, J, Haase, D, Bauer, A, Perpar, A, Grochowski, M, Ravetz, J, Jarrige, F and Aalbers, C, 2012, Dealing with sustainability trade-offs of the compact city in peri-urban planning across European city regions, *European Planning Studies*, 21, 4, 473–97

Wheatley, D, 2011, Work-life balance, travel-to-work, and the dual career household, *Personnel Review*, 41, 6, 813–31

Wilcox, Z, 2014, *Delivering change: Making transport work for cities – practical policy solutions to improving transport in cities*, London: Centre for Cities

Wilkins, RJ, 2008, Eco-efficient approaches to land management: A case for increased integration of crop and animal production systems, *Philosophical Transactions of the Royal Society B: Biological Sciences*, 363, 1491, 517–25

Williams, B and Redmond, D, 2014, Ready money: Residential over-development and its consequences, in A MacLaren and S Kelly (eds) *Neoliberal urban policy and the transformation of the city: Reshaping Dublin*, Basingstoke: Palgrave Macmillan, 107–19

Williams, K, 2014, Urban form and infrastructure: A morphological review, *Foresight future of cities working paper*, London: Government Office for Science

Wilson, W, 2013, The reform of the Housing Revenue Account, SN/SO/4341, 7 February, London: House of Commons Library

Wilson, E and Piper, J, 2010, *Spatial planning and climate change*. Abingdon: Routledge

Wishlade, F, 2015, Another generation in competition policy control of regional development policy, *European Policy Research Paper*, No 89, European Policies Research Centre, Glasgow: University of Strathclyde

Witte, P, Wiegmans, B, van Oort, F and Spit, T, 2014, Governing inland ports: A multi-dimensional approach to addressing inland port–city challenges in European transport corridors, *Journal of Transport Geography*, 36, 42–52

Woltjer, J, Alexander, ER, Hull, A and Ruth, M, 2015, *Place-based evaluation for infrastructure and spatial projects*, Farnham: Ashgate

Wong, C, Baker, M, Hincks, S, Schultz-Baing, A and Webb, B, 2012, Why we need to think strategically and spatially-The 'Map for England' study and the importance of strategic spatial thinking in an era of localism, *Town and Country Planning*, 81, 10, 437.

Woodward, R, 2009, *Organisation for Economic Co-operation and Development (OECD)*, Abingdon: Routledge

Woolcock, S, 2010, EU trade and investment policymaking after the Lisbon treaty, *Intereconomics*, 45, 1, 22–5

World Bank, 2013, *Planning, Connecting, and Financing Cities – Now: Priorities for City Leaders*, Washington, DC: World Bank

Young, AR, 2007, Trade politics ain't what it used to be: the European Union in the Doha round, *JCMS: Journal of Common Market Studies*, 45, 4, 789-811

Zegras, C, Nelson, J, Macario, R and Grillo, C, 2013, Fiscal federalism and prospects for metropolitan transport authorities in Portugal, *Transport Policy*, 29, 1-12

Zonneveld, W and Waterhout, B, 2005, Visions on territorial cohesion, *Town Planning Review*, 76, 1, 15-27

Zucchetti, M, 2013, The Turin–Lyon high-speed rail opposition: The commons as an uncommon experience for Italy, *South Atlantic Quarterly*, 112, 2, 388-95

Index